# DECORATIVE NEEDLEWORK FOR THE HOME

# Woman's Day
# DECORATIVE NEEDLEWORK FOR THE HOME

Edited by Nancy Schraffenberger

Robert J. Kasbar
Book Coordinator/Production Manager

Designed by Allan Mogel Studios

 Columbia House

New York

ISBN: 0-930748-18-2
Printed in the United States of America
Published by Columbia House, a Division of CBS Inc.,
1211 Avenue of the Americas, New York, New York 10036

# CONTENTS

# INTRODUCTION

As a woman who has both pride in her home and skill with a needle, you are fortunate indeed. These days, when adding amenities to the space you live in often involves either a compromise in quality or astronomical expense, you're able to choose exactly what you want and bear only the cost of the materials. Our treasury of decorative needlecrafts is designed especially for you.

Like you, we think that nothing sets off a room like a beautiful handmade that's precisely the right size and color, something beyond price that has been painstakingly created to achieve a certain effect in a certain place. For this collection, we combed the pages of *Woman's Day* to select the most appealing needlecraft projects calling for the broadest range of skills—crocheting, knitting, patchwork, appliqué, needlepoint, embroidery, weaving, macramé, trapunto and of course sewing by machine and by hand.

You'll find afghans, lap throws, quilts, coverlets and spreads in a dazzling range of color combinations, weights and textures. The pillow group includes exquisite Delft-pattern needlepoint, dainty floral embroideries, big, handsome floor pillows, puffs, box shapes, a loveseat ensemble and a unique pillow-hassock. For your walls, there are punch-needle, long-stitch, soft-sculpture and knotted-twine graphics; for windows, dramatic cornice treatments, fragile organdies and rustic jute-strung shutterettes; for floors, Aran-pattern, latch hook, Shaker and woven rugs. Accessories for every room include tablecloths and mats, a Victorian footstool and a bargello desk set, kitchen and closet necessaries, versatile bellpulls and a stunning three-panel macramé screen.

All of these designs are appearing in book form for the first time and all are accompanied by explicit information on tools, materials and techniques. In many cases, diagrams, charts or patterns go with the clearly written instructions.

So turn the pages, pick a project and do yourself—and your house—proud.

# GENERAL INFORMATION

## HOW TO ENLARGE PATTERNS

You will need brown wrapping paper (pieced if necessary to make a sheet large enough for a pattern), felt-tipped marker, pencil and ruler. First connect grid lines or dots across pattern with a colored pencil to form a grid over the pattern. Next cut wrapping paper into a true square or rectangle slightly larger than full-sized pattern. Mark dots around edges, 1" or 2" apart or whatever is indicated on pattern, making same number of spaces as there are squares around edges of pattern diagram. Form a grid by joining the dots across opposite sides of paper. Check to make sure you have the same number of squares as in diagram. With marker, draw in each square the same pattern lines you see in corresponding square on diagram.

If you want to avoid drawing a grid to enlarge the pattern, you can order a package of four 22" x 34" sheets of 1" graph paper for $2 postpaid from Sewmakers, Inc., 1623 Grand Ave., Baldwin, N.Y. 11510.

## ABBREVIATIONS AND TERMS

| | |
|---|---|
| **beg** | Beginning |
| **bl** | Block |
| **ch** | Chain |
| **cl** | Cluster |
| **dc** | Double crochet |
| **dec** | Decrease |
| **dp** | Double pointed |
| **d tr** | Double treble crochet |
| **h dc** | Half double crochet |
| **inc** | Increase |
| **k** | Knit |
| **lp** | Loop |
| **p** | Purl |
| **psso** | Pass slipped stitch over |
| **rnd** | Round |
| **sc** | Single crochet |
| **sl** | Slip |
| **sl st** | Slip stitch |
| **sp** | Space |
| **ssk** | Slip, slip, knit |
| **st** | Stitch |
| **tog** | Together |
| **tr** | Treble crochet |
| **y f** | Yarn in front |
| **y o** | Yarn over hook |
| **\* Asterisk** | Repeat instructions following asterisk as many times as specified in addition to the first time. |
| **[ ] Brackets** | Indicate changes in size. |
| **( ) Parenthesis** | Repeat instructions in parenthesis as many times as specified. |
| **Stockinette stitch** | K 1 row, p 1 row. |
| **Garter stitch** | K each row. |

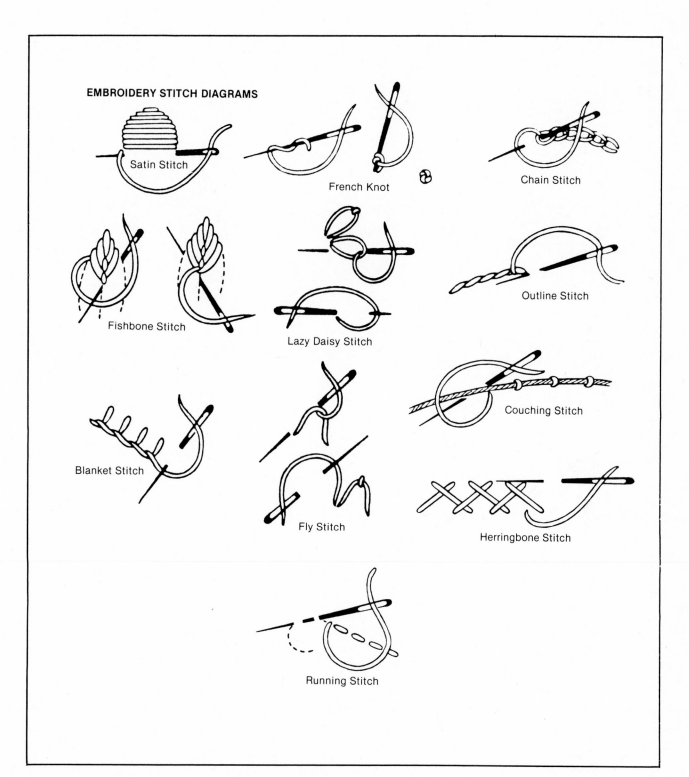

**EMBROIDERY STITCH DIAGRAMS**

Satin Stitch

French Knot

Chain Stitch

Fishbone Stitch

Lazy Daisy Stitch

Outline Stitch

Blanket Stitch

Fly Stitch

Couching Stitch

Herringbone Stitch

Running Stitch

# 1

# BEDCOVERINGS AND WARMERS

# BED OF ROSES CROCHETED COVERLET

The diamond-shaped rose-garden center and the corners are composed of three flower and two bud motifs, all crocheted to reveal their petal shapes against a light brown background.

**SIZE:** 70" x 84" (see note below).

**MATERIALS:** Brunswick Windrush (Orlon acrylic knitting-worsted-weight yarn), 13 (4-ounce skeins light brown No. 9034 (color B), 2 skeins each light cherry No. 9096 (C), peach No. 90090 (P) and medium willow green No. 90862 (G), 1 skein light Imari rose No. 90583 (R); aluminum crochet hook size G (or international hook size 4:50 mm) or the size that will give you the correct gauge; tapestry needle.

**Note :** Instructions are given for afghan to fit flat on double bed as shown. See placement diagram (half of afghan shown; broken line runs along center of middle row of motifs.) Note that the diamond design is not centered top and bottom; an extra row of plain motifs, necessary for the afghan to fit properly on the bed, has been added above the diamond. (For a symmetrical afghan, omit plain row. For afghan to fit over pillows, add more plain rows.) Each 4-ounce skein will make about 16 plain motifs.

**GAUGE:** Each large motif (or 4 small motifs joined to form square) = 4½" square.

**FIRST MOTIF (make 14):** With color P, ch 6. Join with sl st to form ring. **1st rnd:** Work 16 sc in ring; join with sl st in 1st sc **2nd rnd:** Ch 1, sc in same st as sl st, * ch 2, skip 1 sc, sc in next sc. Repeat from * 6 times more; ch 2; join (8 petals) **3rd rnd:** Sl st in 1st lp, ch 2, work (6 dc, h dc) in same ch-2 lp, * in next ch-2 lp work (h dc, 6 dc, h dc). Repeat from * 6 times more; join with sl st in top of ch 2 (8 petals). Break off. **4th rnd:** With C, sc in sp between any 2 h dc between petals, * ch 4, folding petals forward, sc in next sp between 2 h dc. Repeat from * around ending ch 4; join. **5th rnd:** Sl st in 1st lp, ch 2, work (5 dc, h dc) in same ch-4 lp, work (h dc, 5 dc, h dc) in each ch-4 lp around; join. Break off. **6th rnd:** With G, sl st in center dc of any 5-dc petal of last rnd, ch 3, (y o and draw up lp in same place, y o and draw through 2 lps on hook) twice, y o and draw through all 3 lps on hook, ch 1 to fasten (1st dc cl made); ch 4, in center dc of next petal work (y o and draw up lp, y o and draw through 2 lps on hook) 3 times, y o and draw through all 4 lps on hook, ch 1 to fasten (another dc cl made); ch 2, then (y o twice and draw up lp in same st as dc cl, y o and draw through 1st 2 lps on hook, y o and draw through next 2 lps on hook) 3 times, y o and draw through all 4 lps on hook, ch 1 to fasten (tr cl made); ch 2, make another dc cl in same place (this completes corner of dc cl, tr cl and dc cl); * ch 4, make dc cl in center dc of next petal, ch. 4, work corner in center dc of next petal as before. Repeat from * twice more, ch 4; join. Break off.

**SECOND MOTIF (make 18):** With C, ch 6. Join with sl st to form ring. **1st rnd:** (Sc in ring, ch 4) 8 times; join (8 lps). **2nd rnd:**

Work 5 sc in each lp around (8 petals); join. **3rd rnd:** Ch 1, folding petal forward, insert hook behind work and sc in ring between 1st 2 sc of 1st rnd (mark this sc), * ch 5, folding next petal forward, sc in ring between next 2 sc of 1st rnd. Repeat from * around, ending ch 5; join (8 lps behind 1st rnd of lps). Break off. **4th rnd:** With P, starting in 1st lp after marked sc, work (sc, h dc, 3 dc, h dc, sc) in each ch-5 lp; join. **5th rnd:** Ch 1, insert hook behind work and sc in back lp of marked sc of 3rd rnd, ch 6, * sc in back lp of next sc of 3rd rnd, ch 6. Repeat from * 6 times more; join. Break off. **6th rnd:** With R, in each ch-6 lp, work (sc, h dc, 5 dc, h dc, sc); join. Break off. **7th rnd:** Using G, work same as for 6th rnd of First Motif. Break off.

**THIRD MOTIF (make 25):** With R, ch. 6. Join with sl st to form ring. **1st rnd:** Ch 3, work 11 dc in ring; join with sl st in top of ch 3. **2nd rnd:** Sc in same place as joining (mark this sc), * ch 4, skip next 2 dc, sc in next dc. Repeat from * twice more, ch 4; join (4 lps). **3rd rnd:** Work (sc, h dc, 3 dc, h dc, sc) in each lp; join. Break off. Petals will cup. **4th rnd:** Fold petals forward and insert hook behind petals as follows: With C, sc in back lp of marked sc of 2nd rnd (mark this sc), * ch 4, sc in 2nd dc of 2 free dc of 1st rnd below next petal, ch 4, sc in back lp of next sc of 2nd rnd (between two petals). Repeat from * around, ending last repeat with sl st in 1st (marked) sc (8 lps made behind petals). **5th rnd:** Work (sc, h dc, 3 dc, h dc and sc) in each lp; join. Break off. **6th rnd:** With P, folding petals forward, sc in back lp of marked sc of 4th rnd, * ch 4, sc in next sc of 4th rnd. Repeat from * around, ending last repeat with sl st in 1st sc. **7th rnd:** Work (sc, h dc, 5 dc, h dc, sc) in each lp; join. Break off. **8th rnd:** With G, repeat 6th rnd of First Motif. Break off.

**FOURTH MOTIF (make 8):** With C, ch 3. Join with sl st to form ring. **1st rnd:** * Sc in ring, ch 4, sc in 4th ch from hook to form picot. Repeat from * 3 times more; join (4 picots). **2nd rnd:** Sc in back lp of same sc as sl st and mark this sc, * ch 2, folding picot forward, sc in back lp of next sc between picots. Repeat from * around, ending last repeat with sl st in 1st sc (4 lps). **3rd rnd:** In each lp, work (sc, ch 1, 2 dc, ch 1, sc); join. **4th rnd:** Ch 1, sc in back lp of marked sc of 2nd rnd, * ch 2, sc in back lp of next sc of 2nd rnd between petals. Repeat from * around, ending last repeat with sl st in 1st sc. **5th rnd:** Work 4 sc in each lp; join. Break off. **6th rnd:** With G, sl st in joining st of last rnd, make 1st dc cl (see First Motif): * ch 6, work next dc cl between next two 4-sc groups. Repeat from * twice more, ch 6; join to top of 1st cl and break off. **7th rnd:** With B, work 10 sc in each lp; join. Center section will cup. **8th rnd:** Ch 3, work 2 dc in same place as ch 3, * ch 2, skip 4 sc, work (3 dc, ch 3, 3 dc) in next sc (corner made); ch 2, skip 4 sc, work 3 dc in next sc. Repeat from * twice more, ch 2, work corner as before, ch 2; join. **9th rnd:** Sl st in each of next 2 dc, sl st in next ch-2 sp, ch 3, work 2 dc in same sp, * ch 2, work corner of (3 dc, ch 3, 3 dc) in corner ch-3 sp, (ch 2, work 3 dc in next sp) twice. Repeat from * around, omitting last 3 dc on last repeat; join. Break off.

**FIFTH MOTIF (plain motif—make 173):** With B, ch 6. Join with sl st to form ring. **1st rnd:** Ch 3, work 2 dc in ring, * ch 3, work 3 dc in ring. Repeat from * twice more, ch 3; join. **2nd rnd:** Sl st in each of next 2 dc, sl st in ch-3, sp, ch 3, in same sp work (2 dc, ch 3, 3 dc) for 1st corner; * ch 2, work (3 dc, ch 3, 3 dc) in next sp (another corner made). Repeat from * twice more, ch 2; join. **3rd rnd:** Sl st in each st to 1st corner sp, work 1st corner in corner sp as before, * ch 2, work 3 dc in next ch-2 sp, ch 2, work corner in next corner sp. Repeat from * around, ending ch 2, 3 dc in next ch-2 sp, ch 2; join. **4th rnd:** Sl st in each st to 1st corner sp, * work corner in sp, (ch 2, work 3 dc in next ch-2 sp) twice, ch 2. Repeat from * around; join. Break off.

**SIXTH MOTIF (make 32 small motifs):** Repeat Fourth Motif through 1st rnd, marking 2nd sc made. **2nd rnd:** With C, sc in same place as sl st, ch 4, sc in 4th ch from hook, working behind next picot of 1st rnd, sc in back lp of marked sc, * ch 4, sc in 4th ch from hook, working behind next picot, sc in back lp of next sc. Repeat from * once more, ch 4, sc in 4th ch from hook; join (4 picots). Break off. **3rd rnd:** With G, sl st in same place as last sl st, ch 3, dc in same st, * ch 6, work 2 dc in next sc between picots. Repeat from * twice more, ch 6; join. Break off. **4th rnd:** With B, sc between any 2 dc, * work (4 sc, ch 2, 4 sc) in next lp, sc between next 2 dc. Repeat from * around, ending last repeat with sl st in 1st sc. Break off.

**SEVENTH MOTIF (make 96 small motifs):** Repeat Fifth Motif through 2nd rnd. Break off.

**FINISHING:** Using matching colors of last rnd and following diagram for placement, sew motifs together through outer lp of each st on last rnd of each motif (forming a ridge on right side of work). Crochet 1 rnd sc around afghan, matching colors of motifs and spacing sts evenly.

# DELPHINIUM DREAM CROCHETED AFGHAN

Each granny square has a lovely blue flower with a raised popcorn-stitch center floating on a creamy shell background.

**SIZE:** 53" x 63".

**MATERIALS:** Brunswick Windrush (Orlon acrylic knitting-worsted-weight yarn), 7 (4-ounce) skeins ecru No. 90100 (color E), 3 skeins each bright navy No. 9013 (N), medium powder blue No. 90112 (M) and light powder blue No. 90111 (L); aluminum crochet hooks sizes G and H (or international hooks sizes 4:50 mm and 5:00 mm) or the sizes that will give you the correct gauge.

**GAUGE:** Each motif measures 5" square.

**MOTIF (make 120):** Starting at center with color E and size H hook, ch 3. Join with sl st to form ring. **1st rnd:** Work 8 sc in ring; join with sl st to 1st sc. Break off. **2nd rnd:** With M, sl st in any sc, ch 3, work 3 dc in same sc, drop lp from hook, insert hook in top of ch 3 and draw dropped lp through lp on hook so that sts puff out toward you (popcorn made); * ch 1, work 4 dc in next sc, drop lp from hook, insert hook in 1st dc of group and complete popcorn as before. Repeat from * 6 times more (8 popcorns), ch 1; join to top of 1st popcorn. Break off. **3rd rnd:** With N, sl st in any ch-1 sp, work popcorn, (ch 2, popcorn in next ch-1 sp) 7 times, ch 2; join. Break off. **4th rnd:** With E, sl st in any ch-2 sp, ch 3, work 2 dc in same sp, * ch 1, in next sp work (3 dc, ch 3 and 3 dc) for corner, ch 1, 3 dc in next sp. Repeat from * twice more; ch 1, work corner in next sp, ch 1; join. Break off. **5th rnd:** With L, sl st in a corner sp, ch 3, in same sp work (2 dc, ch 3 and 3 dc) for 1st corner, * (ch 1, 3 dc in next ch-1 sp) twice; ch 1, in next corner sp work (3 dc, ch 3 and 3 dc) for another corner. Repeat from * twice more; (ch 1, 3 dc in next sp) twice, ch 1; join. Break off. **6th rnd:** With E, sl st in a corner sp, work corner, * ch 1, 3 dc in next sp. Repeat from * to next corner sp, ch 1, work corner in corner sp. Continue in pattern, ch 1; join. Break off.

**JOINING:** Arrange motifs 10 wide by 12 long and sew tog neatly, working through outer lps only of last rnd.

**BORDER:** With G hook repeat 6th rnd once each with E, L, M and N.

# AUTUMN DAISY
# CROCHETED AFGHAN

Blazing fall colors highlight two flower motifs—one flat, one raised. The golden-eyed daisy has thick popcorn-stitch petals.

**SIZE:** 45½" x 59½".

**MATERIALS:** Brunswick Windrush (Orlon acrylic knitting-worsted-weight yarn). 7 (4-ounce) skeins ecru No. 90100 (color E), 2 skeins each café au lait (medium brown) No. 90290 (C), autumn (orange) No. 9064 (A) and persimmon (gold) No. 9004 (P); aluminum crochet hook size G (or international hook size 4:50 mm) or the size that will give you the correct gauge.

**GAUGE:** Each motif measures 3½" square.

**FIRST MOTIF (make 68):** Starting at center with color P, ch 4. Join with sl st to form ring. **1st rnd:** Ch 3, work 15 dc in ring (16 dc, counting ch 3 as 1 dc); join with sl st in top of ch 3. Break off. **2nd rnd:** With E, sl st in back lp of any dc; ch 4, work 4 tr in same place as sl st, drop lp from hook, insert hook in top of ch 4 and pull dropped lp through lp on hook so that sts puff out toward you (1st popcorn made); ch 2, skip next dc, * work 5 tr in back lp of next dc, drop lp from hook, insert hook in top of 1st tr of group and complete popcorn as before, ch 2, skip next dc. Repeat from * around (8 popcorns); join. Break off. **3rd rnd:** With C, sl st in any ch-2 sp, ch 3, work 3 dc in same sp; work (1 dc, 2 tr, ch 3, 2 tr and 1 dc) in next ch-2 sp (corner made); * work 4 dc in next sp, work corner in next sp. Repeat from * twice more; join. Break off.

**SECOND MOTIF (make 68):** Starting at center with C, ch 6. Join with sl st to form ring. **1st rnd:** Work 16 sc in ring; join. Break off. **2nd rnd:** With A, sl st in any sc; ch 4, y o twice, insert hook in same place as sl st, y o and draw through, (y o and draw through 2 lps on hook) twice, y o twice, insert hook in next sc, y o and drop lp through, (y o and draw through 2 lps on hook) twice, y o twice, insert hook in same st, y o and draw lp through, (y o and draw through 2 lps) twice, y o and draw through all 4 lps on hook (1st cl made); ch 2; * y o twice, insert hook in next st, y o and draw lp through, (y o and draw through 2 lps) twice, y o twice, insert hook in same st, y o and draw lp through, (y o and draw through 2 lps) twice. Repeat from * once more, y o and draw through all 5 lps on hook (another cl made), ch 2. Repeat from * around (8 cl); join. Break off. **3rd rnd:** With E, repeat 3rd rnd of First Motif.

**THIRD MOTIF (make 85):** With E, work as for Second Motif.

**JOINING:** Arrange motifs 13 wide by 17 long, following photograph for placement, and having center area made up of third motifs 5 wide by 9 long. Sew tog neatly, working through outer lp of each st.

# GARDENIA LACE CROCHETED LAP THROW

Two floral granny motifs—one a gardenia with three tiers of rippling petals—are arranged in a checkerboard pattern. Tiny four-leaf clovers form a decorative border.

**SIZE:** About 32" x 50".

**MATERIALS:** Lion Brand Sportelle (acrylic sportweight yarn), 12 (2-ounce) skeins eggshell No. 99; aluminum crochet hook size E (or international hook size 3:50 mm) or the size that will give you the correct gauge.

**GAUGE:** Each motif measures 3" square.

**MOTIF A (make 68):** Starting at center, ch 6. Join with sl st to form ring. **1st rnd:** Ch 5, (dc in ring, ch 2) 7 times; join with sl st in 3rd ch of ch 5 and mark st with pin (8 ch-2 lps). **2nd rnd:** In each lp work (sc, 3 dc and sc). Join with sl st in 1st sc (8 petals). **3rd rnd:** Ch 1, reaching hook behind work, sc in marked st on 1st rnd, * ch 3, fold petal forward and sc in back lp only of next dc of 1st rnd. Repeat from * 6 times more, ch 3; join to 1st sc (8 lps behind petals). **4th rnd:** In each lp work (sc, h dc, 3 dc, h dc and sc); join to 1st sc (2nd rnd of 8 petals behind 1st petal rnd). **5th rnd:** Ch 1, reaching hook behind work, sc in back lp only of 1st sc of 3rd rnd, * ch 4, fold petal forward, sc in back lp of next sc of 3rd rnd. Repeat from * 6 times more, ch 4; join to 1st sc (8 lps behind petals). **6th rnd:** In each lp work (sc, h dc, 5 dc, h dc and sc); join to 1st sc (3rd rnd of petals behind 2nd petal rnd). **7th rnd:** Ch 1, reaching hook behind work, sc in back lp of 1st sc of 5th rnd, * ch 5, fold petal forward, sc in back lp of next sc of 5th rnd. Repeat from * 6 times more, ch 5; join to 1st sc. **8th rnd:** Ch 3, work 8 dc in 1st lp, work 9-dc group in each lp around; join to top of ch 3. **9th rnd:** Sl st to center dc of 1st group, sc in this dc, * ch 7, in center of next group work (3 dc, ch 3 and 3 dc) for corner; ch 7, sc in center of next group. Repeat from * twice more, ch 7, work corner in next group, ch 7; join to 1st dc. Break off.

**MOTIF B (make 67):** Work same as for Motif A through 2nd rnd. **3rd rnd:** Sl st to center dc of next 3-dc group, sc in this dc, ch 5, (sc in center of next group, ch 5) 7 times; join to 1st sc. **4th and 5th rnds:** Work same as for 8th and 9th rnds of Motif A. Break off.

**JOINING:** Neatly sew squares tog, working through outer lps only of last rnd, arranging them as follows: Alternate motifs in checkerboard fashion, 9 squares across and 15 down, placing Motif-A squares in corners.

**BORDER:** First make 128 four-leaf clovers as follows: Starting at center, ch 4, join to form ring. * Ch 2, 3 dc in ring, ch 2, sl st in ring. Repeat from * 3 times more. Break off. Set clovers aside. Now start border: **1st rnd:** Sl st in a corner sp of afghan, ch 3, work 4 dc in corner sp, dc in next 3 dc of motif, 6 dc in each of next 2 lps, dc in next 3 dc, * dc in corner sp of motif, dc corner sp of adjoining motif, dc in next 3 dc, 6 dc in each of next 2 lps, dc in next 3 dc. Repeat from * to next corner sp on afghan, work 5 dc in corner sp. Continue around in this manner, working other 3 edges to match 1st edge; join to ch 3. **2nd rnd:** Ch 5, skip next dc, sl st in next dc (center st of corner), ch 5, skip next dc, sl st in next dc, * ch 5, skip next 3 dc, dc in next dc. Repeat from * to within 2 dc of next 5-dc corner group, ch 5, skip 2 dc, sl st in 1st dc of group, ch 5, skip next dc, sl st in center dc, ch 5, skip next dc, sl st in next dc. Continue around in this manner; join. **3rd rnd:** Sl st to center of 1st ch-5 lp, * ch 5, sl st in center of next lp. Repeat from * around, ending with ch 5; join. **4th rnd:** Work 7 dc in next ch-5 lp (corner), 7 dc in next lp, * skip next lp, 7 dc in next lp. Repeat from * around, ending with ch 5; join. **4th rnd:** Work 7 dc in next ch-5 lp (corner), 7 dc in next lp, * skip next lp, 7 dc in next lp. Repeat from * to lp before next corner lp, skip lp before corner lp, work 14 dc in corner lp, skip next lp, 7 dc in next lp. Continue in this manner, working 7 dc in every other lp along edges, 7 dc in each of the 3 lps around 3rd corner, then working 4th corner as 2nd corner and 7 dc in last lp of rnd; join. **5th rnd:** * Ch 4, sl st in one leaf of clover, ch 1, sl st in center dc of next 7-dc group, ch 1, sl st in adjoining leaf of same clover, ch 4, sl st in next sp between two groups. Repeat from * around. Break off.

# CRESTS AND EMBLEMS CROCHETED AFGHAN

Knights' royal pennants are suggested by an imaginative combination of motifs in four different sizes and designs with two unusual joining bands and chain-loop picoted edging.

**SIZE:** About 46" x 68".

**MATERIALS:** Bucilla Winsom (Orlon acrylic lightweight knitting-worsted-weight yarn), 5 (2-ounce) skeins each black No. 350 (B) and royal blue No. 292 (R), 4 skeins each coffee No. 376 (C) and Lapis Blue No. 310 (P), 3 skeins each white No. 1 (W), almond No. 377 (S) and olive green No. 360 (G); aluminum crochet hook size H (or international size 5:00 mm) or the size that will give you the correct gauge; tapestry needle; 6 bobbins.

**GAUGE:** 4 sc = 1"; 4 rows sc = 1".

**TO CHANGE COLORS:** To attach new color, work last st of old color until 2 lps remain on hook, push both lps far back on hook and make lp on hook with new color. Draw lp of new color through both lps of old color. (If new color has been attached previously, draw it through both lps of old color.) If you are going to use the old color again after next few sts, carry it along top of piece and work over it. If you will not be using that color again until next row, instead of working over it wind yarn on bobbin and let it hang on wrong side of piece until you need it again.

**SQUARE MOTIF No. 1 (make 6):** Work only in back lp of each st throughout. Starting at center with B, ch 6. Join with sl st to form ring. **1st rnd:** Ch 1, work 12 sc in ring; join with sl st to 1st sc. **2nd rnd:** (Ch 7, sl st in same place as last sl st, sl st in each of next 3 sc) 3 times; ch 7, sl st in same place as sl st, sl st in last 2 sc. **3rd rnd:** (Work 11 sc in next ch-7 lp, skip next 2 sl sts, sl st in next sl st) 4 times. Break off B, attach S. **4th rnd:** Skip 1st sc, (sc in each of next 2 sc, h dc in next sc, 2 dc in next sc, 3 dc in next sc, 2 dc in next sc, h dc in next sc, sc in each of next 2 sc, skip next sc, sl st in sl st, skip next sc) 4 times; join to 1st sc. Break off. **5th rnd:** Make lp with P. (Sc in each of next 3 sts, 2 sc in each of next 5 sts, sc in each of next 3 sts, skip next sc, sl st in next sl st, skip next st) 4 times; join to 1st sc (68 sts). Break off. **6th rnd:** Make lp with R. (Sc in each of next 3 sc, 2 h dc in next st, 2 dc in each of next 6 sts, 2 h dc in next st, sc in each of next 4 sts, skip next sl st, sc in next st) 4 times; join (96 sts). Break off. **7th rnd:** With B, sc in each of next 21 sts, (skip last st of petal and 1st st of next petal, sc in next st and mark with pin, sc in next 21 sts) 3 times; skip next 2 sc, sc in next st and mark this st; join (88 sc). Break off. **8th rnd:** With W, sl st in any marked st, ch 4, * dc in next sc, h dc in next sc, sc in each of next 5 sc, h dc in each of next 2 sc, dc in next sc, 3 dc in next sc (corner group), dc in next sc, h dc in each of next 2 sc, sc in each of next 5 sc, h dc in next sc, dc in next sc, tr in next (marked) sc. Repeat from * 3 times more, omitting last tr; join with sl st in top of ch 4 (96 sts). **9th rnd:** Draw up lp in each of next 2 sts, y o and draw through both lps on hook (1st dec), (sc in each st to center st of corner, 3 sc in corner st, sc in each st to within 2 sts of next tr, dec 1 st, sc in tr, dec 1 st) 4 times, omitting last sc and last dec on last repeat; join (96 sts). Break off. **10th rnd:** With R, sc in each st around, working 3 sc in center st of each corner group; join (104 sts). Break off. **11th rnd:** With B, repeat 10th rnd (108 sc). Break off. Block motif 7½" square.

**RECTANGULAR MOTIF No. 2 (make 6):** Work only in back lp of each st throughout. Motif consists of 2 small squares joined to form rectangle.

**Small Square:** Starting at center with C, ch 6. Join with sl st to form ring. **1st rnd:** Ch 1, work 12 sc in ring; join with sl st to 1st sc. Break off. **2nd rnd:** Make lp on hook with W. (With W, sc in each of next 2 sc; with S (see "To Change Colors," page 17), work 3 sc in next sc) 4 times, changing to W in last st (20 sc). **3rd rnd:** (With W, work 2 sc in each of next 2 sc; with S, work 2 sc in each of next 3 sc) 4 times, changing to W in last st (40 sc). Break off S. **4th rnd:** With W only, sc in each sc around; join. Break off. **5th rnd:** Make lp on hook with S, y o, dc in any sc on last rnd, dc in each dc around, increasing 4 dc as evenly spaced as possible (44 dc); join. Break off. **6th rnd:** With P, work dc in any dc, * 3 tr in next dc (corner), dc in each of next 2 dc, h dc in next dc, sc in each of next 5 dc, dc in each of next 2 dc. Repeat from * 3 times more, ending last repeat with 1 dc; join. Break off. Make another small square and sew both squares tog to form rectangle. **Border:** With B, work sc evenly around motif, working 3 sc in each corner. Block motif to 5½" x 10½".

**SQUARE MOTIF No. 3 (make 6):** Work only in back lp of each st throughout. Starting at center with P, ch 6. Join with sl st to form ring. **1st rnd:** Ch 1, work 12 sc in ring; join with sl st to 1st sc. **2nd rnd:** Ch 3, dc in each of next 2 sc, ch 5, (dc in each of next 3 sc, ch 5) 3 times; join with sl st in top of ch 3. Break off. **3rd rnd:** Make lp on hook with R; y o, dc in each of next 2 dc, * dc in each of next 2 ch; in next ch (corner) work dc, ch 3 and dc; dc in each of next 2 ch; dc in each of next 3 dc. Repeat from * 3 times more, omitting last 2 dc on last repeat; join. Break off. **4th rnd:** With S, dc in each of next 4 dc, (dc in next ch; in corner ch work dc, ch 3 and dc; dc in next ch, dc in next 9 dc) 3 times; dc in next ch, work corner in next ch, dc in next ch, dc in next 5 dc; join. Break off. **5th rnd:** With G, dc in each of next 5 dc, (dc in next ch, work corner in next ch, dc in next ch, dc in next 13 dc) 3 times; dc in next ch, work corner in next ch, dc in next ch, dc in next 8 dc; join. Break off. Work triangles on sides of square to form larger squares as follows:

**1st row:** With right side facing you, using C, dc in 1st 17 dc after any corner sp; ch 3, turn. **2nd row:** Skip 1st 3 dc, dc in next 11 dc, skip next 2 dc, dc in last dc; ch 3, turn. **3rd row:** Skip 1st 3 dc, dc in next 7 dc, skip next 2 dc, dc in last dc; ch 3, turn. **4th row:** Skip 1st 3 dc, dc in each of next 3 dc, skip next 2 dc, dc in last dc; ch 3, turn. **5th row:** Skip 1st 2 dc, dc in next dc (corner), skip next dc, dc in last dc. Break off. Work triangle across remaining 3 sides of square.

**Border: 1st rnd:** With right side facing you and starting in any corner, with P (work 3 dc in corner st, 2 dc over end of each next 5 rows, 2 dc in next color G sp, 2 dc over end of each of next 5 rows) 4 times; join. Break off. **2nd rnd:** With W, sc in each st around, working 3 sc in center st of each corner; join. Break off. **3rd rnd:** With R, work dc in each st around, working 3 dc in center st of each corner; join. Break off. **4th rnd:** With B, repeat 2nd rnd. Break off. Block motif to 10½″ square.

**RECTANGULAR MOTIF No. 4 (make 6):** Work in both lps of each st throughout. Starting at 1 long edge of rectangle with R, ch 50 to measure about 13″. **1st row:** Work sc in 2nd ch from hook and in each ch across (49 sc); ch 1, turn. Wind 3 bobbins each W, R and S, and 2 bobbins P. **2nd row:** With ball R, sc in each of 1st 12 sc; with 1 bobbin S (see "To Change Colors," page 17), sc in each of next 2 sc; with 1 bobbin W, sc in each of next 2 sc; with 1 bobbin R, sc in each of next 6 sc; with 1 bobbin P, sc in each of next 5 sc; with another bobbin R, sc in each of next 6 sc; with 2nd bobbin W, sc in each of next 2 sc; with 2nd bobbin S, sc in each of next 2 sc; with 3rd bobbin R, sc in remaining 12 sc, ch 1, turn. **3rd row:** Work 11 R sc, 2 S, 2 W, 6 R, 7 P, 6 R, 2 W, 2 S, 11 R; ch 1, turn. **4th row:** Work 10 R sc, 2 S, 2 W, 6 R, 9 P, 6 R, 2 W, 2 S, 10 R; ch 1, turn. **5th row:** Work 9 R sc, 2 S, 2 W, 6 R, 5 P; with 3rd bobbin S, work 1 sc; with 2nd bobbin P, work 5 sc; work 6 R, 2 W, 2 S, 9 R; ch 1, turn. **6th row:** Work 8 R sc, 2 S, 2 W, 6 R, 5 P, 3 S, 5 P, 6 R, 2 W, 2 S, 8 R; ch 1, turn.

Work 3 more rows, working 2 more center S sts each row and 1 less R st at each end of each row.

**10th row:** Work 4 R, 2 S, 2 W, 6 R, 5 P, 5 S; with 3rd bobbin W, work 1 sc; work 5 S, 5 P, 6 R, 2 W, 2 S, 4 R; ch 1, turn.

Work 3 more rows, working 2 more center W sts each row and 1 less R st at each end of each row.

**14th row:** Work 2 S, 2 W; work 6 R sc; work 5 P, 5 S, 4 W; with B, work 1 sc; work 4 W, 5 S, 5 P, 6 R, 2 W, 2 S; ch 1, turn.

Work 2 more rows, working 2 more center B sts each row and 1 less S st at each end of each row.

**17th row:** Work 1 S, 2 W, 6 R, 5 P, 5 S, 4 W, 3 B, 4 W, 5 S, 5 P, 6 R, 2 W, 1 S; ch 1, turn.

Starting with 14th row, follow pattern back to 2nd row. Break off bobbins. **Next row:** Work with R, sc in each sc across. Break off.

**Border:** With right side facing you and in back lp only of each st. **1st rnd:** With W, work sc evenly around motif, working 3 sc in each corner; join. Break off. **2nd rnd:** With R, work sc in each sc around, working 3 sc in center st at each corner; join. Break off. **3rd rnd:** With B, repeat 2nd rnd. Break off. Block motif to 7½″ x 14½″.

**RIGHT ANGLE MOTIF No. 5 (make 6):** Work in both lps of each st throughout. Motif consists of two 2½″-wide strips joined to form right angle.

**First Strip:** Starting at 1 end of strip with G, ch 8. **1st row:** Sc in 2nd ch from hook and in each ch across (7 sc); ch 1, turn.

**2nd row:** Sc in each of next 3 sc; with P (see "To Change Colors," page 17), sc in next sc; with G, sc in each of next 3 sc; ch 1, turn. Continue to work even in sc as follows: **3rd row:** Work 2 G sc, 3 P, 2 G; ch 1, turn. **4th and 5th rows:** Work 1 G sc, 5 P, 1 G; ch 1, turn. **6th row:** Repeat 3rd row. **7th row:** Work 3 G sc, 1 P, 3 G; ch 1, turn. **8th and 9th rows:** Work 7 G sc; ch 1, turn. Repeat 2nd through 9th rows 3 times more or until strip is same length as 1 side of Motif No. 1 without B border. Break off.

**Second Strip:** Work as for First Strip, repeating 2nd through 9th rows until strip is 2½″ longer than First Strip. Break off. Sew strips tog to form right angle with inner edges same length.

**Border:** With right side facing you, with B, work 1 row sc evenly around angle, working 3 sc in each corner; join. Break off. Block motif 2½″ wide and to fit around 2 adjacent sides of Motif No. 1.

**RECTANGULAR MOTIF No. 6 (make 6):** Work only in back lp of each st throughout. Starting at 1 end of rectangular strip with C, ch 11. **1st row:** Dc in 4th ch from hook and in each remaining ch across (9 dc, counting turning ch as 1 dc); ch 1, turn. **2nd row:** Sc in each of 1st 2 dc, h dc in next dc, dc in next dc, tr in next dc, dc in next dc, h dc in next dc, sc in each of last 2 dc; drop C, attach B and ch 1, turn. **3rd row:** Draw up lp in each of 1st 2 sts, y o and draw through all 3 lps on hook (1 sc dec), sc in each of next 2 sts, 3 sc in next (center) st, sc in each of next 2 sts, dec 1 sc over last 2 sts; ch 1, turn. Repeating 3rd row for pattern, work in stripes of 2 rows each of B and C until strip is ¼″ less than length of Motif No. 4 without B border. Ch 3, turn at end of last row. **Next row:** Skip 1st dc, dc in next sc, h dc in next sc, sc in next sc, sl st in next (center) sc, sc in next sc, h dc in next sc, dc in each of last 2 sc. Break off.

**Border:** With right side facing you, with B, work 1 row sc evenly around strip, working 3 sc in each corner; join. Break off. Block motif to 2½″ x 14½″.

**ASSEMBLING:** Following diagram (page 20), sew motifs tog with B, whipstitching through back lp only of each st.

**BORDER STRIPS:** Work only in back lp of each st throughout.

**SIDE STRIP (make 2):** Starting at 1 end of strip with C, ch 13. **1st row:** Dc in 4th ch from hook and in each remaining ch across (11 dc); ch 1, turn. **2nd row:** Sc in each of 1st 2 dc, h dc in next dc, dc in each of next 2 dc, tr in next dc, dc in each of next 2 dc, h dc in next dc, sc in each of last 2 dc. Drop C, attach B and ch 1, turn. **3rd row:** Dec 1 sc, sc in each of next 3 sts, 3 sc in next (center) st, sc in each of next 3 sts, dec 1 sc; ch 1, turn. Repeating 3rd row for pattern, work in stripes as for Motif No. 6

until border is same length as assembled motifs; ch 3, turn. **Next row:** Skip 1st sc, dc in each of next 2 sc, h dc in next sc, sc in next sc, sl st in next sc, sc in next sc, h dc in next sc, dc in each of last 3 dc. Break off. **Border:** With B, work sc evenly across 1 long edge (inner edge) of strip. Sew inner edge of each strip to long edges of afghan.

**END STRIP (make 2):** Work as for Side Strip until strip is width of assembled piece; ch 3, turn. Repeat last row of Side Strip. Break off. **Border:** Leaving 3" free at each end of 1 long edge of strip, with B work sc evenly across long edge (inner edge). Sew inner edge of each strip to ends of afghan, sewing the 3" areas without border to ends of Side Strips.

**EDGING: 1st rnd:** With right side facing you, with B work sc evenly around afghan, working 3 sc in each corner; join. **2nd rnd:** * Sc in each of next 5 sc, ch 5, sl st in 5th ch from hook (picot). Repeat from * around; join. Break off.

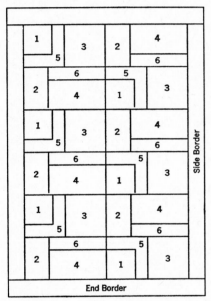

**CRESTS AND EMBLEMS AFGHAN**

# ROMAN-STRIPE CROCHETED AFGHAN

Worked diagonally from one corner, the bold bands of different widths provide a good way to use up odds and ends of yarn.

**SIZE:** About 61" square.

**MATERIALS:** Knitting-worsted-weight yarn, 40 ounces assorted colors, including 8 ounce cream for border and tassels; aluminum crochet hook size K (or international hook size 7:00 mm) or the size that will give you the correct gauge.

**GAUGE:** 3 sts = 1".

Afghan is crocheted on the bias. Work in stripes of 1 to 5 rows in colors of your choice as follows: Starting at corner, ch 2. **1st row:** Work (h dc, sc and h dc) in 2nd ch from hook; ch 1, turn.

2nd row: Work (h dc and sc) in 1st st (1st inc made); h dc in next st, (sc and h dc) in last st (2nd inc made); ch 1, turn. 3rd row: 1st inc in 1st st; work 1 h dc, 1 sc, 1 h dc; work 2nd inc in last st (last st worked is lower edge; mark lower edge with pin); ch 1, turn. 4th row: 1st inc in 1st st; 1 h dc, * 1 sc, 1 h dc. Repeat from * to last st, 2nd inc in last st; ch 1, turn.

Repeating 4th row for pattern st, work until lower edge (marked with pin) measures about 59" from beg, or 2" les than desired finished side to allow for border.

Dec as follows: Next row: Draw up lp in each of 1st 2 sts, y o and draw through all 3 lps on hook (dec made); 1 sc, * 1 h dc, 1 sc. Repeat from * to last 2 sts; dec as before; ch 1, turn. Repeat last row until 3 sts remain. Last row: Draw up lp in each of 3 remaining sts, y o and draw through all 4 lps on hook. Break off.

BORDER: With cream, sc evenly around entire outer edge of afghan, working 3 sc in each corner; at end of rnd, join with sl st to 1st sc. Repeat this rnd 4 times more. Break off.

TASSELS (make 4): Wrap cream 25 times around 7" long strip of cardboard. Cut strands at one end and remove cardboard. Open strands and tie together at center. Fold in half again and tie 1" below folded end. Trim ends to even length.

# FENCED FIELDS CROCHETED AFGHAN

The geometric patterns of flat farmlands seen from the air inspired this design. There are fifteen units with matching borders and the joinings form the "fences."

SIZE: About 52" x 70", not including fringe.

MATERIALS: Knitting-worsted-weight yarn, 12 ounces each pale orange (color A) and pale yellow (B); 8 ounces each tangerine (C) and coffee brown (D); 4 ounces each cream (E), dark brown (F), bud green (G), toast (H), Kelly green (I), gold (J) and aqua (K); aluminum crochet hook size G (or international size 4:50 mm) or the size that will give you the correct gauge.

GAUGE: 9 sts = 2"; 4 rows = 1". Large "field" (or rectangle) with fence measures 7½" x 11¼". Small "field" (or square) with fence measures 3¾" square. Large field plus border, or group of 6 small fields plus border, each measures 13" x 16½".

**Note:** Each st has 2 horizontal and parallel lps on top. Normally, when making a st both of these lps are worked into. When working this afghan, however, in order to form ridges representing "plowed fields," usually only 1 of the 2 lps is worked into. When directions say, "Work into front lp of each st," you must work into the lp that is closest to you. When directions say, "Work into back lp of each st," you must work into the lp that is behind the one closest to you.

**LARGE FIELD (make 8):** With A ch 36. **1st row (right side):** Sc in 2nd ch from hook and in each ch across (35 sc). Drop A lp, do not turn. **2nd row (right side):** Make lp on hook with B and, working in back lp of each st, sc in 1st sc at beg of last row and in each sc across. Drop B lp, pick up A lp; ch 1, turn. **3rd row (wrong side):** With A, working in front lp of each st, sc in each sc across. Drop A lp, pick up B lp at beg of row; ch 1, do not turn. **4th row (wrong side):** With B, working in front lp of each st, sc in each sc across (ridges are forming on right side). Drop B lp, pick up A lp; ch 1, turn. **5th row (right side):** With A, working in back lp of each st, sc in each sc across. Drop A lp, pick up B lp; ch 1, do not turn. **6th row (right side):** With B, working in back lp of each st, sc in each sc across. Drop B lp, pick up A lp; ch 1, turn. Repeat 3rd through 6th rows for pattern until 44 rows have been completed in all. Break off. Block piece to 7¼" x 11".

**Border: 1st rnd ("fence" rnd):** With right side facing you, starting at 1 corner with C and working across end of field, make lp on hook, * sc in each of next 3 sts, insert hook from front to back in st 2 rows below next st, y o and draw up lp so that it lies flat against work, y o and draw through both lps on hook (long sc made); skip st behind long sc. Repeat from * to next corner, working long sc at corner on a diagonal. Working across side of field, ** sc over end st of each of next 3 rows, work long sc over 2 sts of next row. Repeat from ** to next corner, working long sc at corner on a diagonal. Continue in this manner across remaining 2 sides; join with sl st. Break off; turn. **2nd rnd (wrong side):** With E, working in front lp of each st, sc in each st around, working 3 sc in diagonal st at each corner; join. Break off. **3rd rnd (wrong side):** With F, working in front lp of each st, sc in each st around, working 3 sc in center st at each corner; join. Break off. **4th through 12th rnds:** Repeat 3rd rnd once each with G, A, H, B, I, J and K, then twice with D.

**SMALL FIELD (make 42): Note:** Six small fields will be joined to form one large field. Before starting, plan color combin-

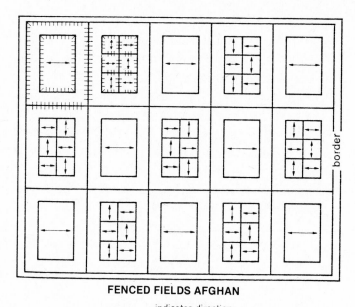

**FENCED FIELDS AFGHAN**

—→ indicates direction of striped rows

+++++++ fence rows

ations as desired, using 2 colors for each small field. With 1st color, ch 17. Work as for large field until 12 rows have been completed. Break off.

**TO JOIN SMALL FIELDS: 1st rnd (fence rnd):** Following diagram for placement, place 6 small fields tog to form a large field. Join adjacent edges as follows: With C make lp on hook. Hold 2 fields with wrong sides tog; working through both thicknesses and starting at one corner, * sc in each of next 3 sts, work long sc 1 row below next st (insert hook right through both pieces), drawing up lp long enough so that long sc will lie flat on each field when pieces are opened and laid flat. Repeat from * twice more, sc in each of last 3 sc. Break off. Join 3rd field to 2nd field to form strip. Make another strip. Join strips with fence pattern along center. Large field formed of 6 small fields.

**Border:** Work as for large field border.

**LARGE FENCES: (to join large fields):** Following diagram for placement of fields, with C join 3 strips of 5 fields each in fence pattern. Then join strips in same manner to form afghan.

**EDGING: 1st rnd:** With C repeat 1st rnd of border. Break off, do not turn. **2nd rnd (right side):** With C, * working in both lps, sc in each sc around, working 3 sc in each corner; join. Break off; turn. **3rd rnd (wrong side):** With D ch 1 and, working in back lp of each st, sc in each sc around, working 3 sc in each corner; join, turn. **4th rnd (right side):** Repeat 2nd rnd, working in both lps. Break off.

Work 2 rows along each end as follows: **1st row:** With wrong side facing you, using D, sc in each sc across; ch 1, turn. Mark last row for placement of 16 tassels, 1 at each end of row and the others evenly spaced between. **2nd row:** Sc in 1st sc, ch 3, but do not skip any sts (this will form lp for tassel), * sc in next sc and in each sc to next marker, ch 3. Repeat from * across. Break off.

**FRINGE:** Make 32 tassels, 1 in each ch-3 sp as follows: Cut ten 12″ strands of D; hold tog and fold in half to form lp. Insert crochet hook from wrong to right side through a ch-3 lp, pull folded end through, draw loose ends through folded end and tighten to form knot. Trim fringe.

# HEXAGON-MOTIF CROCHETED LAP THROW

The six-sided units are worked in single and double crochet and post trebles, creating a three-dimensional effect.

**SIZE:** 36″ x 66″.

**MATERIALS:** Knitting worsted-weight yarn, 4 ounces red, 6 ounces gold, 10 ounces brown, 14 ounces green and 16 ounces blue; aluminum crochet hook size H (or international size 5:00 mm) or the size that will give you the correct gauge; tapestry needle.

**GAUGE:** Hexagon measures 8″ from 1 flat side across to opposite side. Lap robe is composed of 37 hexagons sewn together.

**HEXAGON (make 37):** Starting at center with red, ch 3 loosely. Join with sl st to form ring. **1st rnd:** Ch 3, work 11 dc in ring; join with sl st to top of ch 3 (12 dc, counting ch 3 as 1 dc).

**2nd rnd:** Ch 3, dc in same st as sl st, work 2 dc in each dc around (24 dc); join. Break off, attach gold.

**3rd rnd:** * Work 2 sc in next dc, sc in next dc, skip next dc but work a post tr around corresponding dc 2 rows below on 1st rnd as follows: Y o hook twice, insert hook from front to back and to front again around dc, y o and draw up a lp (hook is now in front of work), (y o and draw through 2 lps on hook) 3 times (post tr completed); sc in next dc. Repeat from * 5 times more (30 sc and 6 post tr); join.

**4th rnd:** Ch 3, dc in same st as sl st, 2 dc in next st, dc in each of next 3 sts, * 2 dc in each of next 2 sts for corner, dc in each of next 3 sts. Repeat from * 4 times more (42 sts); join. Break off gold, attach brown.

**5th rnd:** * Sc in next dc, 2 sc in next dc for corner, sc in each of next 2 dc, work a post tr around each of next 3 sts 2 rows below. Repeat from * 5 times more (30 sc and 18 post tr); join.

**6th rnd:** Ch 3, dc in next st, * 3 dc in next st for corner, dc in each of next 7 sts. Repeat from * 5 times more, ending last repeat with dc in each of last 5 sts (60 sts); join. Break off, attach green.

**7th rnd:** Sc in each of next 2 dc, * 3 sc in next dc for corner, sc in each of next 2 dc, work a post tr around each of next 5 sts 2 rows below, sc in each of next 2 dc. Repeat from * 5 times more, ending with 5 post trs (42 sc and 30 post tr); join.

**8th rnd:** Ch 3, dc in each of next 2 sts, * 3 dc in next st for corner, dc in each of next 11 sts. Repeat from * 5 times more, ending last repeat with dc in last 8 sts (84 dc); join. Break off, attach blue.

**9th rnd:** Sc in each of next 3 dc, * 3 sc in next dc for corner, sc in each of next 3 dc, work post tr around each of next 7 sts 2 rows below, sc in each of next 3 dc. Repeat from * 5 times more, ending last repeat with 7 post tr (54 sc and 42 post tr); join. **10th rnd:** Sc in each st around, working 3 sc in each corner (108 sc); join. Break off.

**ASSEMBLING:** With right sides facing and using blue, whip-stitch hexagons together, alternating rows of 7, 8, 7, 8, and 7 hexagons each.

23

# ROSEBUD PATTERN KNITTED AFGHAN

Seven panels make up this luxuriously textured and fringed design: four with knitted-in rosebuds, three with diagonal cables.

**SIZE:** About 52" x 52", not including fringe.

**MATERIALS:** Knitting-worsted-weight yarn, 29 ounces scarlet (color S) and 11 ounces hunter green (G); 1 pair No. 8 knitting needles (or international needles No. 5) or the size that will give you the correct gauge; for edging and assembly, aluminum crochet hook size G (or international size 4:50 mm).

**GAUGE:** In stockinette st, 4 sts = 1".

**ROSEBUD PANEL:** Starting at lower edge with S, cast on 37 sts. **To Establish Pattern:** Starting with a p row, work in stockinette st for 5 rows. **6th row (right side):** K 9, * p 5, k 9. Repeat from * once more. **7th row:** P 9, * k 5, p 9. Repeat from * once more. **8th row:** K 9, * p 2; in next st work as follows: k 1 (wrap yarn around needle twice when working this k 1), y o, k 1, y o and p 1; p next 2 sts, k 9. Repeat from * once more. **9th row:** P 9, * k 2, p 5, dropping extra wrap; k 2, p 9. Repeat from * once more. **10th row:** K 9, * p 2, k 5, p 2, k 9. Repeat from * once more. **11th row:** P 9, * k 2, p 5, k 2, p 9. Repeat from * once more. Repeat 10th and 11th rows once more. **14th row:** K 9, * p 2, k 2 tog, k 1, sl 1, k 1, psso, p 2, k 9. Repeat from * once more. **15th row:** P 9, * k 2, p 3, k 2, p 9. Repeat from * once more. **16th row:** K 9, * p 2, sl 1, k 2 tog, psso, p 2, k 9. Repeat from * once more. Repeat 7th, then 6th row.

Starting with a p row, work stockinette st for 5 rows. **24th row:** K 16, p 5, k 16. **25th row:** P 16, k 5, p 16. **26th row:** K 16; repeat from * on 8th row, ending repeat k 16. **27th row:** P 16; repeat from * on 9th row, ending repeat p 16. **28th row:** K 16, p 2, k 5, p 2, k 16. **29th row:** P 16, k 2, p 5, k 2, p 16. Repeat last 2 rows once more. **32nd row:** K 16; repeat from * on 14th row, ending repeat k 16. **33rd row:** P 16, k 2, p 3, k 2, p 16. **34th row:** K 16; repeat from * on 16th row, ending repeat k 16. **35th row:** P 16, k 5, p 16. **36th row:** K 16, p 5, k 16.

Repeat these 36 rows for pattern until panel measures about 52" from beg, ending with a 23rd pattern row. Bind off

**Edging:** With S, make lp on crochet hook and, with right side of panel facing you, sc evenly around edges, working 2 sc in each corner; join with sl st to first sc. Break off. Make 3 more panels.

**CABLE PANEL:** Starting at lower edge with G, cast on 23 sts. **1st and 3rd rows:** P across. **2nd row (right side):** K 2; * to work twist over next 2 sts, k 2 tog without slipping sts from left-hand needle, then insert right needle in first st and k, slipping both sts from left needle; k 1. Repeat from * across. **4th row:** * K 1, work twist. Repeat from * across to last 2 sts; k 2. Repeat these 4 rows for pattern until panel measures same as rosebud panel. Bind off.

**Edging:** With G, work same as for rosebud panel. Make 2 more cable panels.

**ASSEMBLING:** Hold 1 S and 1 G panel with wrong sides together. With s, work sc through top lps of matching sts along 1 side edge. Alternating S and G panels, join remaining panels.

**FRINGE:** For each fringe, from S cut eight 10" strands. Work fringe evenly spaced along upper and lower edges, changing colors to match panels.

# BLACK AND OMBRÉ KNITTED AFGHAN

Stockinette and garter stitches are used for a sophisticated, easy design reminiscent of lightning flashes in a dark sky.

stockinette st for 4 rows. Break off ombré; attach black. Continuing to work black rows (always an even number) in garter st and ombré rows in stockinette st, (work 4" black, 4 rows ombré, 1" black, 4 rows ombré, 1" black, 4 rows ombré, 4" black, 4 rows ombré) 4 times, then work 4½" black. Break off.

**SIZE:** About 50" x 65".
**MATERIALS:** Red Heart 4-ply Hand Knitting Yarn, 7 (3½-ounce) skeins black No. 12 and 2 skeins Mexicana (ombré) No. 950; 1 pair No. 10½ knitting needles (or international needles No. 2) or the size that will give you the correct gauge.
**GAUGE:** 3 sts = 1".
Starting at 1 end with black, cast on 150 sts. Work 4½" even in garter st. Break off black, attach ombré and work even in

# PINWHEEL KNITTED BEDSPREAD

Small knitted triangles make up nine-inch squares, which are then joined to form the many-colored pinwheel pattern.

SIZE: 54" x 90".

MATERIALS: Knitting-worsted-weight yarn: 44 ounces black; 3 ounces each lavender (color A), olive green (B), light turquoise (C), light natural (D), melon (E) and atomic pink (F); 2 ounces each burnt orange (G), yellow (H), cobalt blue (I), amethyst (J), taupe (K), medium orange (L), pink (M), emerald (N), eggshell (O), hot orange (P), Oxford grey (Q), dark turquoise (R), dark gold (S) and apple green (T); 1 ounce sapphire blue (U); knitting needles, 1 pair No. 8 (or international needles No. 5) or the size that will give you the correct gauge; aluminum crochet hook size J (or international size 6:50 mm); tapestry needle.

GAUGE: 4 sts = 1"; 8 rows = 1".

Note: Some of the colors specified for our spread can be purchased only in 4-ounce skeins. If you wish to substitute other colors or use other yarns you might have on hand, we give the exact amount of yarn used for each color.

The spread is composed of 15 pinwheels separated by 24 black sections. Each pinwheel consists of 4 squares (see heavily outlined blocks on Diagram 1, page 27). Each square is made up of 2 small triangles and 1 large black triangle.

PINWHEEL 1: Starting with pinwheel at upper left-hand corner of Diagram 1, work as follows:

Square 1: Triangle 1: Starting along edge X with color A, cast on 25 sts. 1st row: K across. 2nd row (right side): K 2 tog, k across. Mark last st for side edge (Y). Repeat first and 2nd rows until 1 st remains. Break off, leaving 18" for sewing. Triangle measures about 6" along side edges X and Y.

Triangle 2: With right side of first triangle facing you, starting at last st completed, with H, pick up and k 25 sts along marked edge. Repeat first and 2nd rows, completing triangle as for triangle 1; break off, leaving 2" end. Large 2-color triangle completed for half of square 1.

Triangle 3 (black): With right sides facing you, starting at last st completed, attach black and pick up and k 50 sts across long edge of 2-color triangle. K 1 row. Working in garter st, k 2 tog at beg of every row until 1 st remains. Break off, leaving 18" for sewing. Completed square should measure about 8½". Set aside.

Square 2: Work triangle 1 with B, triangle 2 with G and triangle 3 with black. Set aside completed square.

Square 3: Work triangle 1 with O, triangle 2 with J, triangle 3 with black. Set aside.

Square 4: Work triangle 1 with I, triangle 2 with T, triangle 3 with black. Set aside.

ASSEMBLING: Block each square to measure 9". Following Diagram 1 for placement, with right sides of squares 1 and 2 facing you, matching "bumps" on edges, weave 2 squares together as follows: Thread yarn remaining from triangle 1 through tapestry needle. Following Diagram 2, weave back and forth through corresponding bumps. Diagram shows three loose sewing sts near needle. Pull yarn after every 2 or 3 sts so as to hide it in the seam. Complete pinwheel in this manner. Weave in ends on wrong side.

Following Diagram 1 for colors and placement, working all unkeyed areas in black, work 14 more pinwheels.

FINISHING: With right sides facing you, following Diagram 1, weave pinwheels together.

With right side of spread facing you, working with black held double, sc evenly around sides, working 2 sc in each corner. Work 1 more rnd sc, increasing at corners to keep them flat. Break off.

**PINWHEEL BEDSPREAD**

[Diagram 1 grid with lettered squares]

| sq 1 | | sq 2 | | | | | |
| X A Y | H B G | J M B | U | D | F C P | P | |
| T I J | O 3 sq | A F Q | A G M | M E S | B | |
| sq 4 | 3 sq | | | | | |

**Diagram 1**

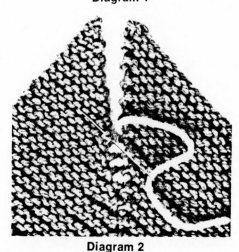

**Diagram 2**

# ROCKING HORSE PATCHWORK QUILT

Tiny florals, plaids and gingham in tones of brown and gold surround a rocking horse appliqué which has embroidered details.

Materials and directions are for a twin size quilt. For a wider quilt, add another row of squares and another band along each of the two side edges, or make the bands wider.

**SIZE:** About 59" x 84".

**MATERIALS:** 45"-wide lightweight, closely woven cottons in assorted harmonizing prints (we used mostly earth tones of browns, creams, rusts and golds), ½ yard for center rectangle (A on Diagram 1, page 28), ⅝ yard for bands B and C, 2 yards of assorted prints for 58 squares, 1½ yard for medium print gingham bands D, E, J and K, 1¼ yard for small print gingham bands F, H, I and patches G, 4 yards large print gingham for backing; 10" x

Diagram 1

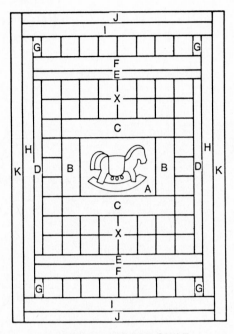

**ROCKING HORSE QUILT**

14" piece of brown velveteen for horse, scrap of raspberry velveteen for saddle blanket, scraps of cotton prints for remaining pieces; 72" x 96" quilt batt, ½" thick.

**CENTER APPLIQUÉ:** Cut one 17½" x 23" center rectangle A. Enlarge pattern, (see How to Enlarge Patterns, page 8). Cut pattern pieces, adding ¼" seams to cotton prints only (velveteen pieces are marked, all others are prints). Cut fabric pieces.

Working on ironing board, assemble and pin pieces to center of rectangle A, lapping raw velveteen edges over print seams. Turn under and press remaining print seams, clipping curves. Baste rocking horse.

Covering all edges, appliqué with close machine zigzag stitches around each piece, or work satin stitch or blanket stitch by hand. Add machine or hand embroidery to saddle blanket and around eye and work hand embroidery for harness and pupil. (See Embroidery Stitch Diagrams, page 9.)

**PATCHWORK:** Cut two 6½" x 17½" B bands and two 6½" x 34" C bands (½" seam allowance included on all patch piece dimensions). Stitch B bands to sides of center and C bands to top and bottom of center and to ends of B bands. Press all seams to one side, not open.

Diagram 2

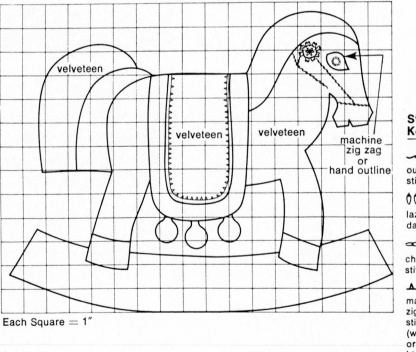

Each Square = 1"

**Stitch Key**

〜〜 outline stitch

◊◊◊ lazy daisy

⬡⬡⬡⬡⬡ chain stitch

▲▲▲ machine zig zag stitch (wide) or hand blanket stitch

28

Cut fifty-eight 6½" squares of assorted prints. Stitch 4 strips of 6 squares each and 2 strips of 9 squares each. Stitch pairs of 6-square strips together to form 2 rectangles (X). Stitch to top and bottom of assembled unit. Stitch 9-square strips to sides of unit.

Cut two 3½"-wide D bands the same length as 9-square strips and stitch in place.

Cut two 3½"-wide E bands to fit top and bottom of assembled unit; stitch.

Cut two 4½"-wide F bands the same length as E bands; stitch.

Stitch 2 strips of 8 squares each. Add 3½" x 6½" patch to ends of strips. Stitch strips to F bands.

Cut two 4"-wide H bands to fit side of unit; stitch.

Cut two 5"-wide I bands to fit top and bottom of unit; stitch.

Cut two 4"-wide J bands to fit I bands; stitch.

Cut two 4"-wide K bands to fit sides of unit; stitch. Patchwork completed.

**BACKING:** Cut 2 pieces 45" x 70". Seam 70" sides to form 70" x 89" backing.

**ASSEMBLING:** The quilt can be assembled on a frame (follow directions that come with frame) or, as the designer did, worked on a large flat surface such as a double bed or the floor.

Spread out backing wrong side up. Smooth quilt batt on top, centering it. Then center quilt top, right side up, on batting. Edges will not be even; trim when quilting has been completed.

Pin layers together in a few places to hold. Baste from center of quilt to a corner, then baste from center to opposite diagonal corner. Always starting from center of quilt to keep fabric from bunching, baste again from center to 2 opposite corners to form X, then add 4 more basting lines from center of quilt to center of each side. Piece is now ready for quilting. This can be done on a frame or in your lap, if you prefer, as the quilting design is simple.

**QUILTING:** Quilt pieces at center first, then work out toward edges. Quilt by hand in small running stitches. Quilt around edge of rocking horse motif then, very lightly with pencil, mark center A background with rows of scallops about ½" apart. Quilt scallops.

Quilt around edges of all squares and bands; quilt an X across each square and a series of X's along length of each band.

**FINISHING:** When quilting has been completed, trim backing and batting to match quilt top. Turn in ½" seam allowance all around and blindstitch. Quilt ¾" from edge to simulate binding.

# NOAH'S ARK APPLIQUÉD QUILT

This crib-size design can be adapted to fit a twin bed—or leave the center area unquilted and use it as a wall hanging.

### GENERAL DIRECTIONS

**SIZE:** The quilt shown in the photograph is crib size. When your child has outgrown a crib you can attach the crib quilt to the center of a regular bedspread by sewing all around outer edge and tacking in a few places in the center area to hold it in place.

We have included directions for making a quilt to fit a twin bed by changing the size of the border.

You can also use just the center design area, with or without a border, leave it unquilted and use it as a wall hanging.

**MATERIALS:** Use closely woven fabrics with soft texture such as calico, broadcloth, percale or muslin. Be sure fabrics are colorfast and preshrunk. It is best not to combine worn fabrics with new ones because the latter will outlast the former.

**CUTTING:** Enlarge individual patterns (see How to Enlarge Patterns, page 8) and use these as your appliqué patterns. Pin actual-size appliqué patterns onto wrong side of fabric. **Note:** In cutting pieces for appliqué, some people prefer to have the pencil line on the right side of the fabric to use as a sewing guide. Cut out pieces adding ¼" seam allowance all around. Follow placement diagram (page 31) and photograph for number of pieces to cut.

Following diagram for size, cut out ark's roof, owl's turret and background blocks or units, adding ½" seam allowance all around.

**APPLIQUÉ:** The neatest method is to press under the seam allowance; slash edges on curves to make them lie flat. Place the appliqué with edges turned under on the background blocks, following diagram for placement, and baste in place. Sew pieces in place using a regular hemming stitch or blindstitch. Use thread in color matching piece you are sewing.

If you are an experienced sewer or after you have practiced awhile, you may use short cuts such as pressing under seam allowance with your thumb and forefinger or simply pinning your appliqué in place and turning under seam allowance as you sew. It is when you use such a short-cut method to appliqué that the pencil lines on the right side of the piece are helpful.

In some places on the designs, pieces are appliquéd onto another appliqué piece such as wings on birds, etc. Sometimes it is easier to appliqué these smaller pieces in place first and then appliqué the unit to the background block. Experiment to see which way is easier for you.

**EMBROIDERY:** Some details of the designs are embroidered. Patterns or placement diagrams show placement of embroidery. The stitches are identified as follows: a black dot—French knot; broken line—chain stitch; dotted line—outline stitch; lightweight lines indicate satin stitch and show the direction the stitch is worked. (See Embroidery Stitch Diagrams page 8.)

**SETTING:** This is the process of assembling the blocks or units of the quilt top and adding any strips or borders. Following placement diagram, join blocks or units from the center out to insure smooth, unwrinkled results. Make ½" seams. Press all seams. For neater results, it is best to press both seam edges to one side instead of pressing them open.

**QUILTING DESIGNS:** You can quilt a top or leave it plain as you prefer. On the crib quilt shown there is very little quilting, just around each background block and ¼" in or out from edge of motifs. Narrow border was not quilted at all. On a twin size, where the border is larger, it would look better to quilt it. When top is completed mark it for quilting lines. You can use any simple quilting design, straight lines or straight diagonal lines ½" to 1" apart,

blocks, triangles or diamonds. Straight lines are drawn with a soft pencil and ruler. Pencil lines can be erased with any good eraser after quilting is completed. It is not necessary to mark the appliqué design area since you simply use the shape of the appliqué piece as your quilting guide. You can quilt ¼" in or out from each stitching line, or if desired quilt ¼" in *and* out from stitching lines.

**QUILTING:** Use a 72" x 90" cotton or polyester quilt batt for interlining. Amounts for backing are given under individual directions. Place quilt backing flat on the floor wrong side up, smoothing it out flat. Place batting on top, smoothing it over the backing with no wrinkles or lumps. Place the quilt top over the batting, right side up and baste all three thicknesses together. Start at the center and baste out to each of the four sides, then starting at center, baste out to the four corners. Baste all outer edges together.

You do not have to use a quilting frame or hoop but it is easier and neater to use one. They hold the work taut while you are quilting. A variety of frames and hoops is sold in art needlework departments of stores with instructions on how to mount the quilt.

If you do not use a frame, baste in several more places than have been described and quilt from the center out. You are now ready to quilt.

Quilting is usually done in the same color thread as the part to be quilted. Use close running stitches. Wherever possible, hold your left hand under quilt to direct right hand which works on top.

**FINISHING:** After quilting has been completed, remove quilt from frame. Trim lining, if necessary. You can turn under edges and slip stitch backing and top together all around or you can bind outer edges. If your top is not quilted, simply hem or bind outer edges.

**SEWING MACHINE QUILTS:** Although classic appliqué and quilting are considered handcrafts, they can be adapted to the sewing machine. When appliquéing by machine, use a zigzag machine or a machine that can do embroidery. Use a zigzag stitch to cover the edge of the appliqué piece. When setting by machine, use regular straight stitching. When quilting, use only simple designs or straight lines.

QUILT

See General Directions, also.

**SIZE:** Crib, 41" x 58"; twin, 70" x 90"; center design area measures 35" x 52".

**MATERIALS: Center design for both sizes:** 1½ yards 36"-wide fabric for background; assorted colors of fabric for blocks

Placement Diagram
Each square equals 2″

THE ARK

Place on fold

**NOAH'S ARK QUILT**

Each square = 1½″

Each square = 1½"

or units and appliqué (see placement diagram to plan amounts needed). **Crib size:** 3⅜ yards 44″-wide fabric for border and backing. **Twin size:** 3⅝ yards 44″-wide fabric for border; 72″ x 108″ sheet or 5⅛ yards 36″- or 44″-wide fabric for backing.

CUTTING: Cut center background area 36″ x 53″. **Crib size:** Cut 42″ x 59″ piece for backing; cut 2 pieces 4″ x 59″ and 2 pieces 4″ x 42″ for border. **Twin size:** Cut sheet or piece fabric so you have a piece 71″ x 91″ for backing; cut 2 side border pieces 18½″ x 91″; 2 end pieces 20″ x 36″. Note that border ends are butted, and not mitered, on twin size.

ASSEMBLING: Cut and appliqué owl, camel, hippo, lion, elephant, portholes and Noah's blocks (except for his sleeve edge and hands), giraffe (except for his neck and head which go through the roof). Embroider any details on these blocks. Embroider words "The Ark" on ship.

Following placement diagram, first join blocks. Appliqué ark to background fabric, then waves (**Note:** Only one wave pattern is given; plan size from placement diagram.) Sew blocks above ark. Appliqué roof in place, leaving opening for giraffe's head. Embroider and appliqué giraffe's head and little bird in place. Close roof opening. Appliqué owl block and his roof in place. Appliqué flag and embroider flag staff. Appliqué Noah's sleeve edge and hands in place. Center design area is now completed.

For crib size: Stitch borders to center section, mitering corners. **For twin size:** Stitch top and bottom borders to center section, then stitch side borders in place.

# PLAID AND WHITE SHEET BEDROOM ENSEMBLE

One queen- and one twin-size sheet, plus a pillowcase and some plaid fabric will produce the coordinated spread and draperies.

SIZE: Bedspread: 82″ x 112″ including 8″ ruffle along sides and foot. **Pillow:** 26″ x 33″ including 3″ ruffle. **Curtains:** Curtains shown fit 36″-wide window. Each curtain is 39″ wide x 84″ long, including 10½″ top border.

MATERIALS: Bedspread: 66″ x 104″ twin flat sheet; 6 yards 45″-wide plaid fabric; 20 yards 1″-wide bias tape. **Pillow:** 20″ x 30″ pillowcase; 1 yard 45″-wide plaid fabric; 3 yards 1″-wide bias tape. **Curtains:** 90″ x 110″ queen flat sheet; 1¾ yards 45″-wide plaid fabric; 6 yards 1″-wide bias tape; 4 small rings; 2 cup hooks; snaps for tie back (optional).

Note: Amounts given are for the actual items pictured. If you wish to make bedspread or pillow a different size or curtains to fit a window with different dimensions, recalculate amounts to suit your particular needs. Dimensions given below include ½″ seam allowance unless otherwise specified.

## BEDSPREAD

From plaid fabric, cut five 9″ x 108″ strips for ruffles and two 7″ x 105″ strips for stripes. Divide sheet into thirds lengthwise (three 22″ sections). Press under ½″ seam allowance along raw edges of each stripe. Center each stripe over 22″ divisions on sheet and stitch. Place tape over each long edge of stripes and topstitch along each edge of tape. Round corners at foot end of sheet by cutting and hemming raw edges. **Ruffles:** Sew ends of 9″ strips together to form one long strip. Make ¼″ hem along one long edge and each short end. Using large machine stitch, sew 2 rows of stitching along remaining long edge, the first ½″ and the second ¼″ from raw edge. Pull up gathers evenly and, placing seam allowance of ruffle on top of right side, pin along side and foot edges of sheet. Stitch in place. Pin tape along side and foot edges, covering seam allowance of ruffle. Turn under ends. Stitch along both edges and ends of tape.

## PILLOW

From plaid fabric, cut four 8″ x 45″ strips for ruffle. Sew ends of strips together to form ring. With wrong sides together, fold in half lengthwise to form 4″-wide ring. Using large machine stitch, sew 2 rows of stitching, the first ½″ and the second ¼″ from raw edge. Pull up gathers evenly. Placing raw edges on top of front of pillow case, pin ½″ in around lower and side edges and 4″ in from edge along open hemmed end (placing outer edge of ring even with hem at open end). Pull up gathers to fit. Baste. Turn pillowcase wrong side out and stitch ruffle along open hemmed end. Turn pillowcase right side out and, stitching through both thicknesses of pillowcase, sew remainder of ruffle in place. Mitering corners, pin and baste tape over seam allowances of ruffle, working through single thickness of pillowcase at open end and through double thickness around remaining sides. Topstitch along both sides of tape in same manner.

## CURTAINS

From sheet, cut two 40½″ x 74″ pieces for curtains, using top hem of sheet for drapery hem, and two 7″ x 12″ strips for tiebacks. From plaid fabric, cut two 14¼″ x 40½″ pieces for top borders and four 11″ x 27″ pieces for bows.

**Curtains:** With right sides together, sew top border to unhemmed 40½″ side of each curtain piece. Press seams toward borders. Make ¾″ hem along each side of each curtain. Turn upper border edges under ¼″, then turn 3″ to wrong side to form casing. Stitch.

**Bows:** With right sides together, stitch short ends of 11″ x 27″ bow pieces together to form two 11″ x 54″ strips (one for each bow). With right sides together, sew each strip lengthwise to form 5″-wide tube. Turn right side out. Fold flat with lengthwise seam along center of back. Pin, then stitch tape along both edges of front side. Cut each end on a diagonal (see photograph), turn raw edges to inside and whipstitch.

**Tiebacks:** With right sides together, sew each piece lengthwise to form tube. Turn right side out, fold flat, turn raw edges at each end to inside and baste. Topstitch around all four sides. Sew small ring to each end. Screw cup hooks into window frame at desired height. Hook rings over cup hooks. After hanging curtains, sew bow to each tieback.

# 2

# PILLOWS FOR ALL PLACES

# TWO NEEDLEPOINT PILLOWS WITH "PATCHWORK" DESIGNS

Surprisingly easy despite their intricate-seeming patterns, this handsome pair of pillows is done with just one stitch, tent.

## GENERAL DIRECTIONS

**TO PREPARE CANVAS:** Fold masking tape over edges of canvas to prevent raveling. Draw outline of square pillow on center of canvas, using a pencil or marker especially made for needlepoint. (**Note:** Do not use other felt-tipped markers, as they may run during blocking.) In same manner outline patchwork sections, following the number of spaces or stitches indicated on charts for individual pillows.

**YARN:** The yarn used to make our pillows is called needlepoint and crewel yarn, and it divides into 3 separate strands. Use 3 strands for canvas with 10 spaces per inch and 2 strands for canvas with 12 spaces per inch. You will need 1¼ yards of yarn to cover one square inch of canvas with 10 spaces per inch and one yard of yarn to cover one square inch of canvas with 12 spaces per inch. Cut yarn into 18" lengths.

**PATCHWORK DESIGNS:** We have given charts for many of the patchwork designs used in the pillows. You can use a design anywhere on the pillow and as many times as desired. In addition to our charts, work some sections or blocks in a solid color or design your own patterns. For example, work patterns of horizontal, vertical or diagonal stripes.

Before stitching, plan placement of designs and colors. This can be done by charting the entire pillow on graph paper, using colored pencils or markers instead of symbols to show color placement.

**TO READ CHARTS:** Each square on the chart indicates one

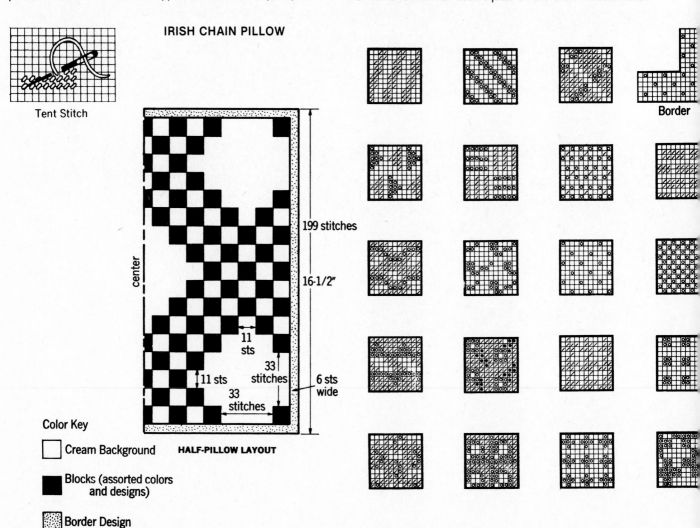

Tent Stitch

**IRISH CHAIN PILLOW**

199 stitches

16-1/2"

11 sts

33 stitches

11 sts

33 stitches

6 sts wide

center

**HALF-PILLOW LAYOUT**

**Color Key**

☐ Cream Background

■ Blocks (assorted colors and designs)

▨ Border Design

Border

IRISH CHAIN

LOG CABIN

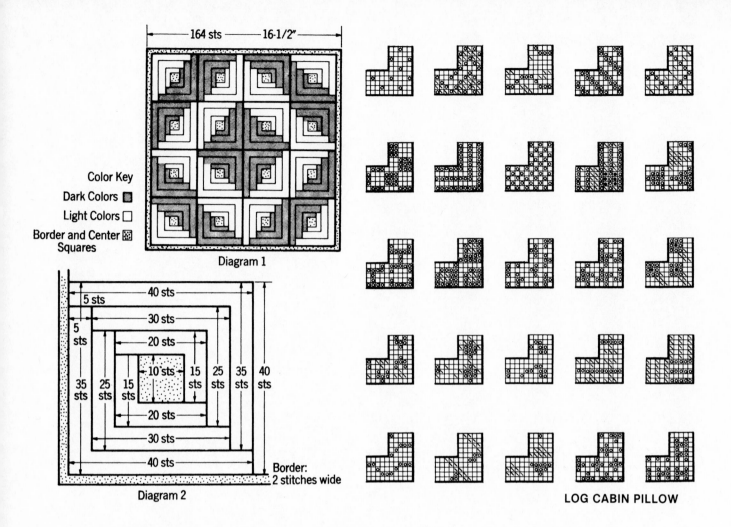

**Color Key**
Dark Colors ▨
Light Colors ☐
Border and Center ▩
Squares

**Diagram 1**

**Diagram 2**

Border: 2 stitches wide

**LOG CABIN PILLOW**

stitch. *Symbols used indicate change in color only. You can use any color combination desired.*

**TO WORK NEEDLEPOINT:** Following stitch diagram, use tent stitch throughout. Work borders first. Whenever possible work light colors before dark colors. Never knot yarn. Draw length through canvas, leaving 1" end on wrong side. Secure end by catching it in next 2 or 3 stitches. To finish yarn run it diagonally through several completed stitches on wrong side and trim.

**TO BLOCK:** Mark brown paper with carefully squared outline of pillow and place on board. Wet needlepoint thoroughly and pin it to board following outline on paper. Pin corners first, then center of each side. Continue pinning until pins are spaced about ½" apart all around. Do not remove until piece is completely dry (at least 2 days).

**TO MAKE PILLOW:** Trim canvas, leaving ½" seam allowance. Use 16" square pillow form or make inner pillow as follows: Cut 2 muslin pieces the same size as canvas. Stitch muslins together, leaving one side open. Turn, stuff and blindstitch opening. With right sides facing, stitch backing fabric to canvas, leaving 12" open along one side. Insert zipper, if desired; turn. Insert inner pillow and close zipper or blindstitch opening.

### IRISH CHAIN NEEDLEPOINT PILLOW

**SIZE:** 16½" square.

**MATERIALS:** 18" square (single-thread) needlepoint canvas with 12 spaces per inch; 3-ply Persian-type needlepoint and crewel yarn, 150 yards cream for background and 150 yards assorted colors for blocks and border; 18" square velveteen or corduroy for backing; 16" square pillow form or polyester-fiberfill stuffiing and ½ yard 45"-wide muslin for inner pillow; tapestry needle; 14" zipper (optional).

**TO START:** See General Directions. Follow diagram (page 36) for layout of half of pillow and to determine number of stitches for border, each square and areas between squares. When following L-shaped chart for border canvas, repeat pattern to next corner.

## LOG-CABIN NEEDLEPOINT PILLOW

**SIZE:** 16½" square.

**MATERIALS:** 18" square single-thread needlepoint canvas with 10 spaces per inch; 3-ply Persian-type needlepoint and crewel yarn, 40 yards of one color for border and center squares and 360 yards assorted colors for L-shaped sections; 18" square velveteen or corduroy for backing; 16" square pillow form or polyester-fiberfill stuffing and ½ yard 45"-wide muslin for inner pillow; tapestry needle; 14" zipper (optional).

**TO START:** See General Directions. Follow Diagram 1 (page 38) for placement of log-cabin motifs and light and dark colors. Follow Diagram 2 to determine number of stitches for border and each section of motif.

When following a chart, turn chart so that corner matches that of L-shaped section. Work chart, then continue to work along lengths of section in established repeat.

# BARGELLO PILLOWS WITH METALLIC ACCENTS

Glinting golden overstitches enhance the beauty of the sunburst and basket-weave patterns worked in bargello stitch.

### GREEN PILLOW (above in picture)

**SIZE:** 14" square.

**MATERIALS:** 16" square double-thread needlepoint canvas with 3 spaces per inch; Bucilla Winsom (Orlon acrylic yarn), 1 (2-ounce) skein each jade green No. 105 (color J), Fern green No. 106 (G), moss (yellow-green) No. 272 (S), emerald No. 297 (E) and almond (light olive) No. 377 (A); Bucilla Spotlight (metallic yarn), 1 (130-yard) ball gold; 16" square green velveteen for backing; 3½ yards matching velveteen piping (or an extra 36" square of velveteen and 3½ yards cord to make piping); 14" pillow form or ½ yard muslin and polyester-fiberfill stuffing to make inner pillow; tapestry needle.

**TO START:** Prepare canvas by folding masking tape over edges to prevent raveling. Find center of canvas by marking 2 crossed lines, starting from center of each side. Canvas is now divided into quarter sections.

Cut yarn into 10″ strands. Work with 6 strands Winsom throughout. Following Diagram 1, work pattern in lower right section (each square on diagram equals 1 space on canvas). Work center stitches over marked lines. Work other quarter sections to correspond, rotating Diagram 1 to follow proper placement of stitches. Then, following Diagram 2, work back stitches (see stitch diagrams) over other stitches with 1 strand of Spotlight.

PIPING: Cut 1″-wide diagonal strips of velveteen (on bias) and

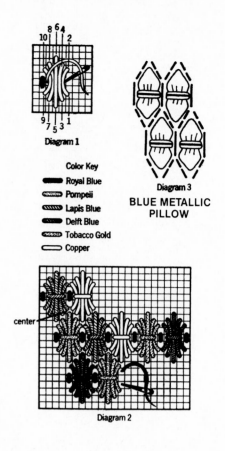

Diagram 1

Color Key
Royal Blue
Pompeii
Lapis Blue
Delft Blue
Tobacco Gold
Copper

Diagram 3
BLUE METALLIC PILLOW

Diagram 2

## GREEN METALLIC PILLOW

Color Key
Moss (S)
Fern Green (G)
Jade Green (J)
Emerald (E)
Almond (A)

Back stitch

Bargello stitch

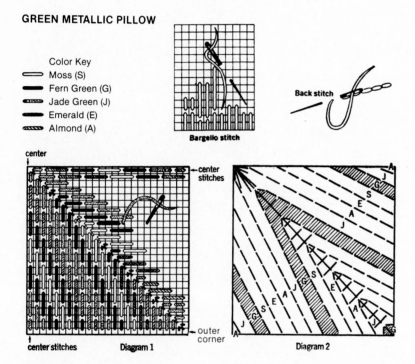

center

center stitches

outer corner

center stitches          Diagram 1

Diagram 2

sew together to make long strip. Fold and stitch over piping cord. Then follow process under Finishing.

INNER PILLOW:: Cut 2 pieces muslin size of bargello. Stitch together along 3 sides, turn, stuff and sew last side.

FINISHING: Block piece if necessary. Pin ready-made piping around bargello piece with raw edges facing outward and piping just overlapping bargello; stitch. Cut and sew ends together. With right sides facing and piping sandwiched between, stitch velveteen backing to bargello, leaving 1 side open. Turn, insert pillow form.

### BLUE PILLOW (below in picture, page 39)

SIZE: About 14″ square.

MATERIALS: 16″ square piece double-thread needlepoint canvas with 3 spaces per inch; Bucilla Winsom (Orlon acrylic yarn),

2 (2-ounce) skeins each Pompeii (rust) No. 339, Delft blue (gray-blue) No. 396, lapis blue No. 310, copper No. 382 and tobacco gold No. 340, 1 skein royal blue No. 292; Bucilla Spotlight (metallic yarn), 1 (130-yard) ball gold; 16″ square piece velveteen for backing; 3½ yards matching velveteen piping (or an extra 36″ square of velveteen and 3½ yards cord to make piping); 14″ pillow form or ½ yard muslin and polyester-fiberfill stuffing to make inner pillow; tapestry needle.

TO START: Prepare canvas as for green pillow.

Following Diagrams 1 and 2, work with 6 strands of Winsom throughout. (Each square on diagrams equals 1 space on canvas.) Then, following Diagram 3, work metallic stitches (bold line) over other stitches with 1 strand of Spotlight.

Finish as for green pillow.

# TEXTURED NEEDLEPOINT PILLOW AND CHAIR SEAT

Against a basket-weave background, you work a variety of needlepoint stitches in wool yarn to create a rich surface-texture and pattern. It's easy to make the designs larger or smaller to adapt to almost any chair seat or pillow size.

## PILLOW

**SIZE:** 18½" square. Size is adjustable.

**MATERIALS:** 23" square single-thread needlepoint canvas with 10 spaces per inch; 3-ply Persian-type needlepoint and crewel yarn, 10 (40-yard) skeins off-white (Note below); tapestry needle; ¾ yard 36"-wide off-white linen for backing; polyester-fiberfill for stuffing; 1½ yards 36"-wide muslin for pillow lining.

**Note:** If you are planning a major change in the size of the pillow, it takes about 1½ yards of yarn to cover one square inch of canvas.

Follow General Directions, chart and stitch diagrams, allowing 2¼" borders on canvas. The chart shows one fourth of pillow. Repeat chart for entire pillow.

### GENERAL DIRECTIONS

**PREPARING CANVAS:** Bind raw edges of canvas with masking tape or overcast them with sewing thread to prevent raveling.

**YARN:** The needlepoint yarn specified separates into three strands. Cut yarn into 18" lengths. **Important:** Use all three strands together for all patterns. Before starting, hold all three strands together at one end and separate them with your fingers; then, holding all three strands together again, thread needle and start your work. This is called separating or stripping yarn; it makes your work much easier and helps the stitches lie smoothly on the canvas.

**FOLLOWING CHART (page 42):** Each graph line on chart indicates one thread of canvas. Stitches indicated are worked over canvas threads. Start at center space and work buttonhole circle (see detail page 43) Work outward from center. Bands with arrows are fern stitch. Shaped motifs are buttonhole stitch, leaf stitch and double leviathan. All fill-in areas are basket weave.

**SIZE:** You can make pillow smaller or larger by working fewer pattern bands for a smaller one or by adding more pattern bands for a larger one.

**TO WORK STITCHES:** All stitch patterns interlock. Never skip a thread of canvas between patterns.

When following stitch diagrams (page 45), bring needle up at A, down at B, up at C and so on in alphabetical order, unless otherwise specified.

Needlepoint stitches used on pillow are basket weave, fern No. 1 and No. 2, leaf, buttonhole circle, half circle, upright Gobelin, and double leviathan. (Other stitches on stitch key are for chair seat.)

**Basket Weave:** See stitch diagrams. We used the basket-weave-stitch method for the background. Each section of this

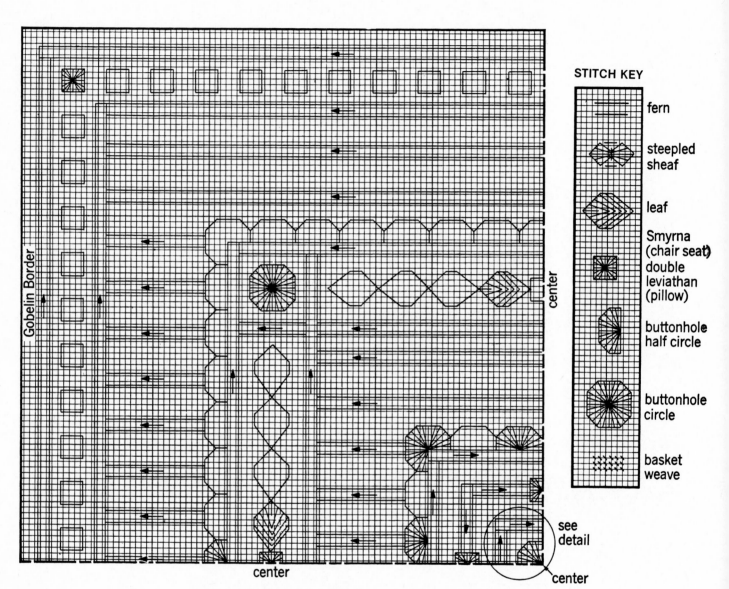

**STITCH KEY**

fern

steepled sheaf

leaf

Smyrna (chair seat)

double leviathan (pillow)

buttonhole half circle

buttonhole circle

basket weave

Gobelin Border

center

center

see detail

center

**TEXTURED PILLOW DIAGRAM**

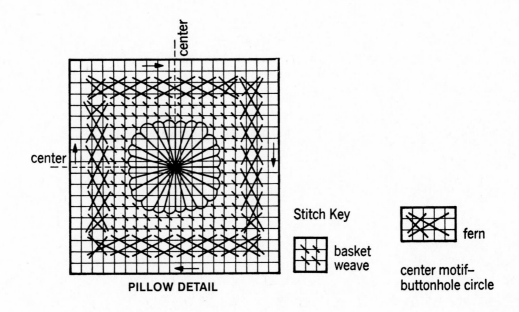

**PILLOW DETAIL**

**Stitch Key**

basket weave

fern

center motif– buttonhole circle

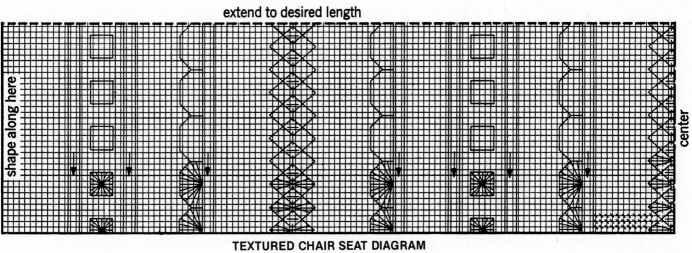

extend to desired length

shape along here

center

**TEXTURED CHAIR SEAT DIAGRAM**

pattern starts at upper left hand corner. It looks the same as half cross-stitch, tent stitch or continental stitch on right side of work, but is worked diagonally. On Diagram 2 the arrows show the direction in which to work each row. When starting a new section of the basket-weave stitch, always make sure that the stitches slant in the same direction as those on previously worked areas. This method forms a padded and durable woven-type backing and will not distort the canvas. It also fits easily around other patterns used in pillow.

**Double Leviathan:** See diagram. This stitch is worked last and is worked on top of basket-weave stitches. It can be omitted if desired, or you can add additional ones.

**Buttonhole Circle:** See diagram. Start in center of canvas for first circle. Before starting this stitch, it is advisable to enlarge center hole so that all the stitches will fit. Use a small round stick or a No. 4 knitting needle; be careful not to break canvas, just enlarge center hole a bit. **To work stitch:** Insert needle from wrong side of work at A, draw needle through to right side; then, leaving a loop of yarn long enough to reach from A to B, insert needle back in A again to wrong side. Bring needle up at B and through loop, holding loop in place.

Insert needle at A and bring out at C and over yarn. Continue working as for last stitch around entire circle. After last stitch, work 1 small stitch from Y to B to complete circle.

**Fern No. 1 and Fern No. 2:** See diagrams and work as shown. Add last 2 short stitches (Q to R and S to T) only after required length of fern stitch has been completed.

**Leaf:** See diagram and work as shown.

**Buttonhole Half Circle:** See diagram for buttonhole circle and work only half of circle. In some places, three fourths of circle is worked.

**Gobelin:** See diagram. Work Gobelin stitch for last row on chart.

**BLOCKING:** If necessary, block pillow as follows: With pencil, ruler and triangle draw the outline of pillow on brown paper; tack paper to a hard board, using rustproof pins or tacks. Dampen needlepoint, then stretch and tack at 1" intervals to the board, following outline on paper. Allow to dry thoroughly (at least 2 days) before removing from board.

**TO MAKE PILLOW:** Trim needlepoint canvas, leaving ½" seam allowance on all four sides. Cut two pieces of muslin same size as trimmed canvas. Stitch seams together, leaving opening for turning. Turn and stuff. Sew opening closed.

**TO MAKE PILLOW COVER:** Cut backing fabric same size as trimmed needlepoint. With right sides together, stitch needlepoint and backing together, leaving one side open. Turn. Insert pillow and sew opening closed.

## CHAIR SEAT

**SIZE:** 18" x 24" or desired size.

**MATERIALS:** 1 piece 25" x 31" (or size needed) single-thread needlepoint canvas with 10 spaces per inch; 3-ply Persian-type needlepoint and crewel yarn, 13 (40-yard) skeins dusty pink (see Note below); tapestry needle; polyester-fiberfill stuffing.

**Note:** If you are planning a major change in the size of the chair seat, it takes about 1½ yards of yarn to cover 1 square inch of canvas.

**TO START:** Make a paper pattern of your chair seat, then add about 1½" seam allowance on all sides. With basting thread, outline the shape and size of pattern on center of canvas. Needlepoint should be worked over entire area to basting line. This allows enough extra to turn under when fastening chair seat to backing.

Follow chart for chair seat, page 43 (see stitch key, and refer to directions for pillow). The chart shows only part of chair seat. Repeat chart to complete seat, shaping along sides to conform to basting lines. Some of the patterns shown on chart may be omitted if necessary to fit your chair seat.

**TO WORK STITCHES:** Needlepoint stitches used on chair seat are basket weave, fern No. 1 and No. 2, buttonhole half circle, Smyrna, and steepled sheaf. These last two stitches are worked on top of basket weave.

**Smyrna.** See diagram and work as shown.

**Steepled Sheaf:** See diagram and work as shown. Shaded stitch indicates first stitch of adjoining sheaf.

See pillow directions for other stitches.

**BLOCKING:** See pillow directions.

**FINISHING:** Folding excess canvas to wrong side over board used for chair seat, nail or staple needlepoint piece to board, leaving one side open. Stuff firmly, then nail last side in place.

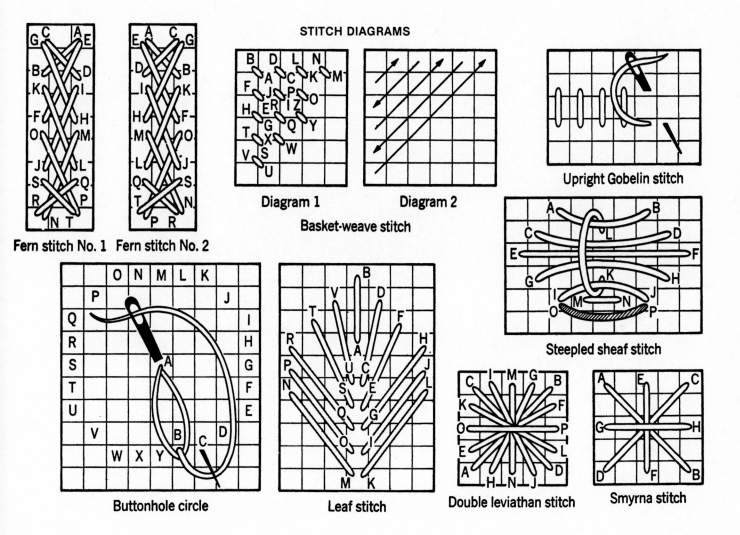

STITCH DIAGRAMS

Fern stitch No. 1    Fern stitch No. 2

Diagram 1        Diagram 2

Basket-weave stitch

Upright Gobelin stitch

Steepled sheaf stitch

Buttonhole circle

Leaf stitch

Double leviathan stitch    Smyrna stitch

# TWO DELFT-PATTERN NEEDLEPOINT PILLOWS

Each soft box pillow is a remarkably exact copy of a charming Delft tile. They're done in tent, mosaic and a few other stitches in Delft's traditional subtle blues on white.

**SIZE:** Each pillow measures about 14½" square.

**MATERIALS:** 21"-square double-thread (penelope) needlepoint canvas with 14 spaces per inch for each pillow; 3-ply Persian-type needlepoint and crewel yarn, for each pillow: 3 (40-yard) skeins grayish-white; 2 skeins each navy blue, royal blue, light blue and pale blue; tapestry needle; 18"-square piece of navy blue linen for backing; ½ yard 36"-wide unbleached muslin for lining; polyester-fiberfill stuffing; 12" zipper (optional).

**TO PREPARE CANVAS:** Tape edges to prevent raveling. Find center of canvas by basting a line from center of one edge to center of opposite edge, being careful to follow a row of spaces. Then baste another line from center of third edge to center of fourth edge. Basting threads will cross at center.

**YARN:** The yarn specified separates into three strands. Use two strands together for both pillows, and cut yarn into 18" lengths.

**STITCHES:** The center bouquet and vase on one pillow and flowers and floral corners on other one are worked mostly in tent stitch (if desired, half cross stitch, which uses less yarn, can be substituted).

The background behind the center designs are worked entirely

MOSAIC

BARGELLO

BARGELLO

PILLOW WITH GEOMETRIC CORNERS

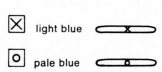

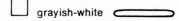
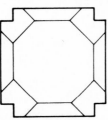

**Placement Diagram**
**Pillow with**
**Geometric Corners**

47

STITCH DIAGRAMS

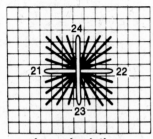

**Large Leviathan Stitch**

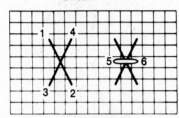

**Tied Oblong Cross Stitch**

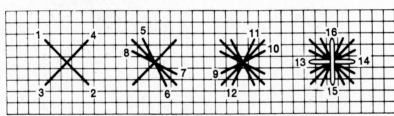

**Small Leviathan Stitch**

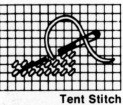

**Tent Stitch**

**Half Cross Stitch**

48

**PILLOW WITH FLORAL CORNERS**

**Color and Stitch Key**

light blue

pale blue

royal blue

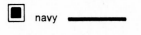
navy

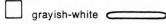
grayish-white

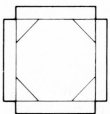

**Placement Diagram**
**Pillow with Floral Corners**

49

in continuous mosaic stitch. Other stitches used for details, bands and borders are bargello, leviathan and tied oblong cross stitches. The mosaic and bargello stitch diagrams are shown on the charts. Separate diagrams are given for all other stitches.

**Following Charts**: Where tent stitch is used, each space on chart indicates one stitch. Where long stitches covering several spaces are used (bargello, mosaic, details on flowers, etc.), each long stitch is indicated by a heavy line on chart or an open oval with color indication mark in center (see color keys).

Stitch diagrams are indicated directly on the charts for continuous mosaic stitch on background, and bargello stitch for part of border on Pillow with Geometric Corners. Outlined areas are marked on vases for bargello, leviathan and tied oblong cross stitches.

One corner for each pillow is given. Repeat it in other three corners. One section of the border for each pillow is given. Repeat the border on all four sides of pillow (see placement diagrams for outline of needlepoint areas).

**TO WORK NEEDLEPOINT**: Find center stitch on chart and work it in center of canvas. Continue to follow chart, working flowers and vase first.

For Pillow with Floral Corners, fill areas A on vase with bargello stitch as shown on the completed righthand area, and the separating bands B as shown on the two completed bands. Then work base of vase, repeating design for left half of base.

For Pillow with Geometric Corners, fill each area A with a small leviathan stitch as follows: Following diagrams (page 48), with navy blue work cross stitch from 1 to 2 and from 3 to 4. Then work 2 more stitches (5 to 6 and 7 to 8), then 2 more stitches (9 to 10 and 11 to 12). Finally, with royal blue make 2 more stitches (13 to 14 and 15 to 16). Fill areas B with same stitch, using pale blue throughout. Fill each area C with a large pale blue leviathan stitch (see diagram). This stitch is similar to small leviathan stitch, but you must make more stitches to cover the larger area. Diagram shows completed stitch with the last 2 stitches numbered. Fill each area D with a light blue tied oblong cross stitch (see diagram). Fill bands E with 1 row each of navy slanting stitches.

When vase and flowers have been completed, work navy octagonal band around design. Fill background with continuous mosaic stitch. Work corners, then borders.

**BLOCKING**: With pencil, ruler and triangle, draw the correct outline of pillow on brown paper; then tack the paper to a hard surface. Dampen needlepoint (or wet it thoroughly if it is badly out of shape). Stretch and tack it at 1" intervals to the board following the outline on paper. Allow to dry for at least 2 days before removing pins.

**TO MAKE PILLOW COVER AND PILLOW**: Trim canvas, following outline of needlepoint and leaving ½" for seams. Cut linen backing and two muslin pieces the same size. Pinch needlepoint corners together and stitch seam at each corner to form box top shape. Repeat with muslin and linen pieces. Stitch muslin pieces together, leaving opening for turning. Turn and stuff. Close opening. With right sides facing, stitch linen and needlepoint together, leaving one side open. Stitch zipper in place, if desired. Turn; insert pillow. Zip or baste closed.

# NOSEGAY PILLOW CROSS-STITCHED ON "VANISHING" CANVAS

You baste the special canvas to fabric, then embroider over the canvas and through the fabric. When you're finished, dampen your work, pull away the canvas threads (they're not interlocked) and the pretty bouquet design remains.

### GENERAL DIRECTIONS

**CANVAS:** The design is worked over special double-thread (penelope) "vanishing" needlepoint canvas that is basted to fabric. Double-thread canvas has 2 vertical and 2 horizontal threads per mesh and there are 2 types: One has interlocked vertical threads and loosely woven horizontal threads; the other has loosely woven vertical and horizontal threads. Be sure to buy the second type of canvas because all the threads must be loosely woven so they can be pulled out ("vanish") when the embroidery has been completed.

You can use any size canvas. We used canvas with 11 spaces per inch (which will make 11 cross-stitches per inch). If you use canvas with fewer spaces per inch than ours, your design will be larger, whereas a canvas with more spaces per inch will produce a smaller design.

**FABRIC:** Use any fabric that is a suitable weight, but it must be washable and colorfast, and not shrink. After the embroidery has been completed, the fabric and canvas will be soaked in order to soften the canvas threads so they can be removed.

**TO WORK CROSS-STITCH:** Cut piece of canvas slightly larger than the size of fabric area to be embroidered. Baste to fabric. Work with an embroidery hoop for soft fabrics and use 3 strands of 6-strand cotton floss throughout. Thread floss in needle and knot 1 end. Starting in center, bring needle, from wrong to right side, through fabric and center of a space in canvas (always work through the large spaces, not through the tiny ones where threads cross). Insert needle in next space diagonally above to the left; bring needle out in space directly below. Continue in this manner, making a row of diagonal stitches; then a row of cross-stitches as shown in diagram (page 52). Be careful not to catch the canvas threads with needle. Fasten on wrong side by weaving floss back and forth 2 or 3 times through stitches on wrong side of work. **Note:** Usually all stitches are crossed in the same direction. Our designer, however, has deliberately crossed some stitches in one direction and some in the opposite direction to give texture to the design.

When embroidery has been completed, soak piece in lukewarm water for a few minutes. While piece is still damp, use tweezers to pull out canvas threads in one direction; then pull out remaining threads. Rinse piece to remove from fabric any trace of "sizing" used to stiffen canvas. Press if necessary.

**TO FOLLOW CHART:** Follow the color key. Most of the colors are represented by a letter and a symbol: A large area worked in a single color is outlined and marked with a letter; a small area is marked with symbols. We have used this method of letters and symbols, as well as shading the background, so that the chart will be easier to follow. Each square in an outlined area or marked with a symbol represents 1 cross-stitch. We have added French knots to the flower centers; these details are worked over the cross-stitches.

Cross-stitch Diagram

### PILLOW COVER

**SIZE:** 13" square.

**MATERIALS:** ½ yard 36"-wide blue colorfast dress-weight linen; 1⅝ yards green piping; 14"-square of "vanishing" canvas with 11 spaces per inch (see Canvas under General Directions); 6-strand cotton embroidery floss, 1 skein each of D.M.C. in the following colors: black, white, light orange No. 972, dark orange No. 608, light pink No. 963, candy pink No. 956, fuchsia No. 601, scarlet No. 666, American beauty No. 815, brown No. 434, light green No. 907, apple green No. 702, forest green No. 904, light olive No. 734, dark olive No. 937; crewel embroidery needle; embroidery hoop; ½ yd. 36"-wide muslin for inner pillow; polyester-fiberfill stuffing; 12" zipper (optional).

See General Directions.

**TO EMBROIDER PILLOW COVER:** Cut 15"-square piece of linen. Center and baste canvas to linen; then mark center of canvas. Follow chart, working center stitch of design (marked with arrow on large B daisy) on center of canvas. Work in cross-stitch throughout; then work brown French knots (see Embroidery Stitch Diagrams, page 9) at dots on center C areas of daisies. When embroidery is completed, remove canvas threads. Trim linen to 14" square.

**TO MAKE INNER PILLOW:** Cut one 14"-square of linen for backing and two 14"-squares of muslin for inner pillow. Stitch muslin

**Color Key**

◼ —black

⊡ A—white

Ⅱ B—light orange

⊙ C—dark orange

⊞ D—forest green

⊘ E—light green

⊡ F—apple green

⊠ G—American beauty

   H—scarlet

⊟ I—light olive

◪ —dark olive

◺ J—fuchsia

⊠ K—candy pink

⊔ L—light pink

pieces together, leaving opening for turning. Turn and stuff; sew opening closed.

**TO FINISH COVER:** With raw edges facing outward and matching raw edges of pillow cover, stitch piping around right side of cover. With right sides facing and piping sandwiched between, stitch cover and backing together around 3 sides. Turn and insert zipper if desired. Insert inner pillow and stitch opening closed.

**NOSEGAY PILLOW**

# FOUR CROSS-STITCH PILLOWS WORKED ON EVEN-WEAVE FABRICS

The stitches in these dramatic, vivid designs are so closely packed that they look like needlepoint—but they're all quick and easy cross-stitch worked on thread-count fabrics.

## GENERAL DIRECTIONS

**TO CUT FABRICS:** See individual instructions for dimensions and cut between threads to keep edges straight. Overcast or pink edges.

If desired, before beginning embroidery, baste guide lines to indicate certain design areas (such as the gingham border on the Gingham Garden Pillow) or the repeated areas.

**CHARTS:** Each square represents one stitch. See individual instructions for following charts. Shaded areas are the fabric background. Where colors are repeated in similar areas, only one area is keyed.

**TO WORK CROSS-STITCH:** For the natural or cream linen, work over 2 horizontal and 2 vertical linen threads with 6 strands of floss. For the gold-colored fabric, work over 3 horizontal and 3 vertical threads with 4 strands of floss.

Thread needle with 20" length of floss. Omitting knot, leave 1" end on under side of fabric. Catch 1" end on back of first few stitches. Following stitch diagram (page 58), work cross-stitches. *All stitches must be crossed in the same direction.* To finish, weave through backs of several stitches.

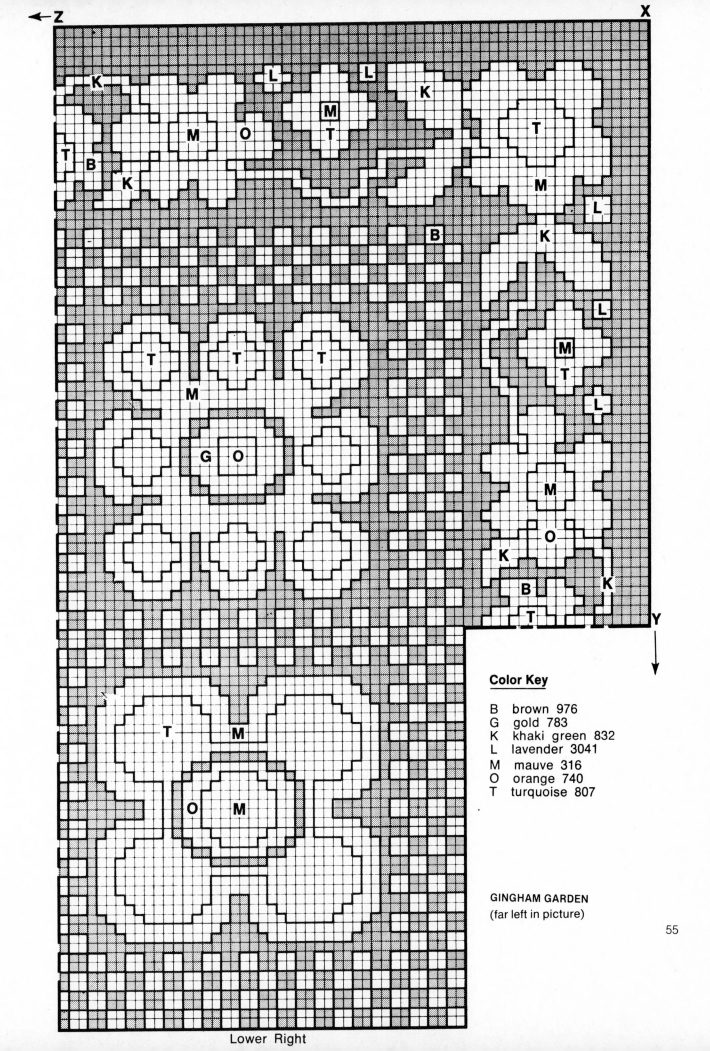

**Color Key**

B   brown 976
G   gold 783
K   khaki green 832
L   lavender 3041
M   mauve 316
O   orange 740
T   turquoise 807

**GINGHAM GARDEN**
(far left in picture)

55

Lower Right

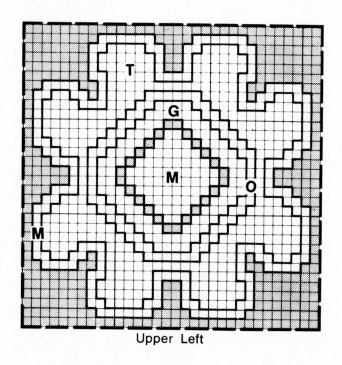

Upper Left

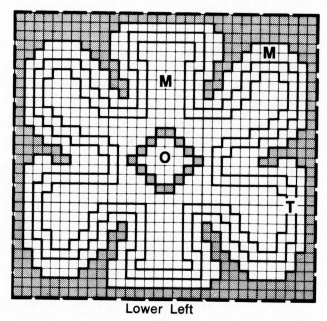

Lower Left

**TO MAKE INNER PILLOW FORM:** Cut 2 pieces muslin same size as embroidered fabric. Stitch 3 sides. Turn and stuff. Stitch last side.

**TO MAKE PILLOW CASE:** Cut fabric same size as embroidered piece. With right sides facing, seam 3 sides. If desired insert a zipper. Turn. Insert pillow form and close.

### GINGHAM GARDEN

SIZE: 18" x 18".

MATERIALS: For pillow cover front, 27" x 35½" even-weave cream-colored linen with 14 threads per inch; D.M.C. 6-strand cotton embroidery floss, 6 (8-yard) skeins brown No. 976 (color B), 5 skeins turquoise No. 807 (T), 4 skeins each orange No. 740 (O) and khaki (Green) No. 832 (K), 7 skeins mauve No. 316 (M), 1 skein each gold No. 783 (G) and lavender No. 3041 (L); tapestry needle; embroidery hoop; 19" x 19" piece of linen or other fabric for pillow cover back; 1¼ yards 45"-wide muslin and 1½ pounds polyester-fiberfill stuffing for inner pillow form.

**TO START:** See General Directions. Cut linen 19" square (including ½" for seams).

**TO WORK CHART (page 55):** Floral Border is shown for top right corner. To complete top and right borders, follow direction of arrows, repeating from Z to X along top and from Y to X along side. Turn chart around and work lower left corner, bottom and left side in same manner. **Gingham Border** is right half of

design. Repeat design for left half, working from center to outer edge. **Large Flower Motifs** (pages 55 and 56) are worked within the squares made by the gingham border. Make sure flowers are in proper squares.

For finishing see General Directions.

### SUNSHINE SAMPLER

SIZE: 16½ x 18".

MATERIALS: For pillow cover front and back, 27" x 35½" even-weave cream-colored linen with 14 threads per inch; D.M.C. 6-strand cotton embroidery floss, 7 (8-yard) skeins orange No. 947 (color O), 6 skeins light blue No. 996 (L), 5 skeins each green No. 700 (G), pink No. 603 (P) and yellow No. 444 (Y), 4 skeins red No. 606 (R), 1 skein each black No. 310 (B) and navy No. 797 (N); tapestry needle; embroidery hoop; ½ yard 45"-wide muslin and 1½ pounds polyester-fiberfill stuffing for inner pillow form.

**TO START:** See General Directions. Cut linen 17½" x 19" (including ½" seam allowance on all sides). Chart shows the whole design except bottom panel, which is a repeat of the top, and the alphabet repeat around 2 sides. Work the chart as shown, then turn embroidery upside down and repeat top panel across bottom. Then repeat alphabet along remaining 2 sides (A at lower right corner and Z near upper left corner are indicated for correct placement of alphabet repeat).

See General Directions for finishing.

**SUNSHINE SAMPLER**

(second from left in picture, page 54)

<u>**Color Key**</u>

B  black  310
G  green  700
L  light blue  996
N  navy  797
O  orange  947
P  pink  603
R  red  606
Y  yellow  444

## FOLK-ART FLORAL

**SIZE:** 11" x 17".

**MATERIALS:** For pillow cover front and back, 1 yard 33½"-wide even-weave gold cotton fabric with 27 threads per inch; D.M.C. 6-strand cotton embroidery floss, 5 (8-yard) skeins No. 892 pink (color P), 4 skeins No. 946 orange (O), 3 skeins each No. 798 blue (B), No. 701 green (G), No. 208 lavender (L), No. 606 red (R) and No. 993 turquoise (T), 2 skeins No. 718 violet (V) and 1 skein No. 971 yellow-orange (Y); tapestry needle; embroidery hoop; ½ yard 45"-wide muslin and 1 pound polyester-fiberfill stuffing for inner pillow form.

**TO START:** See General Directions. Cut fabric 12" x 18" (including ½" seam allowance). Chart indicates half of design. To work other half, repeat design, omitting center stitch. To finish see General Directions.

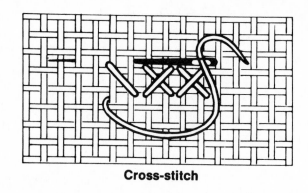

**Cross-stitch**

FOLK-ART FLORAL (below right in picture, page 54)

**Color Key**

| | |
|---|---|
| B | blue 798 |
| G | green 701 |
| L | lavender 208 |
| O | orange 946 |
| P | pink 892 |
| R | red 606 |
| T | turquoise 993 |
| V | violet 718 |
| Y | yellow-orange 971 |

center stitch ↑

58

# GUATEMALA GEOMETRIC

**SIZE:** 13¼″ x 18¼″.

**MATERIALS:** For pillow cover front and back, 27″ x 35½″ even-weave cream-colored linen with 14 threads per inch; D.M.C. 6-strand cotton embroidery floss, 8 (8-yard) skeins each bronze No. 831 (color G) and navy No. 797 (N), 7 skeins each copper No. 920 (C) and purple No. 552 (P), 6 skeins blue (B) No. 995;

tapestry needle; embroidery hoop; ½ yard 45″-wide muslin and 1 pound polyester-fiberfill stuffing for inner pillow form.

**TO START:** See General Directions. Cut linen 14¼″ x 19¼″ (including ½″ seam allowance all around). Chart indicates half of design. To work other half, repeat design, omitting center stitch. See General Directions for finishing.

**GUATEMALA GEOMETRIC** (above right in picture, page 54)

## Color Key

| | |
|---|---|
| B | blue 995 |
| C | copper 920 |
| G | bronze 831 |
| N | navy 797 |
| P | purple 552 |

Y

↑ center stitch

# TILE-MOTIF EMBROIDERED PILLOW

This tiny pillow, just ten inches square, is a lovely example of thread-count embroidery; even-weave linen becomes the tapestry on which you work satin and other simple stitches.

**SIZE:** 10″ square.

**MATERIALS:** 14″ square even-weave linen with 21 threads to the inch and the same number of threads in both directions, made especially for embroidery (see note below); 1 yard 36″-wide velveteen for backing and welting; 1¼ yards welting cord; ½ yard 45″-wide muslin for inner pillow and polyester-fiberfill stuffing or 10″-square pillow form; 6-strand embroidery floss, 3 (9-yard) skeins rose (color R), 2 skeins each pink (P), mauve (M), light blue (B), chartreuse (C) and green (G); embroidery needle.

**Note:** Linen is not stamped with the design. You count the threads to work the stitches.

**PLACEMENT OF MOTIFS:** Following layout diagram (page 62) for placement, work embroidery (see To Work Stitches) in colors specified under directions for individual motifs. The grid lines on Motif Nos. 1 through 5 correspond to threads of the linen. The design lines are the embroidery stitches.

**TO WORK STITCHES:** Use 4 strands of the 6-strand floss throughout.

**Window Stitch:** Following stitch diagram, bring needle up at A, from wrong side of linen to right side, down at B, up at C, down at D, up at B again, down at D, up at B, down at E, up at D, down at F, up at E, down at F. Continue in this manner, making 9 boxes in all (including unfinished 1st box). In order to turn corner, bring needle up at E, down at G, up at F, down at H, up at G, down at H (corner box completed), up at F, down at I, up at H, down at J, up at I, down at J. Continue in this manner to form border, ending with stitch across 1st box from A to C.

**Star Stitch:** Following stitch diagram, bring needle up at A, down in center hole, up at B, down in center hole. Continue around in this manner, following letters.

**Satin Stitch:** Following stitch diagram, bring needle up at A, down at B, up at C, down at D. Continue in this manner around to form square frame, working stitches in corners as shown on diagrams for motifs.

**Diamond Stitch:** Following stitch diagram and working around center hole on motif area, bring needle up at A, down at B, up at C, down at D, up at A again, down at C, up at B, down at D (center diamond completed). Come up at E, down at F, up at G, down at H, up at E again, down at G, up at F, down at H (2nd round completed). Continue in this manner, working outward, for 4 more rounds.

**TO WORK MOTIFS: Motif No. 1:** Find center of linen and mark with pin. There are 5 No. 1 motifs marked on layout diagram. Work first one in center of linen (dot on diagram indicates center

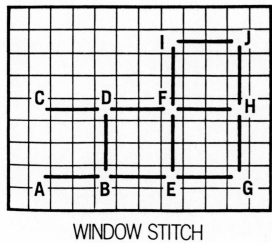

WINDOW STITCH

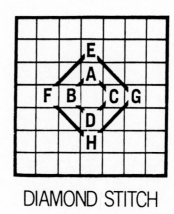

DIAMOND STITCH

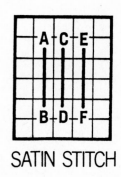

SATIN STITCH

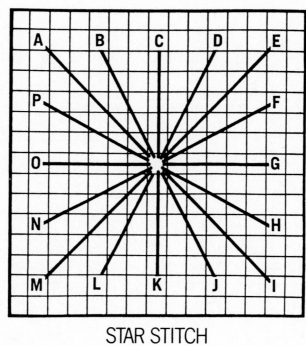

STAR STITCH

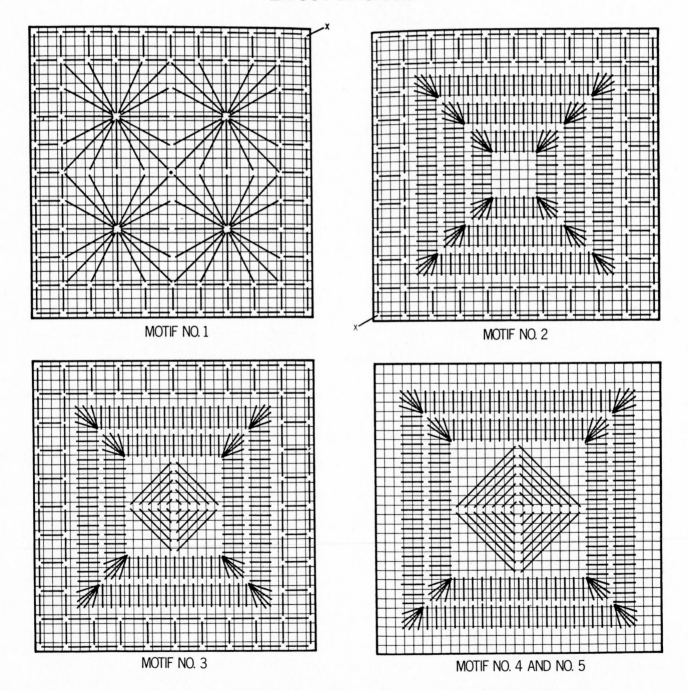

| 1 | 4 | 3 | 4 | 1 |
|---|---|---|---|---|
| 5 | 2 | 4 | 2 | 5 |
| 3 | 5 | 1 | 5 | 3 |
| 5 | 2 | 4 | 2 | 5 |
| 1 | 4 | 3 | 4 | 1 |

LAYOUT DIAGRAM

MOTIF NO. 1

MOTIF NO. 2

MOTIF NO. 3

MOTIF NO. 4 AND NO. 5

point of linen marked with pin). Follow motif chart and work window stitch border with color M. Work 4 star stitch units with R. Work remaining 4 No. 1 motifs later.

**Motif No. 2:** There are 4 No. 2 motifs. Work first one above and to right of center No. 1 motif. Follow motif chart and work window stitch border with M, bringing up needle for 1st stitch in corner marked X on chart for motif No. 1 (corner X on motifs 1 and 2 share the same space). Work outer satin stitch square frame with R, middle and inner satin stitch frames with P. Work other 3 No. 2 motifs, making sure the corner of each that is adjacent to motif No. 1 shares the same space with No. 1. Now work remaining 4 No. 1 motifs in outer corners of design area (they share corner spaces with motifs No. 2).

**Motif No. 3:** There are 4 No. 3 motifs. Follow motif chart and work window stitch border with M (inner corners of motifs share spaces with corners of motifs (No. 2). Work outer satin stitch square frame with R, inner satin stitch frame with P, diamond stitch with R.

**Motifs No. 4 and 5:** These 2 motifs are alike except for color. There are 6 in each color scheme. Unlike other motifs, they are not bordered with window stitch, but are worked in remaining plain areas.

For motif No. 4, follow motif chart and work diamond stitch in center with G. Work inner satin stitch square frame with C, outer satin stitch frame with G.

For motif No. 5, work diamond stitch in center with G. Work inner satin stitch square frame with B, outer satin stitch frame with C.

**FINISHING:** Trim embroidery to 11″ square. Cut velveteen backing same size. **Welting:** Cut 1½″-wide diagonal strips of velveteen and sew together on bias to make strip to fit around linen piece. Fold and stitch over welting cord.

Pin welting around linen, with raw edges facing outward, to form 10″ square. Stitch. Cut and sew welting ends together. With right sides facing and welting sandwiched between, stitch backing and linen, leaving one side open. Turn, insert pillow form or inner pillow (see below) and sew opening closed.

**Inner Pillow:** Cut 2 pieces muslin 11″ square. Stitch together along 3 sides. Turn, stuff and sew last side.

# THREE FLOWER-STREWN EMBROIDERED PILLOWS

Brilliant crewel yarns are worked on solid color linen or homespun using mostly easy satin stitch, lazy daisy and French knots.

### GENERAL DIRECTIONS

**ENLARGING DESIGNS:** See How to Enlarge Patterns, page 8.

**TRANSFERRING DESIGN:** To transfer design to fabric, place dressmaker's carbon paper (it comes in light and dark colors) carbon side down on material. Put full-size design on carbon paper and, using a blunt pencil or knitting needle, outline design to transfer carbon to fabric.

**MAKING THE PILLOW:** Cut 2 pieces of muslin same size as linen. Stitch together along 3 sides. Turn, stuff and sew opening closed. With right sides together stitch linen pieces along 3 sides. Insert zipper, if desired. Turn, insert pillow and sew opening closed.

### PEASANT PLEASANTRY (left in picture)

**SIZE:** 14" square.

**MATERIALS:** ½ yard 45"-wide red suit-weight linen; ½ yard 36"-wide muslin for pillow liner; polyester-fiberfill for stuffing; matching thread; embroidery needle; embroidery hoop; 14" zipper in matching color (optional); dressmaker's carbon paper; smallest skeins available of Bucilla Needlepoint and Crewel Wool in the following colors: white No. 1 (color A), raspberry 100 (B), dark fern 8 (C), spearmint 75 (D), green mint 96 (E), dark peacock 84 (F).

**TO START:** See General Directions.

From linen cut 2 pieces 16" square. Enlarge design; center and transfer it to one piece of linen.

To embroider design, refer to Color Key and photograph. (See color photograph, page 82.) Use all 3 strands of crewel yarn. Where adjacent motifs are the same color, only one is marked with a letter of the alphabet.

Fill in center flower, surrounding leaves, the open tulip shapes and triple leaf buds in corners with satin stitch (see Embroidery Stitch Diagrams, page 9). Small circles are worked in French knots and large ones are worked in satin sh G. titch. Use lazy-daisy stitch to outline corner buds and top motifs of each tulip shape as indicated on pattern.

Block completed embroidered design if necessary, then make pillow, following General Directions.

### NAIVE NOSEGAY (right in picture)

**SIZE:** 12" square.

**MATERIALS:** ½ yard 45"-wide royal blue suit-weight linen; ½ yard 36"-wide muslin for pillow liner; polyester-fiberfill stuffing; matching thread; embroidery needle; embroidery hoop; 12" zipper in matching color (optional); dressmaker's carbon paper; smallest skeins available of Bucilla Needlepoint and Crewel Wool in the following colors: white No. 1 (color A), raspberry 100 (B), apricot brandy 79 (C), bittersweet 94 (D), apricot 78 (E), light peacock 82 (F), medium peacock 83 (G), fuchsia 86 (H), spearmint 75 (I), emerald 68 (J).

**TO START:** See General Directions.

From linen cut 2 pieces 14" square. Enlarge design; center and transfer it to one piece of linen.

To embroider design, refer to Color Key and photograph. (See color photograph, page 82.) Use all 3 strands of crewel yarn. Where adjacent motifs are the same color, only one is marked with a letter of the alphabet. All large flowers, leaves (unless indicated otherwise on diagram), scalloped doily edge and ribbons are worked in satin stitch (see Embroidery Stitch Diagrams, page 9). Work all small circles in satin stitch. Use chain stitch to accent center of flowers, to outline the inside edge of doily scallops and on streamers indicated on diagram. All small flowers are worked in lazy-daisy stitch with French-knot centers in contrasting color. Work remaining leaves in fishbone stitch.

Block completed embroidered design if desired, then make pillow following General Directions.

### FLOWER BEDS (below in picture)

**SIZE:** 12" square.

**MATERIALS:** ½ yard 45"-wide bronze wool homespun; ½ yard 36"-wide muslin for pillow liner; polyester-fiberfill for stuffing; matching thread; embroidery needle; embroidery hoop; 12" zipper in matching color (optional); dressmaker's carbon paper; smallest skeins available of Bucilla Needlepoint and Crewel Wool in the following colors: dark yellow No. 3 (color A), bright yellow 120 (B),

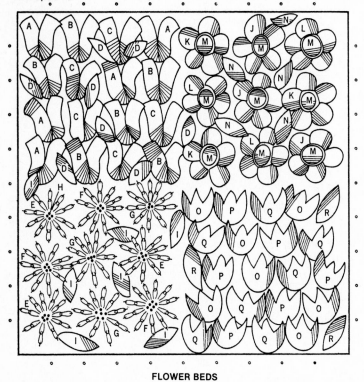

Each square = 1"

**FLOWER BEDS**

dark chartreuse 110 (C), spearmint 75 (D), medium peacock 83 (E), emerald 68 (F), blue 32 (G), royal 33 (H), dark fern 8 (I), raspberry 100 (J), apricot brandy 79 (K), apricot 78 (L), bittersweet 94 (M), medium fern 7 (N), dark lavender 72 (O), plum 87 (P), fuchsia 86 (Q), dark olive 29 (R).

**TO START:** See General Directions.

From linen cut 2 pieces 14" square. Enlarge design; center and transfer it to one piece of linen.

To embroider design, refer to Color Key and photograph. (See color photograph, page 82.) Use all 3 strands of crewel yarn. Where adjacent motifs are the same color only one is marked with a letter of the alphabet.

Work all blue- and green-tone flowers in lazy-daisy stitch (see Embroidery Stitch Diagrams, page 9) with centers worked in French-knot clusters. All remaining flowers and leaves are worked in satin stitch.

Block completed embroidered design, if desired, then make pillow, following General Directions.

Color Key

| | | |
|---|---|---|
| A dark yellow | G bright blue | M bittersweet |
| B bright yellow | H royal blue | N medium fern |
| C dark chartreuse | I dark fern | O dark lavender |
| D spearmint | J raspberry | P plum |
| E medium peacock | K apricot brandy | Q fuchsia |
| F emerald | L apricot | R dark olive |

Each square = 1"

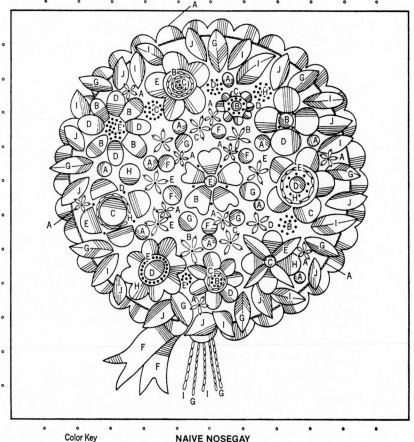

**NAIVE NOSEGAY**

Color Key

| | |
|---|---|
| A white | F light peacock |
| B raspberry | G medium peacock |
| C apricot brandy | H fuchsia |
| D bittersweet | I spearmint |
| E apricot | J emerald |

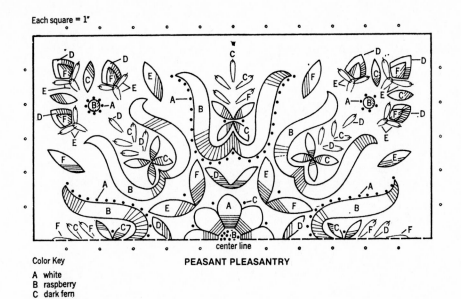

Each square = 1"

**PEASANT PLEASANTRY**

center line

Color Key
A white
B raspberry
C dark fern
D spearmint
E green mint
F dark peacock

# RAINBOW-AND-CREAM AND HONEYCOMB PUFF CROCHETED PILLOWS

Motif for the square pillow is a rainbow circle formed of popcorn stitch in ombré yarn with the granny square completed in natural; round pillow has airy hexagons, just two rounds each.

**RAINBOW-AND-CREAM PILLOW** (above in picture)

**SIZE:** 23" square.

**MATERIALS:** Dawn Sayelle (Orlon acrylic knitting-worsted-weight yarn), 2 (4-ounce) skeins fisherman (natural) No. 336, 2 (3½-ounce) skeins peacock ombré No. 381; aluminum crochet hook size G (or international size 4:50 mm) or the size that will give you the correct gauge; ¾ yard 72"-wide yellow-orange felt; 1⅜ yard 36"-wide unbleached muslin for pillow lining; 3 pounds polyester-fiberfill stuffing; 20" zipper (optional); tapestry needle.

**GAUGE:** Each module measures about 5" square.

Pillow front is composed of 12 square modules, sewn together, and a border.

**SQUARE MODULE (make 12):** Starting at center with ombré and starting to crochet at beg of one of the ombré shades, ch 8. Join with sl st to form ring.

**1st rnd (popcorn rnd):** Ch 3, work 4 dc in ring; remove hook from lp and insert it from back to front through 3rd ch of ch-3, insert hook through dropped lp and draw it through ch st (1st popcorn completed—it will pop out on opposite side of work); * ch 2, work 5 dc in ring, remove hook and insert from back to front in 1st dc of 5-dc group, complete popcorn. Repeat from * 6 times more, sliding popcorns close together so they will all fit on ring (8 popcorns in all), ch 2; join with sl st to top of ch-3 on 1st popcorn.

**2nd rnd:** Sl st in 1st ch-2 sp, ch 3, make 1st popcorn in same sp, ch 2, work another popcorn in same sp; * ch 2, in next ch-2 sp work (popcorn, ch 2 and popcorn). Repeat from * 6 times more (10 popcorns), ch 2; join. Circle should measure about 4″ in diameter. Break off.

Now shape circle to form square. Turn piece over.

**3rd rnd (right side):** Make 1st corner as follows: Make lp on hook with natural, y o, work dc in any ch-2 sp, in same sp work dc, ch 1 and 2 dc (1st corner completed); * work dc in next popcorn, 2 h dc in next ch-2 sp, 2 sc in next sp, 2 h dc in next sp, dc in next popcorn; in next sp work (2 dc, ch 1 and 2 dc—another corner made). Repeat from * twice more; complete 4th side in pattern, ending with dc in last popcorn; join with sl st to 1st dc.

**4th rnd:** Ch 3 and, working in back lp only of each st, dc in each st around and 3 dc in each corner ch-1 sp (60 dc); join. Break off.

**CORNER MOTIF (make 9):** Starting at center with ombré at beg of one of the shades, ch 6. Join with sl st to form ring. Work as for 1st rnd of square until 4 popcorns have been made, ch 2; join and break off.

**ASSEMBLING:** Sew 4 squares together in a strip, using natural yarn and sewing through back lp of each of the 16 sts (from corner to corner) across 1 side of each square. Make 3 more strips. Sew strips together to form large square. Tack a corner motif over each point where 4 squares meet.

**BORDER: 1st rnd:** Make lp on hook with natural, y o, work dc in back lp of any dc on square. Working in back lp of each st, work dc in each dc around, dc in each joining and 3 dc in center dc at each corner (248 dc); join.

**2nd rnd:** Ch 3, dc in back lp of each dc around, 3 dc in center dc at each corner (256 dc); join and break off.

**3rd rnd:** (Work in back lp of each st.) Make lp on hook with natural, y o, work dc in center dc at any corner, work 2 more dc in same place (1st corner made); * dc in next 8 dc, (ch 2, skip next 2 dc, dc in each of next 3 dc) 9 times; ch 2, skip next 2 dc, dc in next 8 dc, 3 dc in next (corner) dc. Repeat from * twice more; complete 4th side in pattern; join to 1st dc. Break off.

**4th rnd:** Make lp on hook with ombré, make 1st corner in center dc at any corner; * dc in back lp of next 9 dc, 3 dc in next sp, (ch 3, skip next 3 dc, 3 dc in next sp) 9 times; dc in back lp of next 9 dc, 3 dc in next (corner) dc. Repeat from * twice more; complete 4th side in pattern; join.

**5th rnd:** (Work in back lp of each st.) Sl st in next (center) dc of corner, ch 2, work 2 h dc in same place; * sc in each of next 2 dc, (3 h dc in next dc, sc in each of next 3 dc) 18 times; 3 h dc in next dc, sc in each of next 2 dc, 3 h dc in next (corner) dc. Repeat from * twice more; complete 4th side in pattern; join and break off.

**TO MAKE PILLOW:** Cut muslin and felt into two 24″ squares each. Stitch muslin squares together across 3 sides. Turn and stuff. Close 4th side. Stitch felt squares together across 3 sides. Insert zipper on center of 4th side, if desired, and stitch felt at each end of zipper. Turn. Insert pillow in case and close zipper or blindstitch opening.

Stretch and pin crocheted piece over one side of pillow, allowing the last 3 rnds to extend beyond pillow. Sew in place.

### HONEYCOMB PUFF PILLOW (below in picture, page 67)

**SIZE:** 28″ in diameter.

**MATERIALS:** Aunt Lydia's Heavy Rug yarn (rayon and cotton), 2 (70-yard) skeins each brick No. 145 and phantom red No. 140, 1 skein each burnt orange No. 320, brown No. 420 and tangerine No. 351; aluminum crochet hook size I (or international size 5:50 mm) or the size that will give you the correct gauge; 1¾ yards 36″-wide burnt-orange velveteen (or 1 yard 72″-wide felt); 1¾ yards 36″-wide unbleached muslin for pillow lining; 3 pounds polyester-fiberfill stuffing; 22″ zipper (optional); tapestry needle.

**GAUGE:** Each hexagonal module measures, when stretched, about 6½″ across from one point to opposite point.

Pillow front is composed of 19 hexagonal modules sewn together.

**HEXAGONAL MODULE:** Starting at center with brick, ch 8. Join with sl st to form ring. **1st rnd:** Ch 6, (work tr in ring, ch 2) 11 times (12 "spokes"); join with sl st to 4th ch of ch-6.

**2nd rnd:** Sl st in next sp, ch 3, in same sp work (dc, ch 2 and 2 dc) for 1st point; * work 4 dc in next sp, in next sp work (2 dc,

68

ch 2 and 2 dc) for another point. Repeat from * 4 times more; 4 dc in next sp; join with sl st to top of ch-3. Break off.

Make 18 more modules, working 5 more with brick, 4 with phantom red and 3 each with burnt orange, brown and tangerine. Following photograph, (page 91) pin modules together. Sew them on wrong side with double sewing thread, working into top lp of each st.

**TO MAKE PILLOW:** From muslin and velveteen, cut two 29" circles and a 3"-wide boxing strip long enough, when pieced, to go around a circle. Piece muslin strips into 1 long strip. Stitch 1 edge of strip around a muslin circle; seam ends of strip. Stitch other edge of strip around other muslin circle, leaving opening for stuffing. Turn and stuff. Assemble velveteen pieces in same way, leaving 22" opening. Insert zipper, if desired. Turn, insert pillow in case and close zipper or blindstitch opening.

Stretch crocheted piece over top of pillow and tack in place.

# COMING-UP-ROSES AND NINE-TIMES-LAVENDER CROCHETED PILLOWS

Full-blown roses form the center of the double and single crochet squares on the pillow on the chair; lush sunset colors are used for the nine lacy squares on the pillow below.

COMING-UP-ROSES PILLOW (above in picture)

**SIZE:** 26" square.
**MATERIALS:** 4-ply knitting-worsted-weight yarn: 1 (4-ounce) skein each rust, gold, dark green, aqua and hot pink; aluminum

crochet hook size H (or international size 5:00 mm) or the size that will give you the correct gauge; 1 yard 72″-wide burnt-orange felt; 1½ yards 36″-wide unbleached muslin for pillow lining; 3 pounds polyester-fiberfill stuffing; 24″ zipper (optional); tapestry needle.

**GAUGE:** Each module measures about 9″ square.

Pillow front is composed of 9 square modules, sewn together, and a picot chain border.

**SQUARE MODULE:** Starting at center of rose with pink, ch 6. Join with sl st to form ring. **1st rnd:** (Ch 4, sc in ring) 7 times; ch 4; join with sl st to base of 1st ch 4 (8 lps).

**2nd rnd:** In each lp work (sc, h dc, dc, h dc and sc) for 8 petals. Piece should measure about 2¾″.

**3rd rnd:** Ch 4, fold 1st petal over to front, work post sc as follows: insert hook under next sc on 1st rnd (sc that was worked into ring), y o and draw lp through, y o and draw through both lps on hook to complete post sc; (ch 4, fold next petal forward, work post sc around next sc on 1st rnd) 7 times (8 lps across backs of petals).

**4th rnd:** In each lp work (sc, h dc, 3 dc, h dc and sc) for 2nd rnd of petals behind 1st rnd of petals.

**5th rnd:** (Ch 5, fold next petal on last rnd forward, work post sc around next sc on 3rd rnd) 8 times (8 lps across backs of petals).

**6th rnd:** In each lp work (sc, h dc, 5 dc, h dc and sc) for 3rd rnd of petals behind 2nd rnd of petals; join with sl st to 1st sc on 1st petal. Break off. Completed rose should measure about 4¼″ in diameter.

Now shape square background as follows: **7th rnd:** (Note: Work all d tr's on this rnd loosely to measure about 2″ when stretched and all d tr cl's to measure about 1¾″.) Make lp on hook with dark green; with right side facing you, fold a petal forward and work d tr as follows: Y o 3 times, insert hook through 1 thread only on back of any sc on 5th rnd, y o and draw lp through (5 lps are now on hook), (y o and draw lp through (5 lps are now on hook), (y o and draw through 2 lps on hook) 4 times to complete d tr; ch 3, work another d tr in same thread; work d tr cl as follows: Working in same thread, make d tr until 2 lps remain on hook, y o 3 times and make another d tr in same place until 3 lps remain on hook, y o and draw through all 3 lps on hook to complete d tr cl (part of 1st corner made); * ch 2, work d tr cl in back thread on next sc on 5th rnd, ch 2, d tr cl in same place (d tr cl group made); ch 2, in back thread of next sc on 5th rnd work corner as follows: D tr cl, ch 2, d tr, ch 3 (corner ch), d tr, ch 2 and d tr cl (corner completed). Repeat from * twice more; ch 2, work d tr cl group, ch 2, complete 1st corner by working d tr cl in thread where 1st corner

was started, ch 2; join with sl st to 1st d tr. Break off.

**8th rnd:** Make lp on hook with gold; make 1st corner as follows: Y o, work dc in and ch-3 corner sp on last rnd, work 2 more dc in same place (shell made), ch 2, work 3 dc in same place (another shell made to complete corner); * (ch 1, shell in next ch-2 sp) 5 times; ch 1, work corner in next (corner) sp. Repeat from * twice more; complete rnd in pattern, ending with ch 1; join with sl st to 1st dc. Break off.

**9th rnd:** Make lp on hook with aqua; y o, work dc in any corner sp, complete corner as for last rnd; * (ch 1, shell in next sp) 6 times; ch 1, work corner in next (corner) sp. Repeat from * twice more, complete rnd in pattern, ending with ch 1; join. Break off.

Make 8 more modules, working pink rose on 4 of them and rust rose on 4.

**ASSEMBLING:** Using aqua, sew 3 modules, 1 with pink rose, 1 with rust rose and 1 with pink rose, together to form strip, sewing through back lp only of each st. Make another strip in same manner. Make strip with rust rose, pink rose and rust rose. Join strips to form square with pink rose in center.

**BORDER:** Make lp on hook with dark green, work sc in any corner sp, ch 6, sl st in 3rd ch from hook (picot made), ch 2, sc in same corner sp (corner lp made); * (ch 6, p, ch 2, sc in next sp) 25 times; ch 6, picot, ch 2, sc in next (corner) sp, make corner lp. Repeat from * twice more; complete rnd in pattern, ending with sl st in 1st sc. Break off.

**TO MAKE PILLOW:** Cut muslin and felt into two 27″ squares each. Complete lining and felt cover as for Rainbow-and-Cream Pillow, page 68.

Stretch and pin crocheted piece over one side of pillow, allowing last rnd to extend beyond pillow. Sew in place.

NINE-TIMES-LAVENDER PILLOW (below in picture, page 69)

**SIZE:** 26″ square.

**MATERIALS:** 4-ply knitting-worsted-weight yarn: 1 (4-ounce) skein each lavender, orange, pink, red and dark red; aluminum crochet hook size H (or international size 5:00 mm) or the size that will give you the correct gauge; 1 yard 72″-wide yellow-orange felt; 1½ yards 36″-wide muslin for pillow lining; 3 pounds polyester-fiberfill stuffing; 24″ zipper (optional); tapestry needle.

**GAUGE:** Each module measures about 7½″ square.

Pillow front is composed of 9 square modules, sewn together, and a border.

**SQUARE MODULE (make 9):** Starting at center with lavender, ch 4. Join with sl st to form ring. **1st rnd:** Ch 1, 8 sc in ring; join with sl st to 1st sc. Turn.

**2nd rnd:** Ch 3, work 2 dc in same place as sl st, * ch 1, 3 dc in next sc. Repeat from * 6 times more, ch 1; join with sl st to top of ch-3. Break off.

**3rd rnd:** Make lp on hook with orange; y o and work dc in any ch-1 sp, work 2 more dc in same sp, * ch 1, 3 dc in next sp. Repeat from * 6 times more (8 shells), ch 1; join with sl st to 1st dc. Break off.

**4th rnd:** Make lp on hook with pink; y o and work dc in any ch-1 sp, ch 1, dc in next dc, * ch 2, skip next dc (center dc on shell), dc in next dc, ch 1, dc in next sp, ch 1, dc in next dc (1st dc on next shell), ch 1, skip next dc, dc in next dc, ch 1, dc in next sp, ch 1, dc in next dc (1st dc on next shell). Repeat from * twice more; ch 2, skip next dc, dc in next dc, ch 1, dc in next sp, ch 1, dc in next dc, ch 1, skip next dc, dc in next dc, ch 1; join.

Now shape background, which will be blocked square, as follows:

**5th rnd:** Sl st in next ch-1 sp, in next dc and in next ch-2 sp; ch 3, 2 dc in same sp, ch 1, 3 dc in same sp (1st corner made); * ch 1, skip next sp, (3 dc in next sp, ch 1) 3 times; skip next sp, work another corner of 3 dc, ch 1 and 3 dc in next ch-2 sp. Repeat from * 3 times more, omitting last corner; join to top of ch-3. Break off.

**6th rnd:** Make lp on hook with red; y o and work dc in any corner ch-1 sp, in same sp work 2 more dc, ch 1 and 3 dc (1st corner made), * (ch 1, 3 dc in next sp) to corner; ch 1, work corner of 3 dc, ch 1 and 3 dc in corner sp. Repeat from * 3 times more, omitting last corner; join to 1st dc. Break off. Block module square.

**7th rnd:** With dark red repeat 6th rnd.

**ASSEMBLING:** Sew 3 squares tog in a strip, using dark red yarn and sewing on right side of squares. Make 2 more strips. Sew strips tog to form square.

**BORDER: 1st rnd:** Make lp on hook with dark red; y o and work 1st corner in any corner sp on square, (ch 1, 3 dc in next sp) 6 times; * ch 1, dc in corner sp at joining, dc in joining, dc in corner sp on other side of joining, (ch 1, 3 dc in next sp) 6 times. Repeat from * twice more; ch 1, work corner. Continue across other 3 sides of square in same manner; join. Break off.

**2nd rnd:** Make lp on hook with lavender; y o and make 1st corner in any corner sp, * (ch 1, 3 dc in next sp) to corner, ch 1, work corner in corner sp. Repeat from * 3 times more, omitting last corner; join. Break off. **3rd rnd:** With pink repeat last rnd.

**TO MAKE PILLOW:** Cut muslin and felt into two 27″ squares each. Complete lining and felt cover as for Rainbow-and-Cream Pillow, page 68. Stretch and pin crocheted piece over one side of pillow; sew.

# STRIPED KNITTED PILLOW

A subtle pattern stitch and fringe add to its dapper looks.

SIZE: 15" square, not including fringe.

MATERIALS: Knitting-worsted-weight yarn, 4 ounces each burnt orange (color A) and dark rose (B), 2 ounces light rose (C), 1 ounce each red (D) and lilac (E); 1 pair No. 9 knitting needles (or English needles No. 4) or the size that will give you the correct gauge; aluminum crochet hook size G (or international size 4:50 mm); 15"-square pillow form.

GAUGE: 4 st = 1"; 6 rows = 1".

PILLOW BACK: With A, cast on 60 st. Work even in stockinette st for 15". Bind off.

PATTERN STITCH: **1st row:** K 4, * p 4, k 4. Repeat from * across. **2nd row:** P 4, * k 4, p 4. Repeat from * across. **3rd and 4th rows:** Repeat 1st and 2nd rows. **5th through 8th row:** Repeat 2nd and 1st rows twice. **9th row:** K across. **10th row:** P across. Repeat 1st through 10th row for pattern st.

PILLOW FRONT: With C, cast on 60 st. Work even in pattern st in color sequence of 8 rows C, 2A, 8C, 2B, 8D, 2E, 8B, 2C, 8B, 2E; work 1st through 4th rows with A, 9th and 10th rows with B; starting with 1st row of pattern st, work 8 rows E, 2D, 8C, 2A, 8C, 2B, 8D. Bind off.

FINISHING: Pin edges of back and front around pillow form. **Edging: 1st rnd:** With B, crochet 1-rnd sc through both thicknesses, working 3 sc at each corner. **2nd rnd:** Sc in each sc around, working 3 sc at each corner; join. Break off. **Fringe:** Work fringe in each sc, using two 4" strands B for each tassel: hold tassel strands together and fold in half. With crochet hook, draw loop end through sc, then draw ends through loop and pull to tighten.

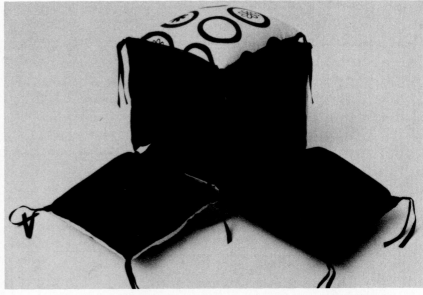

# SIX-PART PILLOW FOOTSTOOL TO SEW

Use the six pyramid-shaped pillows separately or fit them together and tie the corner ribbons for a cube-shaped footstool.

**SIZE:** 10½″ high.

**MATERIALS:** 44″-wide sailcloth or other heavy cotton: ½ yard red, ¾ yard navy and ¾ yard white-navy-red print; 4 pounds polyester-fiberfill stuffing; 8 yards ⅜″-wide grosgrain ribbon for ties.

**Note:** Footstool is composed of six pyramid-shaped pillows.

**TO START:** For peaked sides of pillows cut 3 red and 3 navy 14½″ squares. (All measurements include ½″ seam allowance.) Following diagram, mark darts at each corner; fold and stitch 4 darts on each square. For flat sides of pillows cut 11½″ squares, 4 from print and 2 from navy. For each pillow cut four 12″ ribbon ties.

**ASSEMBLING EACH PILLOW:** Fold ties in half. With right side of flat pillow side facing you, tack 1 tie to each corner with fold on seam line. With right side facing (ties are sandwiched between), stitch flat pillow piece to darted piece, catching ties and

leaving a long opening for stuffing. Turn and stuff very firmly; sew opening closed.

To assemble footstool, tie all 6 pillows together at each corner with peaked surfaces inside.

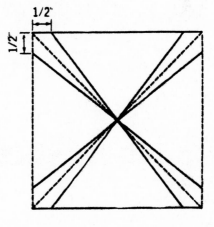

**SIX-PART PILLOW FOOTSTOOL**

# QUICK-CHANGE FLOOR PILLOW TO SEW

The tie-on cover reverses from a solid color to a small print.

**SIZE:** 22" square.

**MATERIALS:** 1½ yards 45"-wide solid-red cotton fabric; 1½ yards 36"-wide muslin for pillow liner (optional); 1 yard each 45"-wide solid-orange and orange-red-yellow print cotton fabrics; matching thread; 3 to 4 pounds polyester-fiberfill stuffing.

**TO START:** Pillow is box-edge type without separate boxing strip. Cut two 27"-square red pieces that allow for half the depth of boxing plus ½" seam allowance. Round corners slightly. Pin inverted pleats at each corner, then, with right sides facing, stitch top and bottom pieces together, leaving one side open. If desired, also make a muslin pillow liner in the same way. Stuff muslin liner and close opening. Insert stuffed liner in red cover and close opening.

For reversible quick-change squares cut two 17" squares from both orange and print fabrics. Also from orange cut eight 2" x 13" strips for ties. Fold each tie in half lengthwise and stitch along end and open long side; turn and press. With raw edges matching, pin a tie at each corner on right side of a print square. Pin orange square on top of print, right sides facing and ties sandwiched between. Stitch squares together, leaving an opening to turn. Turn and press; close opening. Repeat to make second reversible square.

Following photograph, position a square so that corners with ties fall centered on each side of pillow. Carefully turn pillow over and position second reversible square. Tie bows at sides of pillow.

# COTTAGE CUSHIONS TO STITCH AND GLUE

Two whimsical designs in felt-covered foam are fun and quick to make.

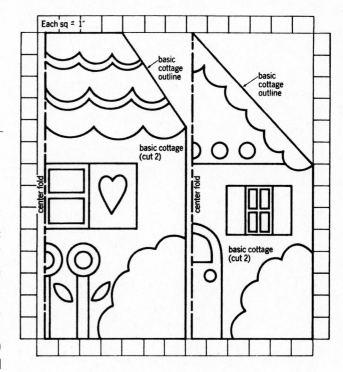

**SIZE:** About 14″ tall.

**MATERIALS:** ½ yard 45″-wide red or yellow felt for basic cottage; felt scraps for details (see photograph page 82 for colors); 3″-thick foam cushion about 14″ square for each pillow; fabric glue; pinking shears; long sharp kitchen knife.

**PATTERNS:** Enlarge patterns (see How to Enlarge Patterns, page 8), and cut out patterns for basic cottage and details, adding ¼″ for seam allowance to all sides of cottage but not to details. Where one piece appears on top of another, cut the full background piece (for example, 1 rectangular window frame on which 4 windowpanes are glued). From felt, cut out front and back cottage and detail pieces, using pinking shears for cottage.

**PILLOW SHAPE:** Cut seam allowance from cottage pattern. Lay pattern on foam cushion and, using ruler and long, sharp kitchen knife, cut out cottage shape. (If knife is long and sharp enough, you should need only 1 or 2 cuts for each foam edge.)

**ASSEMBLING:** Using pinking shears, cut 3½″-wide felt boxing strip 1″ longer than measurement around pillow. Making ¼″ seam, stitch strip around 1 cottage piece; stitch end of strips together. Stitch other edge of strip to other cottage piece, leaving bottom open. Insert pillow in case and stitch opening.

Following photograph and pattern for placement, glue to both sides of pillow. If desired, add green bush-shaped pieces to boxing strip.

# LOVESEAT PILLOWS AND SEAT CUSHIONS TO SEW

Make saucy pillows from pillowcases and shams, using extra fabric to trim a side stand and matching paint to spruce up worn spots.

**SIZE: Ruffled pillow;** 17" x 30" plus 4" wide ruffle. **Round pillows:** about 15" diameter. **Seat cushions:** about 18" square.

**MATERIALS:** We used standard-size pillowcases and ruffled envelope-style pillow shams (about 19" x 30" plus 4"-wide ruffle) to make our pillows: 1 sham for ruffled pillow, 1 sham for 2 round pillows, 1 pillowcase per seat cushion. You will also need **for ruffled pillow,** 2 bags polyester-fiberfill; **for each round pillow,** 1½ yards welting, cover-a-button kit with two 1½"-diameter button molds and 14" diameter foam pillow form; **for each seat cushion,** 2⅛ yards welting and 3"-thick foam pad about 18" square **for wicker furniture;** acrylic paint to harmonize with one color in pillows, paintbrush, scrap fabric left from pillows, tape or fabric glue.

**RUFFLED PILLOW:** We made our pillow narrower by sewing 2" fold on one long side. Stuff sham with polyester and sew opening closed.

**ROUND PILLOWS:** One sham will make 2 round pillows. Open seams and hem of sham and remove ruffle; press. Cut 4 circles about 15" in diameter. Following directions with button kit, cover

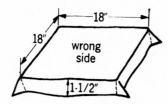

18"

18"   wrong
      side

1-1/2"

2 buttons for each pillow with contrasting part of print. Save excess fabric to cover table legs, if desired.

With raw edges matching, pin and stitch welting around right side of pillow piece, making ½" seam. Join ends of welting neatly. With right sides facing and welting sandwiched between, stitch pillow pieces together, leaving 12" opening for turning. Turn and insert pillow form. Blindstitch opening closed.

Placing a button on each side of pillow, sew buttons together through center of pillow.

**SEAT CUSHIONS:** Use one pillowcase for each cushion. Open seams and press. For each pillow, cut 2 pieces about 21" square (full width of opened case). Following diagram, pleat and stitch corners on each piece to form box top shape. Follow paragraph two of Round Pillows, above, to complete cushion.

**TO TRIM WICKER FURNITURE:** Use acrylic paint on braided trim and any other details desired. To cover table leg or brace with fabric, cut fabric strips about 1½" wide. Glue or tape one end to leg, then wind strip tightly to cover leg; glue or tape other end.

# BURLAP FLOOR PILLOWS WITH WOVEN TRIM

Scrap yarn is woven through the burlap and knotted for fringe.

**SIZE:** 28" square.

**MATERIALS:** For each pillow cover: 1 ¾ yards 48"/50"-wide burlap and a variety of yarns in colors to harmonize with color of burlap; for each inner pillow: 1¾ yards 38"/39"-wide muslin and 6 pounds polyester-fiberfill stuffing; large-eyed tapestry needle.

### GENERAL DIRECTIONS

Pillows are worked by pulling threads in one direction from the burlap, then weaving yarn in place of the pulled threads. In order to have a firm base on which to work, the pillows are sewn and stuffed first, then decorated afterward. Proceed as follows:

**INNER PILLOW:** With right sides facing, stitch together two 29" squares of muslin with ½" seam, leaving 1 side open. Trim

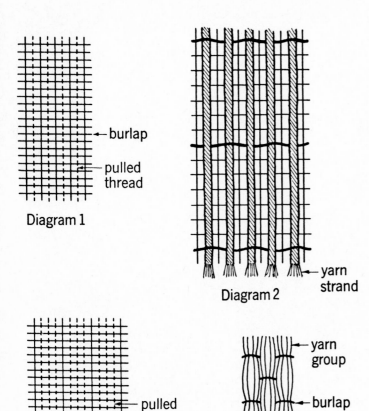

Diagram 1

Diagram 2

yarn strand

Diagram 3

Diagram 4

yarn group

burlap

seams. Turn, stuff and sew last side closed.

**PILLOW COVER:** With right sides facing, stitch together two 30″ squares of burlap with 1″ seam, leaving 1 side open. Trim seams. Turn, insert inner pillow and sew opening closed.

**TO PREPARE BURLAP:** Following detailed instructions below for specific weaving techniques, mark off the areas on the pillow top where you will place the strips of your design.

Pull out rows of burlap threads, clipping them if they are caught in the stitching. Save threads to secure knots after yarn has been woven and knotted.

**TO PREPARE YARNS:** The yarns can be a mix of many weights, ranging from fingering to knitting worsted to bulky; combine strands of thinner and thicker yarns in similar color ranges to add to the texture. Picking colors at random, cut strands of yarn about 2 feet longer than the width of the piece of burlap (about 1 foot extra on each side—3″ for the knot and 9″ for the fringe). On stripes with more than 1 knot allow about 3″ extra for each additional knot.

**TAN PILLOW TOP (page 77, right):** Mark along 1 edge for stripes as follows: 2″ to be pulled and rewoven, 1″ burlap, 3¼″ rewoven, 1½″ burlap, 2″ rewoven, 1½″ burlap, 5½″ rewoven, 1½″ burlap, 2″ rewoven, 1½″ burlap, 3¼″ rewoven, 1″ burlap and 2″ rewoven. Pull out alternate threads from burlap across stripes marked for reweaving (broken lines on Diagram 1, indicate pulled threads). Thread yarn in tapestry needle. Following Diagram 2, weave yarn to replace pulled threads. Following photograph, knot ends. Trim fringe.

**CREAM PILLOW TOP (page 77, left):** Mark along 1 edge for stripes as follows: ½″ burlap, 1″ to be pulled and rewoven, 1½″ burlap, ½″ rewoven, 1½″ burlap, 1″ rewoven, 1″ burlap, 2″ rewoven, 1″ burlap, 1½″ rewoven, ½″ burlap, 3½″ rewoven, ½″ burlap, 2″ rewoven, 1″ burlap, 2½″ rewoven, 1″ burlap, 1″ rewoven, 1½″ burlap, ½″ rewoven, 1″ burlap, 1½″ rewoven. For 3½″ slightly off-center stripe to be rewoven, pull out alternate threads from burlap and weave as for Tan Pillow Top (Diagrams 1 and 2). For the other stripes to be rewoven, work as follows: Depending upon the number of strands of yarn to be held together in the weaving, pull 3 to 5 adjacent threads of burlap (Diagram 3). On narrower stripes pull only 1 set of adjacent threads and weave only 1 group of yarn strands. Knot these strands as desired while weaving. On wider stripes weave 2 or 3 yarn groups, alternating the spacing of the threads worked under on adjacent rows to create woven effect (Diagram 4). Begin and end narrower stripes at random as shown in photograph. Knot strands of yarn at ends of woven sections. Tack knots with threads pulled from burlap. Trim fringe.

# 3

# WALL HANGINGS, WINDOW TREATMENTS AND RUGS

# PUNCH-NEEDLE WALL HANGING AND PILLOW

Even beginners find a punch needle great fun to use. First, you transfer the design for the Sierra Nevada hanging or Salinas pillow to burlap and put the fabric on a stretcher frame. Then, working from the back, you punch-needle up and down in a rhythmic motion that leaves a row of thick loops on the right side.

**SIZE:** Pillow measures 16″ square. Hanging measures 24″ x 36″.

**MATERIALS: For pillow:** Aunt Lydia's Heavy Rug Yarn (75% rayon, 25% cotton), 2 (70-yard) skeins original cream No. 558 (color A), 1 skein each lilac No. 010 (B), national blue No. 715 (C), mint green No. 645 (D), medium blue No. 710 (E), orchid No. 025 (F), medium pink No. 105 (G), peacock No. 740 (H), grass green No. 615 (I), watermelon No. 135 (J), peach No. 305 (K), spring green No. 605 (L) and emerald No. 655 (M); 20″ square piece of burlap; 20″ square of fabric for pillow back; 16″ pillow form. **For hanging:** Aunt Lydia's Heavy Rug Yarn, 2 (70-yard) skeins each light blue No. 705 (color A), turquoise icing No. 735 (B), navy No. 725 (C) and spring green No. 605 (D); 1 skein each medium blue No. 710 (E), white No. 805 (F), peacock No. 740 (G), buttercup No. 540 (H), coral No. 130 (I), peach No. 305 (J), light orchid No. 020 (K), emerald No. 655 (L), phantom red No. 140 (M) and lavender No. 005 (N); 28″ x 40″ piece of burlap. **For both items:** adjustable rug punch needle (such as Hero Adjusto-matic Rug Punch Needle No. 6); stretcher frame; waterproof felt-tipped marker; tracing paper; carbon paper; dressmaker's tracing wheel.

### GENERAL DIRECTIONS

Cut a sheet of tracing paper, piecing it if necessary, to exact size of pillow or hanging. Enlarge diagram for piece you are making (see How to Enlarge Patterns, page 8) on the tracing paper. Grid will cover entire sheet.

Rug punching is done from wrong side of fabric so, to reverse pattern, turn tracing over and pin it to burlap. Slide piece of carbon paper between a section of tracing and burlap and go over lines firmly with tracing wheel. Trace all pattern lines in this manner, checking occasionally to make sure burlap is marked (the markings will be faint). When entire design has been transferred, remove tracing and carbon and go over all lines on burlap with felt-tipped marker.

Mount burlap on stretcher frame with marked side facing upward. Following directions that come with rug punch needle, fill in each area with ½″ loops of color specified.

**FINISHING: For pillow:** Remove work from stretcher frame. With right sides together, sew pillow back to front on 3 sides. Trim seams and turn right side out. Insert pillow form and sew open side closed. **For hanging:** Remove work from stretcher frame. Turn raw edges to wrong side, mitering corners, and hem in place. **(Note:** If you wish to use hanging as a rug, brush on a liquid antiskid rug backing, following directions on container.)

CORNICE COVER AND DRAPERIES (page 107)

TEXTURED NEEDLEPOINT PILLOW (page 41)

FLOWER-STREWN EMBROIDERED PILLOWS (page 65)

COTTAGE CUSHIONS
(page 75)

QUICK-CHANGE FLOOR PILLOW (page 74)

IRISH CHAIN NEEDLEPOINT PILLOW (page 36)

WOVEN NEEDLEPOINT CANVAS PLACE MAT (page 136)

NOAH's ARK APPLIQUED QUILT (page 29)

DELFT-PATTERN NEEDLEPOINT PILLOWS (page 46)

STUFFED-SHIRT SOFT SCULPTURES (page 114)

LOVESEAT PILLOWS AND SEAT CUSHIONS (page 76)

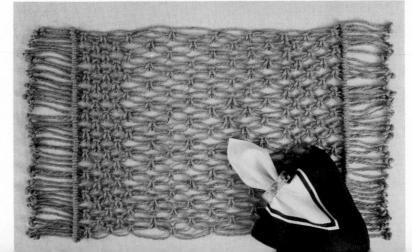

JUTE MACRAMÉ PLACE-MAT (page 135)

NOSEGAY CROSS-STITCH PILLOW (page 51)

BARGELLO-TRIMMED DESK SET (page 141)

PUNCH-NEEDLE WALL HANGING AND PILLOW (page 80)

CUT-OUT AND SCALLOPED PLACE MAT (page 138)

CROCHETED SLEEVE FOR POT HANDLES (page 143)

EMBROIDERED PLACE MAT AND NAPKIN (page 134)

**LACY KNITTED PLACE MAT** (page 139)

**VINYL PICNIC PLACE MAT WITH POCKETS** (page 140)

**COMING-UP-ROSES AND NINE-TIMES-LAVENDER PILLOWS** (page 69)

ROMAN-STRIPE
CROCHETED AFGHAN (page 20)

DELPHINIUM DREAM
CROCHETED AFGHAN (page 14)

ROSEBUD PATTERN
KNITTED AFGHAN (page 24)

MORNING GLORY EMBROIDERED SHEET
AND PILLOWCASE (page 153)

CRESTS AND EMBLEMS CROCHETED AFGHAN (page 17)

WINDOW "VINE" WITH ORGANDY LEAVES (page 121)

LONG-STITCH STARBURST MOTIF
FOR PICTURES OR PILLOWS (page 100)

YARN-WOVEN-CANVAS WINDOW PANEL (page 112)

JUTE-STRUNG SHUTTERETTES (page 111)

BURLAP FLOOR PILLOWS (page 77)

WINDOW AND PILLOW ENSEMBLE
ADAPTED FROM SHEETS (page 120)

SHAKER DESIGN RUG TO KNIT (page 130)

WOVEN UPHOLSTERY WEBBING-RUG (page 125)

LATCH HOOK GRANNY RUG (page 122)

ROCKING HORSE PATCHWORK QUILT (page 27)

TEXTURED NEEDLEPOINT CHAIR SEAT (page 41)

CONCENTRIC SQUARES KNITTED HANGING
(page 102)

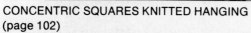

RAINBOW-AND-CREAM
AND HONEYCOMB
PUFF CROCHETED PILLOWS (page 67)

DRAPERIES AND TABLECLOTH
ADAPTED FROM SHEETS (page 118)

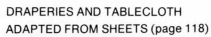

MACRAMÉ HANGING
OR WINDOW BLIND (page 104)

APPLIQUÉD AND EMBROIDERED
BELL PULLS (page 148)

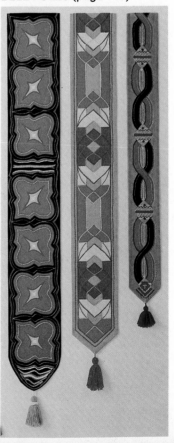

BED OF ROSES CROCHETED COVERLET
(page 12)

BURLAP DRAPERY (page 110)

HEXAGON-MOTIF CROCHETED
LAP THROW (page 23)

TILE-MOTIF EMBROIDERED PILLOW (page 60)

MACHINE APPLIQUÉD GLASS CURTAINS (page 116)

LACK AND OMBRÉ KNITTED AFGHAN (page 25)   AUTUMN DAISY CROCHETED AFGHAN (page 15)

NCED FIELDS CROCHETED AFGHAN (page 21)   GARDENIA LACE CROCHETED LAP THROW (page 16)

"GALWAY BAY" ARAN RUG (page 126)

MOSAIC-TILE-MOTIF
CROCHETED RUG (page 123)

CROSS-STITCH PILLOWS (page 54)

NEEDLEPOINT-COVERED FOOTSTOOL (page 155)

STUFFED-SHIRT SOFT SCULPTURES (page 114)

LOG CABIN NEEDLEPOINT PILLOW (page 36)

NEEDLEPOINT STRAWBERRIES PICTURE (page 98)

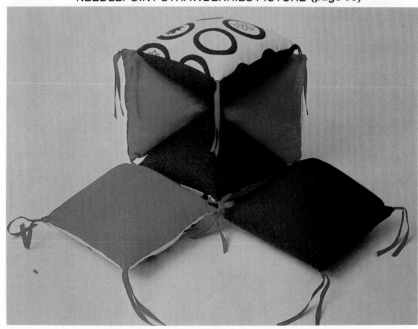

SIX-PART PILLOW FOOTSTOOL (page 73)

PLAID AND WHITE SHEET BEDROOM ENSEMBLE (page 33)

Each sq. = 1"

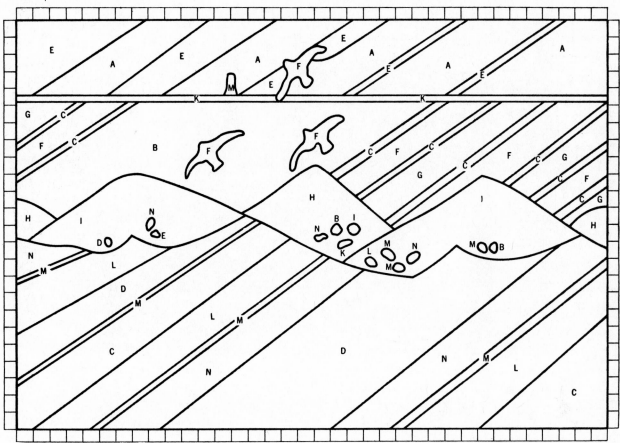

**SIERRA NEVADA WALL HANGING**

**SALINAS PILLOW**    Each sq. = 1"

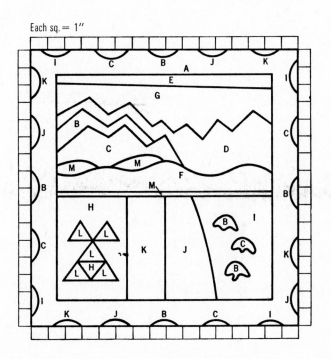

97

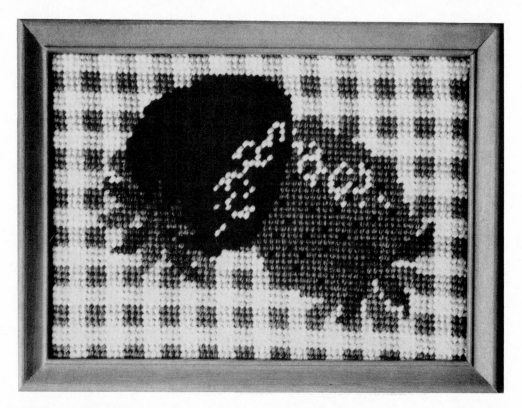

# NEEDLEPOINT STRAWBERRIES PICTURE

Berries on a basketlike background are worked in half cross-stitch.

**Half cross-stitch**

**SIZE:** 5″ x 7″.

**MATERIALS:** 8″ x 9″ piece double-thread (penelope) needlepoint canvas with 10 spaces per inch; 3-ply, Persian-type needlepoint and crewel yarn, 13⅓ yards light yellow, 8⅓ yards dark yellow, 6⅔ yards white, 5 yards red, 3 yards pink, 2⅓ yards each medium and dark green and 1⅓ yards brown; tapestry needle; masking tape; 5″ x 7″ heavy cardboard; 5″ x 7″ unfinished picture frame without glass; pigmented-shellac primer; enamel or acrylic paint; screw eyes; picture wire.

**TO PREPARE CANVAS:** Tape edges to prevent raveling. Find center of canvas by basting a line from center of one edge to center of opposite edge, being careful to follow a row of spaces. Then baste another line from center of third edge to center of fourth edge. Basting threads will cross at center.

**YARN:** Do not separate yarn; use 3 strands throughout. Cut yarn in 20″ lengths.

**STITCHES:** The entire design and background are worked in half cross-stitch (see diagram).

**TO WORK NEEDLEPOINT:** Each space on chart indicates one stitch. Find center stitch on chart and work it on center of canvas. Continue to follow chart, working strawberries and leaves first, then background.

**FINISHING:** Wet canvas and block to 5″ x 7″. Allow it to dry thoroughly at least 2 days before removing blocking pins. Apply pigmented-shellac primer to frame; let dry. Paint frame with enamel or acrylic; let dry. Center cardboard backing on wrong side of canvas and wrap excess canvas to back, taping in place. Insert needlepoint in frame and add glazier tips or small brads to hold in place. Add screw eyes and picture wire to hang.

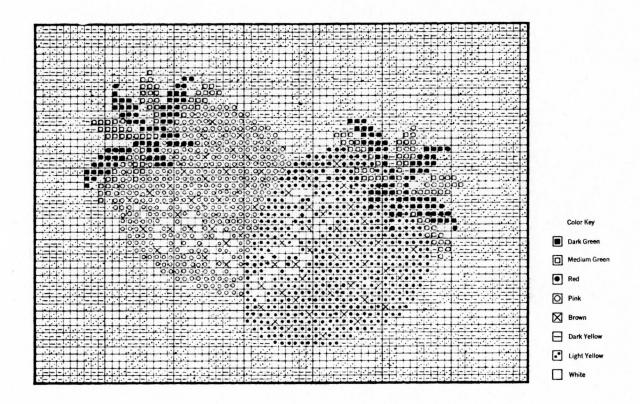

Color Key

- ■ Dark Green
- ▣ Medium Green
- ◉ Red
- ◯ Pink
- ⊠ Brown
- ⊟ Dark Yellow
- ⊡ Light Yellow
- ☐ White

# LONG-STITCH STARBURST MOTIF FOR PICTURES OR PILLOWS

Four different color schemes give four distinct looks to a single sophisticated design pattern to frame or face a pillow.

**SIZE:** Design measures 15½" square.

**MATERIALS:** 20"-square double-thread needlepoint canvas with 12 spaces per inch; waterproof needlepoint pen; 18"-square needlepoint stretcher frame; tapestry needle; thumbtacks or staple gun; 3-ply Persian-type needlepoint and crewel yarn, 40-yard skeins in the following colors:

**Rust-beige scheme:** 3 skeins medium beige; 2 skeins light rust; 1 skein each light beige, dark rust and light rust.

**Black and white scheme:** 4 skeins each black and white.

**Rainbow scheme:** 2 skeins each orange and red; 1 skein each yellow, dark magenta, medium magenta, dark purple, medium purple, medium blue, light blue, medium green and light green.

**Pastel scheme:** 4 skeins cream; 2 skeins mint green; 1 skein each yellow, pale orange, baby pink, baby blue and lavender.

## GENERAL DIRECTIONS

Using thumbtacks, center canvas and fasten to stretcher frame, pulling it taut. Mark center hole on canvas. Following diagram (one fourth of design given), mark design on canvas with waterproof pen. **(Note:** The grid on the diagram corresponds to the meshes of the canvas.)

Following photograph, page 95, for color, start by working shapes within triangular section at the center of each side. For these sections *only,* the stitches run *parallel* to the meshes so the color areas must be worked twice for the yarn to cover adequately. First, work stitches to fill color area parallel to nearest side of canvas (A on diagram), then work stitches over the same area perpendicular to the nearest side (B on diagram). The design covering the remainder of the canvas is worked with stitches running *diagonal* to the mesh and the color areas need to be worked only once for the yarn to cover the canvas.

After the triangular sections have been completed, work the 8 star points at center (see diagram for stitch direction). Start first star point with first stitch through center hole, then complete point by working 14 more stitches. Work adjacent star point with 14 stitches *only* (do not work through center hole). Continue in this manner, working first stitch of every alternate star point through center hole (4 stitches worked through center hole). These star points establish the direction of the stitches for the long parallelograms on the diagram. Each parallelogram is divided into diamonds of 14 stitches each (for some designs, 2 adjacent diamonds may be the same color). Complete these parallelograms next, working from center line out. Finally, work the squares at each corner (see diagram for stitch direction).

To block canvas, remove from stretcher frame, wet thoroughly, then tack to a board. Let dry for several days.

Frame needlepoint again or make into pillow.

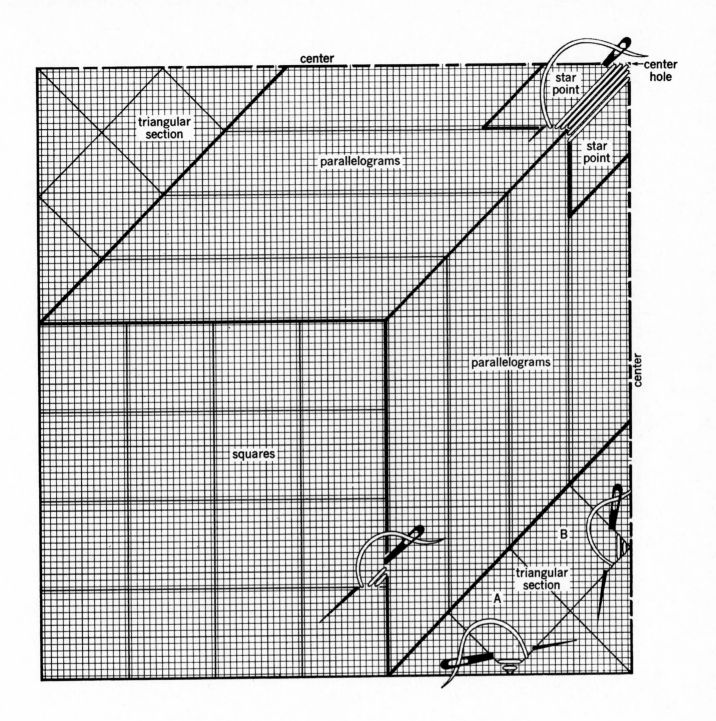

center

triangular
section

parallelograms

star
point

star
point

center
hole

squares

parallelograms

center

B

triangular
section

A

# CONCENTRIC SQUARES KNITTED HANGING

Worked in stockinette stitch, the tubular sections for this unusual wall hanging are stuffed with muslin "pillows" as you go.

**SIZE:** About 47" square.

**MATERIALS:** Wool sport yarn, 11 ounces yellow, 24 ounces yellow-green, 27 ounces green-blue, 26 ounces green, 23 ounces blue; knitting needles, one 14"-long pair No. 3 and one 29" circular needle No. 3 (or international needles No. 11) or the size that will give you the correct gauge; 4 yards 36"-wide muslin and polyester-fiberfill stuffing for inner pillows; one 48" dowel 1" in diameter for rod; 2 wooden finials.

**GAUGE:** 7 stitches = 1"; 9 rows = 1".

**Note.:** Wall hanging is composed of knitted tubes filled with stuffed muslin "pillows." The following information will help if you plan to adjust the size. One (100-yard) ounce of sport yarn will make a piece of knitting about 5" x 18". Each tube is 5" wide before it is folded in half to form tube.

**CENTER SECTION A:** (See Diagrams 1 and 2.) Starting at center of wall hanging with yellow and 14" needles, cast on 35 sts. Work in stockinette st for 9". Bind off. Fold in half right side out to form 4½" x 5" rectangle. Seam sides; turn. Make pillow (see To Make Inner Pillow, below) and insert it in knitted center section. Sew opening.

**TO MAKE INNER PILLOW:** For center section A cut 2 pieces muslin 5½" x 6". Sew together, leaving 1 side open. Turn, stuff and sew open side. Make pillows for tubes as you need them, as follows: Cut 2 muslin pieces 3½" x length of tube, adding ½" seam allowance at each end. Seam ends and 1 side; turn. Place a roll of stuffing in tube, turn in edges at open side and sew.

The remainder of hanging can be made in either of the following 2 methods. The designer used the Pick-Up Stitches Method, but the Sew-Together Method can be used if you wish a more portable, easy-to-handle construction.

You will find it easier to knit the longer tubes by working back and forth on the circular needle.

**PICK-UP STITCHES METHOD: Tube B:** (See Diagram 1.) Pick up a st in each st across folded edge of center section A. Attach yellow-green and work in stockinette st for 5", ending with a p row. Make inner pillow and place it on wrong side of piece. Fold piece over pillow (sts are still on needle). With free needle pick up a st at fold where tube was started, slide it into needle with sts and K 2 tog.

*Pick up next st at start of tube, slide it onto other needle and k 2 tog. Repeat from * across. Break off. Tube with pillow inside is completed. Work another B tube across opposite edge of A.

Across one side of B-A-B unit work C tube with yellow-green by picking up a st for each row on A section and ends of both B tubes. Work in stockinette st for 5". Bind off. Complete as for B. Work another C tube across opposite edge of B-A-B.

With green work a D tube by picking up a st for each row on ends of C tubes and in each st along fold of B tube. Complete as before. Work another D tube across opposite edge.

Continue working tubes, following Diagram 2 for placement and colors.

**Corners:** Starting with small square (X on diagram), make corner sections separately and sew in place. The color of each tube is a continuation of the color used on sides of square

**SEW-TOGETHER METHOD:** For each B tube cast on 35 sts with yellow-green and work in stockinette st for 5″. Bind off. Fold in half lengthwise right side out and seam ends; turn. Make and insert inner pillow. Lining up sts, carefully sew open side of tube to A (See Diagram 1).

For remaining tubes determine number of sts to cast on by measuring edge to which the new tube will be sewn and multiply by 7. For example, a C tube will measure 2½″ (end of B) plus 5″ (A) plus 2½″ (end of other B). This adds up to 10″. 10 times 7 equals the 70 sts to be cast on. Work as for B tube, following Diagram 2 for color and placement.

**Corners:** See corners for Pick-Up Stitches Method.

**TUBES FOR HANGING ROD:** With blue make 2 empty tubes 8″ long and 1 empty tube 25″ long. Sew to wrong side of work, between last 2 rounds of tube sections (broken lines on Diagram 2). Insert rod through tubes and attach a finial to each end.

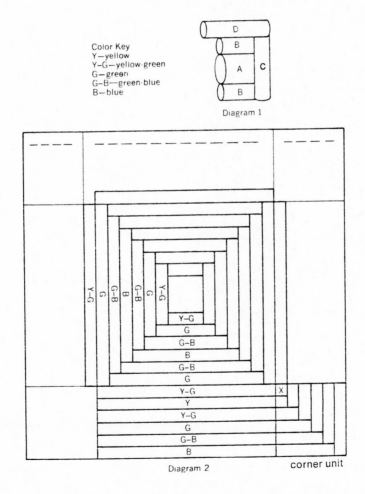

Color Key
Y—yellow
Y-G—yellow-green
G—green
G-B—green-blue
B—blue

Diagram 1

Diagram 2          corner unit

# MACRAMÉ HANGING OR WINDOW BLIND

Make the design any size, depending on your window or wall area. Worked with jute in rust and natural, it's mostly square knots.

**SIZE:** Approximately 30″ wide; length adjustable.

**MATERIALS:** 2½′ length ¾″-diameter dowel; 15 heavy-duty ½″ inside-diameter and 1½″ outside-diameter flat steel washers; 14 heavy-duty 7/16″ inside-diameter and 1″ outside-diameter flat steel washers; two 4-ounce (70-yard) tubes Lily Jute-Tone in burnt orange; four 4-ounce (70-yard) tubes Lily Jute-Tone in natural color; scissors; T-pins; C-clamps; yardstick; 20″ x 30″ piece of Homoste for knotting board; small jar of white glue, diluted half and half with water; small brush; 2 large-eyed tapestry needles; brown wrapping paper; pencil; clear spray lacquer; black felt-tipped marker.

**PREPARATION:** Measure window inside casing and cut dowel to length. Sand smooth and spray with clear lacquer for a protective finish; let dry. Also spray all washers with lacquer if they do not already have a protective finish.

Curtain is worked on 20″ x 30″ knotting board with a grid of 1″ squares ruled off on brown wrapping paper taped in place (to make grid cut paper to 20″ x 30″ size then mark dots at 1″ intervals around edges. Join dots across opposite sides of paper using black felt-tipped pen). Tape grid in place.

To measure out cord lengths, set up two C-clamps so that cord can be wrapped between them. Set clamps 7′ 6″ apart and measure off 29 lengths of burnt orange; cut cord at first clamp for 29 lengths of 15′ orange cord. Reset clamps to measure 15 lengths of 35′6″ natural jute. If your window is unusually long, move clamps farther apart to cut longer cords. Keep center fold in each cord.

**Note:** The curtain is made up of two repeated vertical arrangements which are referred to as A and B in Diagram A. There are 15A groups alternating with 14B groups.

**TO START:** Referring to Diagram B, Steps 1 through 4, fold a natural jute length in half and attach to dowel as shown. Continue adding remaining lengths, using 31′ lengths for A groups and the 35′ 6″ lengths for B groups. Lift the natural jute loop over as shown and pull the doubled strand through enough to permit the dowel to be run through the formed loop. When dowel is picked up, each group will have four strands—two orange holding cords that form core of each group flanked by two natural jute knotting cords. Arrange groups of cords evenly (approximately 1″ apart) across dowel and tighten up. Fold each group of cords into bundle and bind with rubber band until ready to use.

Secure dowel at top of knotting board and as you work, pull knotted design over top edge of board to line up on grid.

**TO WORK A GROUP:** Work across as follows: With natural, tie two square knots as in Diagram A (See Diagram D for making

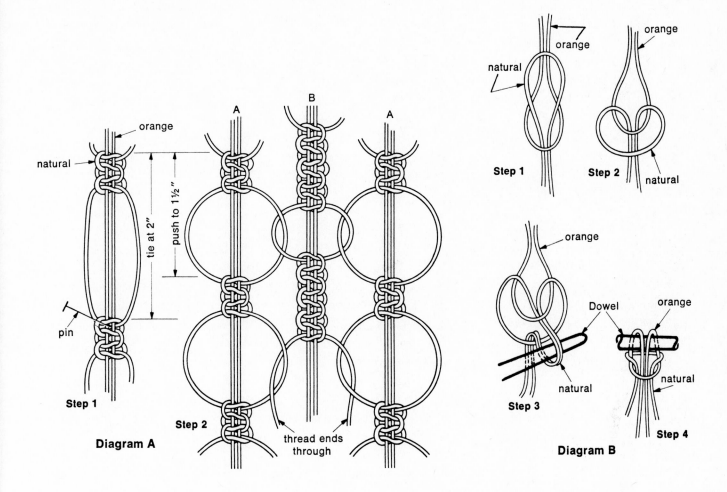

**Diagram A**

Step 1

orange

natural

pin

tie at 2"

Step 2

A  B  A

push to 1½"

thread ends through

orange

natural

**Step 1**  **Step 2**

orange

natural

orange

Dowel

orange

natural

**Step 3**  **Step 4**

natural

**Diagram B**

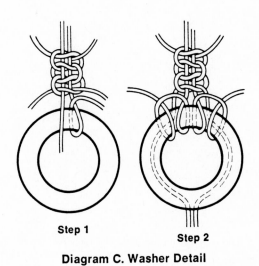

Step 1  Step 2

**Diagram C. Washer Detail**

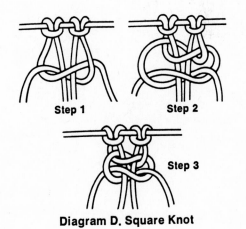

Step 1  Step 2

Step 3

**Diagram D. Square Knot**

square knot) over orange holding cords. Push knots up tight against dowel and hold in place with T-pin. Measure down 2" from dowel, insert T-pin. Tie two more square knots, pushing tightly against pin as shown in Diagram A page 105. Coming down 2" from knots, insert pin, tie two more square knots and push tight against pin. Repeat, working down each A group until you run out of room on board. Push natural jute up orange as shown in Step 2 of Diagram A, hold orange holding cords taut as you do this, and arrange natural jute to form open circles 1½" apart. Repeat above procedure 28 times on each A group, moving your work as required by size of board, or until shade is desired length before bottom border.

**TO WORK B GROUP:** Tie three square knots as in Step 2, Diagram A. Push knots up tight against dowel and pin. Coming down about 1" or a little more, insert pin on centerline. Thread the left hand cord of the B group through the adjacent loop of the A group, going from the front to back as shown in Step 2, Diagram A. Now tie four square knots, bringing them up tightly to the pin. Remove the pin and push natural jute up orange, holding it taut as you do so, to form small circle. Make sure each small circle is of sufficient size so that it does not draw two A groups together. See relationship of size in Diagram A. (**Note:** As you work you will find that you will tie the B groups by eye, probably without pinning, and allow automatically for slight variations in thickness of jute.) Plan to use your 1" grid on knotting board to help you plan size of small circles. When all B groups are knotted, begin bottom border as follows:

To make bottom borders you will continue to maintain A and B groups. Beginning with A groups first, align the bottom row of large circles accurately. Make any necessary adjustments to even design. On each A group tie eight square knots and form large circle as before, then tie two more square knots. Thread orange jute on two tapestry needles. Referring to Diagram C, hold natural jute at back of large washer, one strand on each half as shown, and bring right orange cord over washer. Go through center hole and up, coming over orange cord from left to right. Go back behind washer, come forward through center hole, up front of washer and under loop previously formed, along side orange cord where it started. This makes double reversed half hitch (a Lark's Head) around washer, covering natural jute. Do a total of eight Lark's Heads around right side of washer, then, repeating technique, cover left side of washer with eight more, using left strand of orange. Repeat border on all 15 A groups, making certain to set in washer equally on all groups.

Proceed to tie border on all B groups. Check alignment of all B groups; adjust if necessary. Tie four square knots down from last small circle. Attach small washer, following procedure described for A groups. Cover washer with six Lark's Heads on right half, then six on left. Tie two square knots using orange as knotting cords. Then, thread ends of orange cords through adjacent A circles as shown. Tie eleven more square knots. Continue to work all B groups in same manner and push last eleven knot units up or down for an even border. Remove curtain from knotting board and turn face down on floor or table. Apply glue-water mixture to last square knots on B groups and bottom edge of large washers on A groups. Let dry. Comb tassel ends. Steam ends or pull straight if they curl. Hang curtain by most feasible means in window and trim ends even.

# CORNICE COVER AND DRAPERIES TO SEW

The fabric on the cornice is padded in a trapunto design, then stretched over a curved plywood frame and stapled. The draperies are pinch-pleated and suspended from a rod and the sheer curtains are hung behind from a separate rod.

**SIZE:** 24" high x 49" wide x 6" deep. (Our window is 48" wide; cornice will fit windows from 45" to 48" wide. Adjustments can be made for other dimensions (see To Build Cornice).

**MATERIALS:** One 4' x 8' sheet of ½" plywood. **For cornice only:** 2 yards 48"-wide antique satin decorator's fabric; 1½ yards 45"-wide organza; 1½ yards muslin (optional—to cover inside of cornice); 2 yards of 45"-wide, ¾"-thick cotton or polyester padding; 2 yards ½"-thick and 3½ yards of 1½"-thick upholstery welting; 1 bag polyester-fiberfill; 3 yards ½"-wide decorative braid (optional); yarn needle; cloth tape measure; wood glue; staple gun and ½" staples; pushpins; safety pins; carbon paper; saber saw; hammer; 1½" finishing nails; scissors; 2 L-shaped corner braces with screws; fabric glue; drill; brown paper; pencil; ruler; try square. (**Note:** We made matching draperies out of the same fabric, with pale-green sheer curtains underneath. To make draperies—sateen lining optional—and curtains, you'll need fabric twice the length of measurement from floor to ceiling plus 20" for hem and ¼ yard for tiebacks; pale-green sheer of same length but without the additional ¼ yard; 6 yards drapery pleating tape; triple-pronged drapery pleating hooks.)

**TO BUILD CORNICE:** Measure width of outside window frame. Add 1" window clearance at sides. Use figure obtained and see Cutting Diagram (page 108) for plywood construction of cornice frame. The width can be made wider or narrower at center of pattern to fit your window. Enlarge pattern (see How to Enlarge Patterns, page 8) on brown wrapping paper, piecing if necessary to make a full-size pattern for front of frame. Hold in place at top of window to check dimensions and adjust if necessary. Make patterns to fit top and sides of frame (depth is 6", but it can be as much as 8", depending on your window). The sides should remain the same as ours in length to match the sides of the front piece.

Mark pattern on plywood with carbon paper. Cut out with saber saw. Following diagram, build frame, butting, gluing and nailing with 1½" finishing nails.

**TO DO TRAPUNTO:** As shown, fabric is 67" x 36". Measure width and height of cornice frame. Add 1" allowance for padding, 18" to width for sides and wrap to back, and 12" to height for top and wrap to back. If you can't get fabric wide enough, piece as needed, matching the fabric's pattern at seams. (Ours is pieced at sides, with seams covered by decorative braid.) If you are using fabric without a visible grain direction or pattern that must run horizontally, use the fabric lengthwise to obtain necessary width. Do not cut the curve at bottom; it is cut later.

Enlarge Trapunto Pattern (see How to Enlarge Patterns, page 8) on brown wrapping paper, piecing if necessary. Test full-size

Each sq = 1"

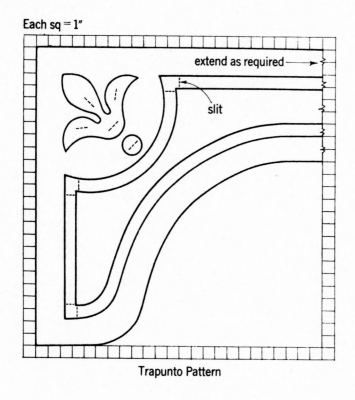

extend as required →

slit

Trapunto Pattern

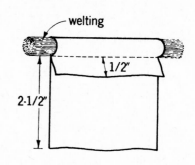

welting

1/2"

2-1/2"

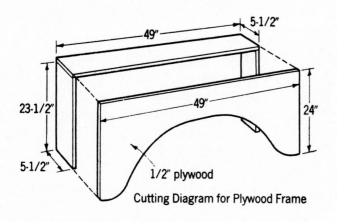

49"

5-1/2"

23-1/2"

49"

24"

5-1/2"

1/2" plywood

Cutting Diagram for Plywood Frame

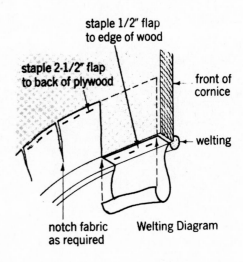

staple 1/2" flap
to edge of wood

staple 2-1/2" flap
to back of plywood

front of
cornice

welting

notch fabric
as required

Welting Diagram

pattern on wood frame; add or subtract from center of pattern to fit your frame, adjusting curve if necessary.

Cut organza to fit entire pattern area, adding 2″ all around. Pin organza on paper pattern. Trace design motifs on organza with pencil. (Since design is symmetrical, it is right side up as traced.) Baste organza to wrong side of center of fabric.

Machine-stitch on scrap pieces of organza and fabric to test bobbin tension. (Stitching lines are worked on the wrong side, so the bobbin tension must be correct for the right side of work to look even.) Follow pencil lines on organza to stitch 1⅛″-wide channels and side corner motifs.

Carefully cut slits in organza within channel stitching as indicated by dotted lines on trapunto pattern. Attach large safety pin to the end of 1½″-wide upholstery welting. Use one of the threads on welting to wrap around pin and end so that they form a point. Work pin end into channel at one end. Inch pin through channel to other end and out through slit. Cut welting at each end, leaving ½″ extra. Push extra bit into end of channel beyond slit to fill. Repeat to fill all channels in same manner. Check the right side as you go, making sure that the ends of channels are neatly filled.

Cut slits as indicated within motifs. Stuff motifs with polyester, using a yarn needle to push padding into all areas of each motif. Slit openings in organza can be sewn closed by hand or left open.

**TO MOUNT TRAPUNTO:** Pad frame front, sides and top with 1½″-thick padding, filling as needed and stapling to inside of frame.

Position fabric with trapunto on padded frame. Hold with pushpins and adjust until fabric covers frame smoothly. Cut curve along bottom, 3″ below wood edge. Clip notches in 3″ excess as needed and staple fabric to inside of frame at sides and bottom. At top, miter corner and staple to inside of frame.

Make welting for bottom as follows: Cut fabric 4½″ wide x 84″ long, piecing as needed for length. Following Welting Diagram, wrap lengthwise around ½″ welting, leaving ½″ flap and 2½″ flap. Stitch in place.

Following diagram, staple welting to bottom edge of wood frame through ½″ flap of fabric in welting piece. Place staples near front edge of frame to keep welting from slipping downward and leaving gap. Start at the lower inside edge of one side section of frame and staple along side, up curve, down to other side and to edge. To end off, cut welting about ½″ within fabric, fold fabric neatly to back and staple to frame. Then take 2½″ flap of fabric welting and staple to inside of frame, covering first line of staples; notch fabric at back, as required, to lie flat.

Following photograph, (pages 81 and 107) lay out optional length of decorative braid. (If fabric is not pieced, or seams are unobtrusive, omit braid.) Cut braid ½″ longer than needed and pushpin in place. Wrap end with small piece of masking tape so that it doesn't unravel. Glue in place with fabric glue, dotted underneath braid. Tuck taped ends into welting at each end. Let dry. Cover inside of frame with muslin stapled in place if desired.

Following directions on package, attach L-shaped corner braces to inside of frame with screws.

To make matching draperies, cut two lengths of fabric floor to ceiling height plus allowance for hem and top. Turn under and press ½″ along top edge. (If draperies are to be lined, cut lining same size. Turn under top and side edges ½″ and blindstitch to back of panels.) Cut pleating tape to fit top edge of each panel, spacing pockets for end hooks same distance from each side edge. Pin tape to wrong side of panel with top edge slightly below top edge of panel. Topstitch along both edges of tape. To pleat, follow manufacturer's directions.

Hem draperies and linings separately, making linings a little shorter. Follow photograph to make tiebacks.

To make sheer curtains, cut fabric as for draperies. Fold ½″, then 1½″ at top for casing. Insert rod in casing to gather curtains. Make hems the same depth as draperies.

# BURLAP DRAPERY WITH PULLED-THREAD PATTERN

An unexpectedly delicate design is created on a rustic fabric by pulling threads and using them to tie groups of warp strands.

**MATERIALS:** 3 yards 72″-wide natural burlap; 72″ strip 2½″- to 3½″-wide buckram or drapery-heading tape; 72″ weighted cloth strip (available in drapery-supply departments), 13 wooden curtain rings; 6′ wooden curtain rod; 2 finials and brackets; 1¼″ dowel; cup hook.

**HEADING:** Fold 1 cut edge of burlap about 1″, folding it exactly along a crosswise thread; press. Pin buckram to wrong side of burlap ½″ from fold line. Topstitch across both long edges of buckram.

**PULLED WORK:** Measure 15″ down from fold line and mark side edge of burlap with pin. Starting at pin, measure ¼″ in from edge of burlap and clip crosswise thread. Pull thread gently and follow it along to other side of burlap; clip other end ¼″ from edge and remove thread. Clip and pull next thread in same manner. Continue removing threads until you have a 4½″ pulled area. Skip first 2″ of warp (lengthwise) threads in pulled area; tie a pulled strand of burlap around middle of next 2″ of warp threads. Continue across pulled area in this manner (see photograph).

Measure 4½″ down from lower edge of pulled area and pull a 3″ band of threads. Measure 4½″ down from lower edge of last pulled area and pull a 4½″ band of threads. Tie threads as for first band. Alternate bands of untied and tied warp threads twice more.

Measure desired length of drapery; add 5″ or 6″ for hem and cut excess along a crosswise thread. Turn under ½″ and press. Mark hemline along a woven thread and lay weighted cloth strip along hem with one edge at hemline. Tack in place. Fold hem over weighted strip and topstitch.

Sew rings to heading. If necessary, cut rod to size. Attach brackets to wall. Slide rings on rod, attach finials to ends and rest on brackets. Screw cup hook into dowel end and insert hook into last curtain ring; use dowel to open and close drapery.

# JUTE-STRUNG SHUTTERETTES

Ready-made unfinished wood shutters come fitted with small curtain rods on which you knot and wind the natural jute twine.

**SIZE:** 36″ x 53″ as shown.

**MATERIALS:** 2 large balls of jute twine (available at hardware stores); 8 unfinished wood shutter panels with open center area (shutter panels come in many sizes; see Note below); four plastic or ceramic knobs; four 1″ x No. 6 roundhead wood screws; sixteen 1½″ hinges (if not packaged with screws, buy ¾″ x No. 6 butt screws); ebony wax stain; drill.

**Note:** Our shutter panels are 9″ x 26½″ each. Measure inside sill of your window and adjust individual panel size as needed, using the same layout.

**TO START:** Following directions on can, stain all shutter panels.

Cut 4- to 5-foot lengths of jute. Knot one end to top rod at back of one shutter panel. Wrap jute between top and bottom rods, half-hitching jute around each rod (see diagram) as you come to it. Maintain even tension throughout wrapping. Use additional lengths of jute as required, knotting end to rod. Wrap all shutter panels.

Following photograph for placement, mark backs of shutters for hinge placement, drilling pilot holes ½" deep. Following directions on package to attach hinges.

Mark placement of knobs; drill pilot holes and screw knobs in place with 1½" x No. 6 screws.

With helper, place shutter panels in windows, marking through hinges for placement. Drill pilot holes and attach hinges to window with screws provided in package.

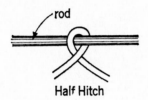

Half Hitch

# YARN-WOVEN-CANVAS WINDOW PANEL

The upper panel—needlepoint canvas with a pattern worked with a weaving needle—coordinates with the café curtains below.

**SIZE:** Panel is 24" x 35". Adjustments can be made for other dimensions (see Note below).

**MATERIALS: For panel:** ¾ yard of 57"-wide nylon mesh canvas with 10 spaces per inch (we used Dritz Nylon Knit needlepoint canvas); three 2-ounce skeins of rayon yarn (we used Kentucky All-Purpose Yarn, 100% rayon); 5" weaving needle; graph paper with 10 squares per inch; pencil. **For curtain:** One twin-size flat sheet. (**Note:** Amounts given are for our panel and curtain. Adjust amounts as needed to fit your window.)

**WOVEN PANEL:** Measure width and height of top half of your window. If width is between 32" and 40", make panel as shown, and weave more or fewer rows of border pattern to modify size. For a larger panel, plan pattern on graph paper (see right), repeating diamond motifs as needed and adding borders to fit.

Use graph paper, pieced to the same size as your window measurements. (Ten-squares-to-the-inch graph paper is actual size.) Mark off 1″ at side and bottom—areas to be left unworked.

Start at lower left corner. Copy pattern (one quarter of design is given) onto graph paper. Repeat pattern across lower edge until three large diamond motifs have been completed.

Copy fourth large diamond motif and then complete right corner, following same pattern as for left corner, transposing border and pattern.

Hold paper pattern up to your window to check placement of diamond motifs—they must be centered. Rearrange by adding or subtracting border rows if necessary.

Side pattern repeats border and triangles. Following photograph, continue pattern up sides. When the last triangle is no less than 2″ from the upper edge, draw upper corners. Top corners are the same as bottom corners but without diamond motifs. Complete triangle motifs along upper edge. Outermost top border does not have zigzag-stitch row; draw remaining border pattern to within 1 graph square of upper edge.

For panel, cut mesh canvas to dimensions of graph-paper pattern, carefully following line of mesh (hemming is unnecessary). For curtain-rod casing, cut strip 1½″ x width of panel.

Thread weaving needle with a 36″ length of yarn. Starting at lower left corner, follow graphed pattern to weave design. Complete graphed pattern, weaving one stitch for every line drawn on paper. (**Note:** To begin yarn on canvas, leave a 3″ end on wrong side of canvas. Work over the end for first few stitches, then clip off excess. To secure end of yarn, run it under the last few stitches on the wrong side and clip off. Start new length by running under a few stitches on the wrong side; trim.)

Handstitch top edge of casing strip to wrong side of canvas, 1″ below top edge of panel. Stitch lower edge of strip 1″ below upper edge of strip, easing casing to allow for thickness of rod.

**TO MAKE CURTAIN:** Use window measurement to make curtain. Wide hem of sheet is bottom edge of curtain; selvages are side edges. Cut sheet desired length plus 3″ for casing.

Turn cut edge under ½″; press; then turn under 2½″ hem. Topstitch two lines: one through fold; one 1½″ above first, to form casing.

Each pattern line = 1 stitch

# STUFFED-SHIRT SOFT SCULPTURES TO SEW

To the shirts you add cloth faces with felt features and hands made from dyed cotton gloves. All the pieces are stitched down on background fabric, stuffed and mounted on canvas stretcher strips. Appropriate accessories complete the family portraits.

**SIZE:** Dad and Mom, 18″ x 30″; children, 14″ x 23″.

**MATERIALS: Dad:** Man's shirt; hanky; felt scraps for hair, mustache and eyes. **Mom:** Woman's blouse; 18″-square piece of felt for hat and purse; felt scraps for hair and features; 3″ x 20″ fabric for hatband and purse button; artificial flowers; 1 yard narrow ribbon. **Each child:** Child's knit turtleneck shirt (about size 4); felt scraps for hair and features; row of cutout paper dolls and pinwheel. **For all sculptures:** 36″-wide fabric for background, ⅝ yard for Mom or Dad, ½ yard for each child; ⅜ yard 36″-wide flesh-colored cotton will make all 4 heads; white cotton gloves (adult's and child's); flesh-colored dye for gloves; fabric glue; matching sewing threads; polyester-fiberfill stuffing; 1¾″-wide canvas stretcher strips, 2 strips each 18″ and 30″ for each grown-up, 2 strips each 14″ and 23″ for each child; staple gun; tailor's chalk.

**Note:** You can use any blouse or shirt that you have on hand. For the new round-collar look on Dad's shirt, just remove old fold-down collar and add a 1″-wide strip of white cotton and a button.

## GENERAL DIRECTIONS

Tint gloves to match flesh color of fabric for head and allow to dry.

Assemble stretcher strips to form frame. Center and lightly mark with chalk the dimensions of frame (see "size") on fabric.

Enlarge diagrams (see How to Enlarge Patterns, page 8), and cut out pieces from fabric and felt, adding ½" seam allowance to sides and top of head; do not add to felt. Sections of some pieces are behind others, as shown by broken lines. Follow complete outline when cutting.

Following photograph for placement, pin top (blouse or shirt) and head to background. Topstitch along shoulders and sides of top. (For Mom, slide hat piece A behind head at slight angle and glue to background.) Turn in seam allowance on sides and top of head; blindstitch.

Fold excess background fabric over top and sides of frame and staple to back.

Insert polyester-fiberfill through neck to pad head, gather slightly at neck, then tuck excess into neck section of top. Stuff sleeves and gloves; insert open ends of gloves into sleeves and sew around wrists. Pad body of top, fold lower edge under and sew to background, then staple lower edge of background to back of frame; or stretch background and top to back of frame and staple.

Glue features and hair to head.

**For Mom:** Glue hat piece B over top of head, overlapping top edge of hat piece A. Cut 3" from hatband fabric and reserve for purse button. Fold remaining fabric in half lengthwise and cut ends diagonally for hatband. Turn in all edges ½" and topstitch. Cut 5" piece from one end; wrap cut end of short piece around long piece 3" from diagonal end and sew to simulate knot. Tack band and flowers to hat as shown. Tack on ribbon.

**Mom's purse:** Cut 7" x 16" felt. Fold up one end 6" and topstitch sides to form pocket; stuff slightly. Trim flap into curve, fold down and tack in place. For button, cut 3" diameter fabric circle, gather edges to form pouch, stuff and flatten slightly; sew to purse.

Fold arms as shown and tack with a few secure stitches to hold position. Tuck purse in Mom's arm; cut a string of paper dolls and tack between girl's fingers; slide pinwheel through boy's fingers; glue upper end. Tuck hanky in Dad's pocket and newspaper in hand.

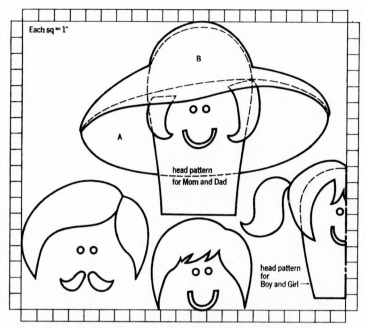

# MACHINE-APPLIQUÉD GLASS CURTAINS

Double-layered organdy appliqués of rolling hills and long-stemmed tulips create a lovely shaded effect on plain panels.

SIZE: 108″ wide x 84″ long.

MATERIALS: 2 glass-curtain panels, each about 108″ wide x 84″ long; 45″-wide organdy, 1¾ yards each of 2 shades green, 1⅛ yard yellow, ¼ yard each of 2 shades blue; matching sewing threads.

TO START: Enlarge patterns (see How to Enlarge Patterns, page 8). Cut out patterns but do not add seam allowance.

Following solid lines, cut 2 dark-green hills. Following solid lines, cut 2 of each tulip; repeat, following broken lines. Following solid lines, cut 4 leaves; repeat, following broken lines. From dark green cut four 23″ stems and two 10″ stems all ¾″ wide.

Pin dark-green hill to a curtain panel, placing end X at front edge and Y at lower edge (allow about 1″ to extend beyond edges for hems). Pin light-green hill over dark green in same manner. Fold hems of both hills over edges of curtain and press. Hem by hand. Machine-appliqué rolling edges of hills, using zigzag stitch. Following photograph, pin stems and flowers in place, placing larger section of each tulip over smaller section. Pin a large leaf to each yellow tulip stem and 2 small leaves to blue tulip stem. Zigzag-stitch all pieces in place (for the flowers, first remove larger section, stitch smaller section, then replace larger section and stitch).

Arrange and stitch pieces to other curtain, reversing hills so that they match at center where curtains meet.

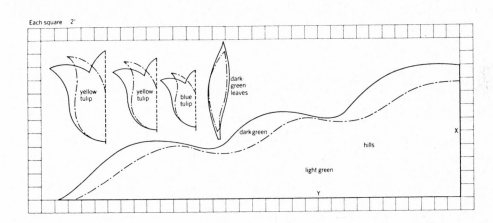

Each square 2″

yellow tulip

yellow tulip

blue tulip

dark-green leaves

dark green

hills

light green

X

Y

# DRAPERIES AND TABLECLOTH ADAPTED FROM SHEETS

Three twin-size sheets in green and yellow are all you need to make the complete ensemble, including the puffed tulips that decorate the cornice and form a jaunty bouquet for the table.

**MATERIALS:** Two solid-green twin-size flat sheets and 1 solid-yellow twin-size flat sheet to make all accessories shown here. **Draperies:** Matching thread; 10"-wide cornice board; small amount of polyester-fiberfill stuffing; 2 small drapery rings. **Tulips:** #18- and #12-gauge covered floral stems; floral tape; white glue.

**DRAPERIES:** Cut a green sheet in half lengthwise. Using top hem of sheet for drapery hem determine length for drapery panels and cut, allowing 2" at top for heading. From yellow sheet cut two 5"-wide strips the length of drapery panels. With right sides facing, pin yellow strip across long cut edge of each panel; stitch. Fold over and bind raw edge, leaving a 2"-wide contrasting edge; blindstitch. Fold over 2" heading at top of each panel; stitch.

For tiebacks cut two 6" x 27" strips from yellow sheet. With right sides facing, fold each tieback in half lengthwise and stitch. Turn and press so that seam falls centered on one side. Turn in and stitch raw edges at ends. Add small drapery rings at ends to hold tieback loop in place.

To upholster cornice board cut fabric to cover front and side pieces, allowing enough excess to wrap all edges, as follows: Cut green for background and bind bottom edge with 3"-wide band of yellow. Pin and stitch background and band together. Following photograph, cover cornice board with pieced fabric, wrapping excess around edges; staple in place. Following directions below, make 3 padded tulips without stems and leaves. Tack tulips, evenly spaced, on cornice face as shown.

**ROUND TABLECLOTH:** Make a pattern from brown wrapping paper for a 60"-diameter semicircle, using pencil, bank pin and long piece of string for a compass. Using pattern, fold remaining green sheet in half, pin pattern on fold and cut out circular cloth. Turn up and stitch ½" hem. From yellow sheet cut 29"-square handkerchief. Fold over and stitch ½" hem to finish raw edges. Place handkerchief on tablecloth as in photograph.

**PADDED TULIPS:** Enlarge patterns for tulip petal and leaf shapes (see How to Enlarge Patterns, page 8). Cut out patterns, adding ½" to all edges for seam allowance. Each tulip has 3 padded shapes tacked together to form complete flower. For each flower cut 6 petals from yellow fabric. With right sides together, stitch pairs of petals together, leaving 1" to 2" open for padding. Turn petals and pad each lightly; close opening. Following photograph, arrange petals and tack together.

For leaves shape #18 wire stem into leaf shape. Cut a rectangular piece of scrap green sheet slightly larger than wire shape. Stretch and glue fabric to wire; let dry. Trim away excess fabric. Insert #12 wire stem in seam of tulips and hold securely with floral tape. Add 1 or 2 leaves along stem with floral tape. Make as many tulips as desired.

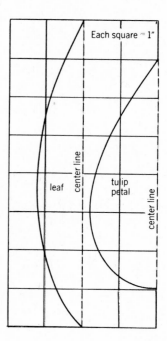

# WINDOW AND PILLOW ENSEMBLE ADAPTED FROM SHEETS

The café curtains and three pillows are made from one king-size tan flat sheet and a generous frosting of ecru lace.

**SIZES: Pillows:** 10" x 15" rectangle, 14" square, 14" square plus 4" ruffle. **Curtains:** Those shown fit 36" x 52" window. Each curtain measures 28" long x 39" wide.

**MATERIALS:** We used the following laces: 2¾"-wide (lace A), 2¼"-wide (B), 1¼"-wide (C), 1"-wide (D), 2"-wide (E). **Pillows:** 66" x 104" tan twin-size flat sheet; cotton/nylon ecru laces: 1 yard lace A (see above), 1 yard B, 1½ yards. C, 1½ yards D, ¾ yard E; 3¼ yards ¾"-wide pink satin ribbon; 3¼ yards

¼"-wide piping cord; sewing thread to match lace and sheet; ½ yard muslin and 1 pound polyester-fiberfill to make each inner pillow. **Curtains:** 66" x 104" tan twin-size flat sheet; cotton/nylon ecru laces: 8 yards lace A, 7 yards. C. **Pillows and curtains:** 108" x 110" tan king-size flat sheet; cotton/nylon ecru laces: 9 yards lace A, 1 yard B, 8½ yards C, 1½ yards D, ¾ yard E.

**Note:** Amounts given are for the actual items pictured. If you wish to make pillows another size or curtains to fit a window with different dimensions, recalculate amounts to suit your particular needs.

## PILLOWS

For rectangular pillow cut two 11" x 16" pieces from sheet. For square pillows cut two 15" squares for each pillow. For ruffle cut 9" x 204" strips, piecing as necessary. To cover piping cord, from remaining fabric cut 1½" x 54" bias strip for rectangular pillow and 1½" x 60" bias strip for square pillow without ruffle, piecing as necessary. (Seam allowance of ½" is included in these measurements.)

Lace strips are machine-sewn along edges with ribbon inserted under lace, if specified, before stitching.

**RECTANGULAR PILLOW:** Following photograph, pin 2 narrowest lace strips (C), with ribbon underneath, at an angle to pillow-cover front. Pin widest strip (A) across center and 1 medium-width strip (B) at each end of cover. Stitch laces in place.

**Finishing:** Fold and stitch bias strip over piping cord. With raw edges facing outward, pin around right side of pillow-cover front. Cut off excess and sew ends together. With right sides facing and piping sandwiched between, stitch front to back, leaving one side open. Turn, insert inner pillow (see below) and sew opening closed.

**Inner Pillow:** Cut two pieces of muslin size of pillow front. Stitch together along three sides. Turn, stuff and sew last side.

**SQUARE PILLOW WITH PIPING:** Following photograph, pin widest lace strip (B) across center of pillow-cover front. Mitering corners, pin 2 narrowest strips (D), then pin 2 medium-width strips (E) with ribbon underneath. Stitch laces in place. Finish as for rectangular pillow.

**SQUARE PILLOW WITH RUFFLE:** Following photograph, pin widest lace strip (A), with ribbon underneath, diagonally across center of pillow-cover front. Pin medium-width strips (C) and narrowest strips (D). Mitering corners, pin strip (C), with ribbon underneath, around cover ¾" in from raw edges. Stitch laces in place.

**Finishing:** Make inner pillow (see Rectangular Pillow). With right sides together, stitch pillow front to back along three sides.

Turn, insert pillow and sew opening closed.

**Ruffle:** Stitch ends of 9"-wide strip together to form large ring. Press under raw edges. With wrong sides together, fold in half lengthwise to form 4"-wide ring; baste turned-under edges together. Machine-stitch with large stitches ¼" from turned-under edges. Pulling up stitching to form gathers, pin this edge around pillow front; then stitch in place.

### CURTAINS

Dimensions given below are for cafe curtains to fit 36" x 52" window. If your window is of other dimensions, follow the same general procedure but adjust the length (allowing about 2" for overlap) and the width (figure about 2½ times the width of the window for each set of curtains to give sufficient fullness).

**CAFE CURTAINS:** Cut four pieces each 40¾" wide x 33" long with selvage at one end of each piece (3¼" allowed for casing along upper edge of each piece and 1¾" for hems on center and lower edges—selvage is side edge of curtain).

Mitering corners, turn center and lower edges of each curtain 1¾" to right side and topstitch. Lapping outer edge of wider lace strip (A) over line of stitching and mitering corners, stitch lace 1½" in from center and lower edges of curtains. Stitch narrower strip (C) about 1½" in from A. Turn in and press ¼" along top edge. Turn same edge 3" to wrong side and topstitch. Stitch again 1½" from folded top edge to form two lengthwise pockets in hem. When hanging curtains, run curtain rod through lower pocket (casing); top pocket forms ruffle.

# WINDOW "VINE" WITH ORGANDY LEAVES

Adjustable to fit any window, the "vine" is made of white netting to which green organdy leaves of assorted sizes are glued.

**SIZE:** Adjustable to fit any window. Ours measures 40" wide x 45" long.

**MATERIALS:** A piece of white netting same size as window (allow 1½" extra top and bottom for rod casings and ½" each side edge for hems); 45"-wide organdy for leaves; ½ yard dark green, ⅝ yard light green (for larger window than ours you may need more fabric); spray adhesive by 3M; 2 lengths ⅝"-diameter Plexiglas rods for curtain rod and weight (available at plastic supply houses); 2 sets rod brackets; waxed paper.

**TO START:** Enlarge diagram (see How to Enlarge Patterns, page 8), and cut 1 pattern for each of the 3 leaves; then cut as

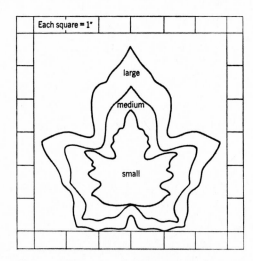

Each square = 1″

large

medium

small

many leaves as desired in assorted sizes from both shades of organdy (we used 6 large, 22 medium and 13 small dark-green leaves; 14 large, 17 medium and 15 small light-green leaves).

Fold over ½″ at sides of netting and stitch hems. Fold over 1½″ at top and bottom and stitch ¼″ from folded edges to form rod casings.

Spread waxed paper on flat surface. Lay netting over paper. Arrange leaves on netting, overlapping them as shown in photograph. When you have a pleasing arrangement, carefully remove the top layer of leaves in a small area; lift up the bottom leaf, spray the back of it with adhesive and press it back in place on netting. Then, a leaf at a time, spray the removed leaves and press them back in place. Continue to next area in this manner until all leaves have been attached.

Slide rods into casings. Attach brackets to window frames and insert rods.

# LATCH HOOK GRANNY RUG

You can work this project on your lap because the hooking is done on handy sections of canvas that you sew together later. Enlarge the rug simply by adding more granny-square sections (one section alone is just the right size for a large pillow).

**SIZE:** 32″ x 48″.

**MATERIALS:** 3 yards double-thread (penelope) rug canvas with 4 spaces per inch; pre-cut rug yarn, 34 packs of black, 5 packs each of pink, purple, blue, and yellow, 4 packs each of green and red, and 3 packs of orange (see Note below); lachet hook; black waterproof marker; heavy-duty sewing thread and blunt-tipped needle.

**Note:** You can also use up any rug yarn you have on hand; the single background color will unify the pattern. Rug is made in six 18″ x 18″ sections with four 8″ x 8″ granny motifs on each section. For each section you need 6 packs of yarn in background color and 1 pack each of 6 other colors.

**TO PREPARE CANVAS:** Cut canvas into six 18" squares. Tape edges to prevent raveling. On each canvas section, mark off a centered 16" square in black (1" left all around). Then within 16" square, mark off four 8" squares, for size of each granny motif.

**TO HOOK:** On each section, work rows one at a time from the bottom up. Follow the chart to fill each 8" square and do each row completely before going on to the next row (do not work small areas separately). Chart shows representative colors; you can make up your own combinations or follow photograph on page 90.

Sew complete sections together with right sides facing, then fold excess canvas to back of rug and overcast in place. Coat back with liquid latex rug backing, following directions on container.

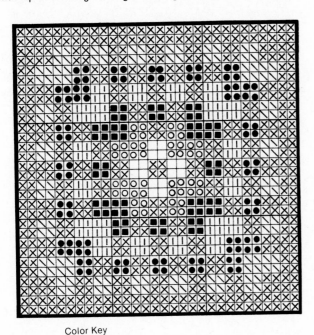

Color Key

- ⊠ Black
- ⧄ Pink
- ⊙ Green
- ⫿ Orange
- ⊡ Blue
- ⊚ Red
- ☐ Yellow

# MOSAIC-TILE-MOTIF CROCHETED RUG

Squares in two sizes are worked in single crochet resembling stockinette stitch and joined with a decorative whipstitch.

**SIZE:** About 40" x 56" without fringe.

**MATERIALS:** Aunt Lydia's Heavy Rug Yarn (rayon/cotton), 14 (2.5-ounce/70-yard) skeins antique gold No. 565 (main color-MC), 6 skeins each sunset No. 550 (S), red No. 120 (R) and brown No. 420 (B); aluminum crochet hook size K (or international size 7:00 mm) or the size that will give you the correct gauge; tapestry needle.

**GAUGE:** 3 V sts=1"; 3 rnds=1". Large square measures 7¼" square; small square measures 3½" square.

## GENERAL DIRECTIONS

We suggest making a sample square in MC first to get the right

123

gauge and learn the stitch. **To work squares:** Always work with right side facing you. Mark beg of rnds. **To work V sts and corners:** A V st is a sc worked to look like a stockinette st. Work V sts along sides of square by inserting hook into center of V formed by st below. Corners are scs worked in usual manner by inserting hook in top lps of st below. (See stitch diagram.) Always pull up sts to form a long V shape. **To change colors:** Work last st of old color until there are 2 lps on hook. Drop old color; draw new color through the 2 lps of old color. After 1st rnd always carry colors not in use across back of piece, working sts over them to give rug body. Pull these strands every 3 or 4 sts to keep the tension even and the square firm.

**LARGE SQUARE (make 19):** Starting at center with MC, ch 3. Join with sl st to form ring.

**1st rnd:** Work 7 sc in ring; insert hook in center of ring, y o and draw up lp; break off MC. With R make lp and draw through both lps on hook (8 sc).

**2nd rnd:** With R work V st in next sc (dot in shaded st on diagram for 2nd rnd), V st in next sc (next dot), changing to S; with

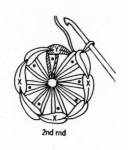

2nd rnd

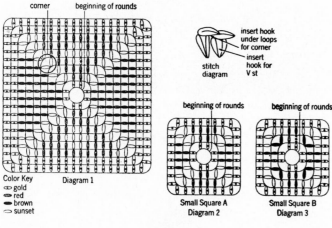

Color Key
⊃ gold
⊃ red
⊃ brown
⊃ sunset

Diagram 1

insert hook under loops for corner
insert hook for V st

stitch diagram

beginning of rounds

Small Square A
Diagram 2

beginning of rounds

Small Square B
Diagram 3

Joining Diagram

S work 2 sc in next st for corner (under lps marked X), changing to B; with B work V st in each of next 2 dots, changing to S; with S work corner, changing to R. With R work V st in each of next 2 dots, changing to S; with S work corner, changing to B; with B work V st in each of next 2 dots, changing to S; with S work corner in top lps (Y) of 1st st, changing to R (16 sts, including 1st st, where last S st was worked).

**3rd rnd:** * With R work 3 V sts, changing to S; with S work corner, changing to B; with B work 4 V sts, changing to S; with S work corner, changing to R; with R work V st. Repeat from * once more changing to S at end of repeat (24 sts).

**4th through 7th rnds:** Following Diagram 1 from 4th rnd for color placement, work V st in each st across to corner (1st of these sts is marked with black dot), * work 2 sc in corner, V st in each st across to next corner. Repeat from * twice more; work corner, work V st (56 sts at end of 7th rnd). Break off R, S and B; attach 3 strands MC.

**8th and 9th rnds:** Working with 1 strand MC (carry other 2 strands across back of piece and crochet over them), work around as before with 1 color only (72 sts at end of 9th rnd). Break off all 3 strands.

**SMALL SQUARE A (make 36):** See Diagram 2. Work as for large square through 3rd rnd. Break off R, S and B; attach 3 strands MC. **4th rnd:** Repeat 8th rnd of large square (32 sts). Break off all 3 strands.

**SMALL SQUARE B (make 28):** Starting at center with MC, ch 3. Join with sl st to form ring. **1st rnd:** Work 8 sc in ring, changing to R. Break off MC. Following Diagram 3 from 2nd rnd (1st st of 2nd rnd is marked with black dot), complete square (use 3 strands MC on last rnd as before). Break off.

**FINISHING:** Following photograph for placement, arrange all squares as shown. When joining, hold 2 squares with right sides facing; using MC and tapestry needle, whipstitch together on wrong side through back lps only. A ridge is produced around each square on right side. With right side of rug facing you, crochet sl sts with B, R or S to form a chain along seams shown in those colors in photograph (see page 94). Sl st with MC along all other seams. Whipstitch sl sts to ridge sts on each side of the R, B and S seams (see Joining Diagram; the sl sts are shaded for clarity).

**Border:** With right side of rug facing you and using MC, work 1 rnd V sts around rug, working 2 sc in each corner.

**Fringe:** For each tassel cut two 9½" strands MC. Holding strands tog, fold in half. Draw folded end through a st on short edge of rug; draw loose ends through fold and tighten. Work a tassel in every other st across both short edges of rug.

# WOVEN UPHOLSTERY WEBBING RUG

The jute strips used for this sturdy, reversible rug are stapled or pinned together after being woven, then machine-stitched.

**SIZE:** 36″ x 63″.

**MATERIALS:** 32 yards 3½″-wide jute upholstery webbing, available from upholstery-supply houses or mail-order catalogs; desk stapler or bank pins; heavy-duty beige thread.

Cut webbing in nine 63″ and sixteen 36″ pieces.

**TO START:** Lay 63″-long pieces side by side on floor for warp. Make certain that all ends are even and square, then place a 3′ length of straight lumber on ends to keep them aligned. Begin weaving a 36″ long piece under and over 2″ in from end of warp and so that 2″ of the woven ends extend on sides. To prevent sections from slipping use staples or bank pins.

Weave remaining 15 lengths, keeping webbing square at crossings with staples or pins as needed. When weaving is complete, use a heavy-duty needle for leather or canvas to machine-stitch along the red bands of webbing *in both directions* to hold weaving permanently. Remove staples or pins.

Machine-stitch a row of stay-stitching across base of extended webbing ends; fringe.

# TWO ARAN RUGS TO KNIT

Traditional stitches originated by seafaring families on Ireland's Aran Islands are worked in rug yarn. You can increase the rugs' sizes to fit in larger areas simply by repeating the motifs.

**GALWAY BAY**

Galway Bay Rug

**SIZE:** 45″ x 72″.

**MATERIALS:** Elsa Williams Rug Wool, 38 (4 ounce) skeins turquoise (R513); 1 36″-long circular knitting needle No. 10½ (or international needle No. 3), or the size that will give you the correct gauge; 1 double-pointed needle for cables; aluminum crochet hook size J.

**GAUGE:** 3 sts = 1″; 3 rows = 1″ in border pattern.

## STITCH PATTERNS FOR GALWAY BAY RUG

**Pattern A (Border)**

PATTERN A (Border Pattern): Worked on a multiple of 5 sts, plus 1; 4 row repeat.

**1st row (right side):** * P 1, slip next st to dp needle and hold in back of work, k 1, k st from dp needle (back twist made), slip next st to dp needle and hold in front of work, k 1 k st from dp needle (front twist made). Repeat from * across, ending p 1. **2nd row:** * K 1, p 4. Repeat from * across, ending k 1. **3rd row:** * P 1, make front twist, make back twist. Repeat from * across, ending p 1. **4th row:** Repeat 2nd row. Repeat first through 4th rows for pattern.

PATTERN B (Blarney Kiss Pattern): Worked on 12 sts and a 12 row repeat.

**1st row (right side):** P 2, k 8, p 2. **2nd row:** K 2, p 8, k 2. **3rd row:** P 2, slip next 2 sts to dp needle and hold in back of work, k 2, k 2 sts from dp needle (back twist made), slip next 2 sts to dp needle and hold in front of work, k 2, k 2 sts from dp needle (front twist made), p 2. **4th row:** Repeat 2nd row. **5th row:** Repeat first row. **6th row:** Repeat 2nd row. **7th row:** Repeat first row. **8th row:** Repeat 2nd row. **9th row:** P 2, make front twist, make back twist, p 2. **10th row:** Repeat 2nd row. **11th row:** Repeat first row. **12th row:** Repeat 2nd row. Repeat first through 12th rows for pattern.

**INISHERE**

Pattern C (Trinity)　　　　Pattern B (Blarney Kiss)

Pattern D (Arrow)

**Galway Bay Rug**

| 16 | 12 | 11 | 19 | 11 | 12 | Stitches |
|----|----|----|----|----|----|----------|
| A | B | C | D | C | B | Patterns |

**Diagram for First Strip**

**Galway Bay Rug**

| 16 | 12 | 11 | 19 | 11 | Stitches |
|----|----|----|----|----|----------|
| A | B | C | D | C | Patterns |

**Diagram for Second Strip**

**PATTERN C** (Trinity Pattern): Worked on 11 sts and a 4 row repeat.

**1st row (right side):** P 11. **2nd row:** K 1, (work k 1, p 1, k 1 in next st, p 3 tog) twice; work k 1, p 1, k 1 in next st, k 1. **3rd row:** P 13. **4th row:** K 1, (p 3 tog, work k 1, p 1, k 1 in next st) twice; p 3 tog, k 1. Repeat first through 4th rows for pattern.

**PATTERN D** (Arrow Pattern): Worked on 19 sts and a 14 row repeat.

**1st row (right side):** K 7, slip next 2 sts to dp needle and hold in front of work, k next 3 sts, k 2 sts from dp needle, k 7. **2nd row:** P 19. **3rd row:** K 6, slip next st to dp needle and hold in back of work, k 2, p st from dp needle (back twist made), k 1, slip next 2 sts to dp needle and hold in front of work, p 1, k 2 sts from dp needle (front twist made), k 6. **4th row:** P 8, k 1, p 1, k 1, p 8. **5th row:** K 5 make back twist, k 1, p 1, k 1, make front twist, k 5. **6th row:** P 7, k 1, (p 1, k 1) twice; p 7. **7th row:** K 4, make back twist, k 1, (p 1, k 1) twice; make front twist, k 4. **8th row:** P 6, k 1, (p 1, k 1) 3 times; p 6. **9th row:** K 3, make back twist, k 1, (p 1, k 1) 3 times; make front twist, k 3. **10th row:** P 5, k 1, (p 1, k 1) 4 times; p 5. **11th row:** K 2, make back twist, k 1, (p 1, k 1) 4 times; make front twist, k 2. **12th row:** P 4, k 1, (p 1, k 1) 5 times; p 4. **13th row:** make back twist, k 1,(p 1, k 1) 5 times; make front twist, k 1. **14th row:** P 3, k 1, (p 1, k 1) 6 times; p 3. Repeat first through 14th rows for pattern.

**Note:** Rug is made in two strips, then sewn together down the center. Work each strip back and forth on circular needle.

**FIRST STRIP:** Cast on 81 sts. Work in pattern A for 24 rows.

Now start patterns as follows: **Next row (right side):** Work pattern B over first 12 sts, place a marker on needle; work pattern C over next 11 sts, place a marker on needle; work pattern D over next 19 sts, place a marker on needle; work pattern C over next 11 sts, place a marker on needle; work pattern B over next 12 sts, place a marker on needle; work pattern A over last 16 sts. Follow each pattern separately, using diagram as a guide. Work even until 20 repeats of pattern B have been completed. Now work in pattern A for 24 rows. Bind off.

**SECOND STRIP:** Cast on 71 sts. Work in pattern A for 24 rows, decreasing 2 sts on last row (69 sts). Now start patterns as follows: **Next row:** Work pattern C over first 11 sts, place a marker on needle; work pattern D over next 19 sts, place a marker on needle; work pattern C over next 11 sts, place a marker on needle; work pattern B over next 12 sts, place a marker on needle; work pattern A over last 16 sts. Follow each pattern separately, using diagram as a guide. Work even until 20 repeats of pattern B have been completed. Inc 2 sts on last row. Work pattern A for 24 rows. Bind off.

**FINISHING:** Sew strips together joining pattern B of one strip to pattern C of other strip (pattern D will run in opposite directions—see photograph). **Fringe:** For each fringe use one 18″ strand of yarn. Double strand to form loop. Insert crochet hook from wrong side through first st on one short end of rug. Pull loop through to wrong side, draw ends through loop to form knot. Work a fringe in every third stitch across. Then take one strand of yarn from first fringe and tie knot with strand of yarn from next fringe ¾″ below edge of rug. Continue across edge. Using alternate strands, continue to knot fringe ¾″ below last row of knots. Trim fringe evenly. Work fringe on other end of rug in same manner.

## INISHERE OATLAND RUG

**SIZE:** 30″ x 50″.

**MATERIALS:** Elsa Williams Rug Wool, 19 (4-ounce) skeins gold (R33); 1 36″-long circular knitting needle No 10½ (or international needle No. 3), or the size that will give you the correct gauge; 1 double-pointed needle for cables; aluminum crochet hook size J.

**GAUGE:** 3 sts = 1″; 3 rows = 1″ in border pattern.

**PATTERN A** (Border Pattern): Worked on a multiple of 4 sts and a 4 row repeat.

**1st row (right side):** * Slip 1 st to dp needle and hold in back of work, k 1, k st from dp needle (back twist made), slip next st to dp needle and hold in front of work, k 1, k st from dp needle (front twist made). Repeat from * across. **2nd row:** P across. **3rd row:**

* Make front twist, make back twist. Repeat from * across. **4th row:** P across. Repeat first through 4th rows for pattern.

## STITCH PATTERNS FOR INISHERE OATLAND RUG

Pattern A (Border)

Pattern B (Cable)

128

**Pattern C (Trellis)**

| 12 | 20 | 40 | 20 | 12 | Stitches |
|----|----|----|----|----|----------|
| A | B | C | B | A | Patterns |

**Inishere Oatland Rug**

PATTERN B (Cable Pattern): Worked on 20 sts and a 4 row repeat.

1st row (right side): P 2, * slip next 2 sts to dp needle and hold in back of work, k 1, k 2 sts from dp needle, k 1, slip next st to dp needle and hold in front of work, k 2, k st from dp needle, p 2. Repeat from * once more. 2nd row: K 2, (p 7, k 2) twice. 3rd row: P 2, (k 7, p 2) twice. 4th row: Repeat 2nd row. Repeat first through 4th rows for pattern.

PATTERN C (Trellis Pattern): Worked on 40 sts and a 16 row repeat.

1st row (right side): * P 3, slip next st to dp needle and hold in back of work, k 1, k st from dp needle, p 3. Repeat from * across. 2nd row: * K 3, p 2, k 3. Repeat from * across. 3rd row:

* P 2, slip next st to dp needle and hold in back of work, k1, p st from dp needle (back twist made); slip next st to dp needle and hold in front of work, p 1, k st from dp needle (front twist made); p 2. Repeat from * across. 4th row: * K 2, p 1, k 2, p 1, k 2. Repeat from * across. 5th row : * P 1, make back twist, p 2, make front twist, p 1. Repeat from * across. 6th row: * K 1, p 1, k 4, p 1, k 1. Repeat from * across. 7th row: Make back twist, p 4, make front twist. Repeat from * across. 8th row: * P 1, k 6, p 1. Repeat from * across. 9th row: K 1, * p 6, slip next st to dp needle and hold in back of work, k next st, k st from dp needle. Repeat from * across, ending p 6, k 1. 10th row: * P 1, k 6, p 1. Repeat from * across. 11th row: * Make front twist, p 4, make back twist. Repeat from * across. 12th row: * K 1, p 1, k 4, p 1, k 1. Repeat from * across. 13th row: * P 1, make front twist, p 2, make back twist, p 1. Repeat from * across. 14th row: * K 2, p 1, k 2, p 1, k 2. Repeat from * across. 15th row: * P 2, make front twist, make back twist, p 2. Repeat from * across. 16th row: * K 3, p 2, k 3. Repeat from * across. Repeat first through 16th rows for pattern.

RUG: Cast on 104 sts. Work back and forth on circular needle. Work in pattern A for 24 rows. Now start patterns as follows: Next row: Work pattern A over first 12 sts, place a marker on needle; work pattern B over next 20 sts, place a marker on needle; work pattern C over next 40 sts, place a marker on needle; work pattern B over next 20 sts, place a marker on needle; work pattern A over last 12 sts. Follow each pattern separately, using diagram as a guide. Work even until 9 repeats of pattern C have been completed. Continue patterns A and B and C as established for 2 more rows. Then work in pattern A for 24 rows. Bind off.

FINISHING: Fringe: For each fringe cut one 18″ strand of yarn. Double strand to form loop. Insert crochet hook from wrong side through first st on one short end of rug. Pull loop through to wrong side, draw ends of yarn through loop to form knot. Work a fringe in every third stitch across. Then take one strand of yarn from first fringe and tie knot with strand of yarn from next fringe ¾″ below edge of rug. Continue across edge. Using alternate strands, continue to knot fringe ¾″ below last row of knots. Trim fringe evenly. Work fringe on other end of rug in same manner.

# SHAKER DESIGN RUG TO KNIT

Reflecting Shaker thriftiness, the rug is knitted of worn-out garments—dress-weight cottons cut into inch-wide bias strips and sewn into lengths (other material can be used). Worked with large needles and just five garter stitches to a row, the color bands grow quickly; a child could easily knit them.

**SIZE:** About 47" x 68".

**MATERIALS:** The rug shown is knitted with strips of printed and plain cotton fabrics, similar in weight to percale. However, lightweight woolens, used garments and even nylon stockings and tights can be substituted if desired. Make sure that the garments are clean and that the fabric is in good condition. Excellent sources for inexpensive fabrics are factories selling mill ends or Salvation Army stores where bundles of garments can be purchased. Suggestions for estimating amounts needed are under Preparing Fabrics; 1 pair knitting needles, No. 9, (or international needles No. 4) or the size that will give you the correct gauge; upholstery needle; carpet thread.

**GAUGE:** 3 sts = 1"; 6 rows (3 ridges) = 1".

**PREPARING FABRICS:** Cut fabric into strips 1"wide, stockings and tights somewhat wider. Cut woven fabrics on the bias and jersey knits on the straight grain. One yard of 36" fabric cut into strips will make a 5-stitch knitted band about 27" long.

Join strips by overlapping ends and stitching. Fold and press strips as for double-fold tape to ¼" width; wind strips into balls for ease in handling.

**CENTER PANEL:** With a fabric strip, cast on 5 sts and k 12 rows. * Break off, attach another color and k 12 rows. Repeat from * 12 more times (14 color blocks). Bind off. Make another band in same manner, using a different color arrangement. Sew bands together along one long edge, using an invisible weaving stitch (rug will then be reversible). Using one color, make 2 bands the same size as before. Sew one on each side of first 2 bands.

**BANDS:** Cast on 5 sts. Work in garter st (k every row) with one color until band is long enough to fit around center panel. Before binding off, lay center panel on a flat surface and pin the band around it, easing it around the corners so that it lies flat. Adjust length of band if necessary, then bind off. Sew band in place and join ends. Make 10 more bands in the same manner. Lay rug on a flat surface and sew each band in place before starting next one.

**SAWTOOTH BORDER:** Cast on 2 sts. **1st row:** K 1, inc 1 st in next st. **2nd row:** K 3. **3rd row:** K 2, inc 1 st in next st. **4th row:** K 4. **5th row:** K 3, inc 1 st in next st. **6th row:** K 5. **7th row:** K 3, k 2 tog. **8th row:** K 4. **9th row:** K 2, k 2 tog. **10th row:** K 3. **11th row:** K 1, k 2 tog. **12th row:** K 2. Repeat first row through 12th row for desired length. Sew in place as for bands.

# 4

# ACCESSORIES FOR EVERY ROOM

# THREE TABLECLOTHS OF APPLIQUÉD ORGANZA

Simple patterns are repeated on the round, square and rectangular shapes so that you can easily extend them for larger sizes and, artistlike, blend or contrast your own selection of colors.

### GENERAL DIRECTIONS

Silk organza, which is used for these tablecloths, is usually 42" wide but can vary slightly in width, depending on color and manufacturer. We chose colors from the same or related families. However, because of the transparency of organza, which subtly blends the colors, other tones can be used instead of ours.

Because our designs have a fresh, free look, you can follow our diagrams exactly or use them simply as guides to cutting your own motifs.

Appliqué motifs and the plaid design are shown on graphs; enlarge them square by square and draw on tracing paper. (See How to Enlarge Patterns, page 8.) Slip paper under organza and trace design with pencil. *Add ⅛" allowance to appliqué* before cutting fabric. A ¼" (or ½") allowance for seams and hems is included in measurements.

Press under all allowances on appliqué; pin or baste to cloth, if necessary, and blindstitch in place.

### PLUM PUFF (left in picture)

**MATERIALS:** For cloth 66" in diameter; 42" silk organza: 5½ yards of purple, 1¾ yards of chartreuse, 1¼ yards of royal blue and ¾ yard of hot pink.

**TO START:** Follow cutting plan to mark 42"-diameter half circle for center of cloth and 66"-diameter half ring for 12" border. Using pencil and string or yardstick as a compass, draw patterns on separate sheets of paper; add ¼" seam and hem allowances. **Note:** If your organza is too narrow for seam allowance, cut half-circle pattern to fit fabric and adjust inner circumference of border pattern.

Slip each pattern under organza, trace and cut two half circles on fold for center and two half rings for border. So that border can be adjusted at end seams, carefully pin one half ring around the purple circle and ease fabric, if necessary; stitch in place. Repeat for second half ring, matching end seams. Place joining seam up, for right side; press toward center. Then join border pieces at their ends; hem outer edge. Appliqué blue circle to purple one, covering joining seam.

Enlarge appliqué motifs; each square equals 1″ square. Transfer motifs to paper; adding ⅛″ allowance, cut organza.

Following placement diagram, pin 12 chartreuse motifs to border and appliqué. Add pink motifs along joining seam and appliqué.

## PLAID RIFFLE (below right in picture)

**MATERIALS:** For cloth 60″ x 82″: 42″ silk organza: 9½ yards of light blue, 2⅜ yards of dark blue, 1¾ yards each of dark green and chartreuse.

**TO START:** For tablecloth and its lining, cut four 30½″ x 82½″ strips from light blue organza, using selvages for seam

**PLUM PUFF**

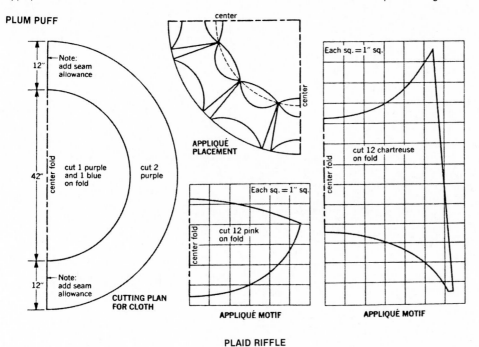

center

Note: add seam allowance

12″

center fold

42″

cut 1 purple and 1 blue on fold

cut 2 purple

Note: add seam allowance

12″

CUTTING PLAN FOR CLOTH

center

APPLIQUÉ PLACEMENT

Each sq. = 1″ sq.

cut 12 pink on fold

center fold

APPLIQUÉ MOTIF

Each sq. = 1″ sq.

cut 12 chartreuse on fold

center fold

APPLIQUÉ MOTIF

**PLAID RIFFLE**

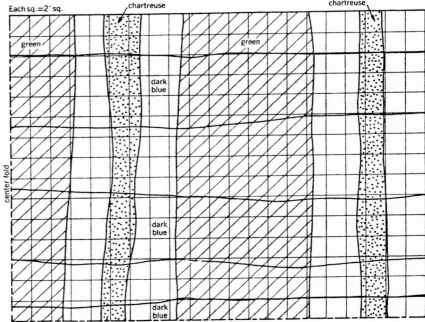

Each sq. = 2″ sq.

chartreuse

chartreuse

green

green

dark blue

center fold

dark blue

dark blue

center fold

APPLIQUÉ DESIGN, one quarter shown

**GOLDEN ZEPHYR**

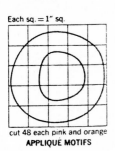

Each sq. = 1″ sq.

cut 48 each pink and orange
**APPLIQUE MOTIFS**

edges; ¼" seam allowances included. Join pairs of strips along length and press seams open.

Enlarge diagram (page 133), showing one quarter of design, for plaid appliqué; each square equals 2" square. Add ⅛" allowance when cutting organza.

Cut one narrow and four wide dark blue bands 82½" long. Appliqué to one light blue piece.

To complete plaid, cut three dark green bands and four chartreuse bands 60½" long. Appliqué to cloth and over dark blue bands.

With right sides together, stitch lining to cloth, leaving an opening for turning; turn and press seam. Appliquéd strips are now on outside of cloth. Blindstitch open edges together.

GOLDEN ZEPHYR (above right in picture, page 132)
MATERIALS: For cloth 55" square: 42" silk organza: 3¼

yards of yellow, 1¼ yards each of green, hot pink and orange.

**TO START:** For cloth cut a 36" x 55½" center and two 10¾" x 55½" side strips from yellow; measurements include ½" seam and ¼" hem allowances. Matching 55½" edges, join strips to center with French fell seams. Sew ¼" hem around cloth. Using pencil and ruler, lightly mark three rows of 5"-square blocks along each edge.

For appliqué, cut forty-eight 5¼" squares from green and mark ⅛" allowances. Enlarge patterns (page 133) for large and small disks; each square equals 1" square. Adding ⅛" allowances, cut disks: 48 large and small from pink and 48 large and small from orange.

Appliqué a large pink disk, then a small orange disk to each green square; appliqué a small pink disk to each large orange disk. Beginning at a corner of cloth, appliqué a green square in every other block in a checkerboard design; appliqué orange disks to yellow blocks between.

# EMBROIDERED PLACE MAT AND NAPKIN

Herringbone, French knot, lazy daisy and straight stitches are embroidered around stripes of rickrack on sunny yellow linen.

SIZE: Width of decorative band is 3¼". Place mat measures 13" x 19"; napkin measures 16" x 21".

MATERIALS: To make 1 place mat and napkin: 1 yard 45"-wide yellow linen; Wrights rickrack, 1 (2½-yard) package each ½"-wide Yale blue No. 78 and jumbo width (⅝"-wide) bright pink No. 22; 6-strand embroidery floss, 2 (8-yard) skeins each pink and blue, 1 skein rose; embroidery needle.

For place mat cut 2 pieces linen 14" x 20" (½" seam allowance included). Set one piece aside for back. On other piece lightly mark with pencil or chalk the position for two 3¼"-wide bands 2" in from each side edge.

For napkin cut 1 piece linen 18" x 23" (1" hem included). The decorative band will run diagonally across 1 corner. To mark position of band place a pin in top edge of linen 6¼" from upper left corner and another pin in left edge 6¼" from same corner. Connect pins with light pencil or chalk line. Mark another line parallel to first and 3¼" from it.

**TO MAKE BAND:** Center and pin pink rickrack between marked lines on place mat or napkin. Pin blue rickrack on each line.

Using 3 strands pink floss on blue rickrack and 3 strands blue floss on pink rickrack, make a small straight stitch at each tip. Using 6 strands pink floss, work herringbone stitch on blue rickrack (see Diagram 1). Using pink floss, work a modified herringbone stitch on each side of pink rickrack, following Diagram 2 and weaving floss under the straight stitches. Using 5 strands blue floss, work 3 lazy daisies (see Embroidery Stitch Diagrams, page 9) at each dot on Diagram 2. Work a French knot with 4 strands rose floss at base of each lazy-daisy group.

**FINISHING: Place Mat:** With right sides facing, stitch front and back pieces together on 3 sides. Turn and blindstitch last side. **Napkin:** Blindstitch ¾"-wide finished hems, mitering corners.

**PLACE MAT AND NAPKIN**

Diagram 1

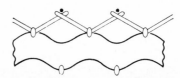

Diagram 2

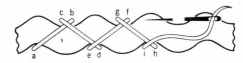

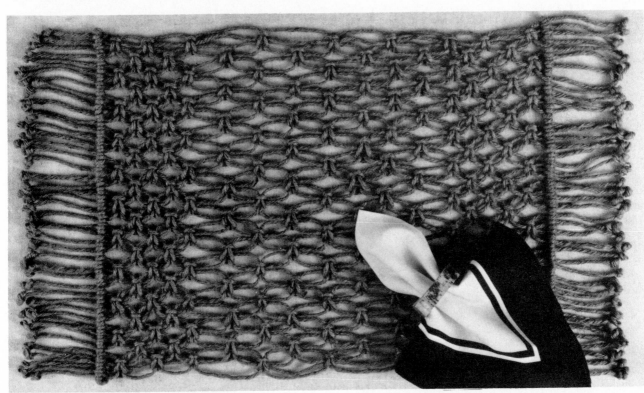

# JUTE MACRAMÉ PLACE MAT

Three knots are used: clove hitch, overhand and alternating square.

**SIZE:** 13" x 24" including fringe.

**MATERIALS:** Large ball 3/16"-diameter jute twine (available in hardware stores); knotting board; T-pins; white glue.

**TO START:** Cut 42 lengths of twine each 8' long for tying cords. Cut 1 strand 16' long for first anchor cord. Tie overhand knot (see diagrams, page 136) near one end of each tying cord and, laying cords adjacent and parallel, pin through knots to top of board. Center anchor cord across tying cords 3" below overhand knots; pin taut on both sides. Work a row of Clove Hitches across anchor cord. Unpin anchor cord and let free ends hang down both sides to become outermost tying cords.

CENTER SECTION: Working alternating square knots, knot 5 rows with knots of each row ½″ below knots on previous row. Work 8 rows 1″ apart and then 4 rows ½″ apart. Cut second

anchor cord the width of center section plus 6″ and pin across cords ½″ below last row of knots. Work another row of Clove Hitches over anchor cord. When row is completed, unpin anchor cord and glue ends to back of Clove Hitches. Work overhand knot on each cord 3″ from last Clove-Hitch row. Remove mat from board. Trim ends. Glue overhand knots.

**MACRAMÉ PLACE MAT**

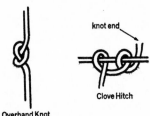

Overhand Knot

knot end

Clove Hitch

Alternating Square Knots

# WOVEN NEEDLEPOINT CANVAS PLACE MAT

A crisply formal pattern of rayon yarn is woven through the mesh.

SIZE: 13″ x 19″.

MATERIALS: Kentucky All-Purpose Yarn(100% rayon), 1 (2-ounce) skein dusty rose No 729; one 14″ x 20″piece Dritz Nylon Knit needlepoint canvas (single thread with 10 spaces per inch); 5″ weaving needle.

YARN: Cut yarn into 36″ lengths before starting to weave.

TO WEAVE: Thread 36″ length of yarn in weaving needle. Following diagram (one quarter of design given), center design on canvas, leaving small unworked border on all 4 sides for hems. To

begin, leave 6″ end on wrong side of canvas. (Work over this end for the first few stitches, then clip off excess.) To end off, run yarn under last few stitches on wrong side of canvas. Start new length of yarn by running yarn under a few stitches on wrong side.

**Note:** Follow diagram carefully, as some spaces on the canvas are occupied by more than one stitch.

**FINISHING:** After weaving is completed, turn canvas edges to wrong side and hem.

**CANVAS PLACE MAT**

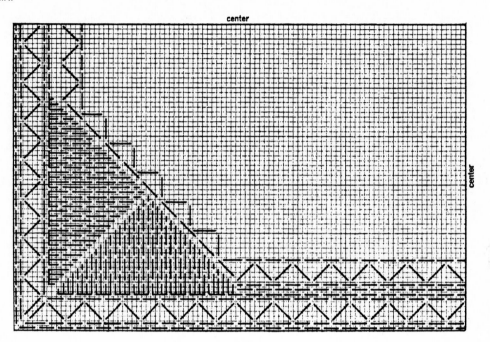

# CUT-OUT AND SCALLOPED PLACE MAT

For this round design, you satin stitch the fabric by machine, then cut out holes and trim scallops around the outer edge.

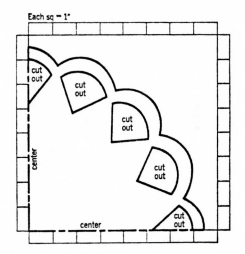

**SIZE:** 15″ diameter.

**MATERIALS:** ½ yard firmly woven fabric; dressmaker's carbon paper.

**TO START:** Enlarge pattern, (see How to Enlarge Patterns, page 8). Using dressmaker's carbon paper, transfer pattern onto fabric. With white thread, work ⅛″-wide zigzag satin stitch along lines on fabric. Cut out sections and cut around outer line of stitching.

# LACY KNITTED PLACE MAT

The airy, open pattern is worked in cotton yarn, then starched.

**SIZE:** 12" x 18".

**MATERIALS:** Lily Sugar-'n-Cream (100% cotton yarn), 1 (125-yard, 2.5-ounce) ball light blue No 26; 1 pair knitting needles No. 10½ (or international needles No. 2) or the size that will give you the correct gauge;  spray starch; 1 yard 45"-wide heavy cotton fabric for backing (enough for 4 mats).

**GAUGE:** 3 sts = 1" when stretched.

**TO START:** Starting at one end, cast on 34 sts loosely.

**1st row (right side):** K across. **2nd row:** K 2, * p 3, y o, p 3 tog, y o. Repeat from * across ending k 2. **3rd row:** K across. **4th row:** K 2, * y o, p 3, tog, y o, p 3. Repeat from * across, ending k 2.

Repeat 1st through 4th row for pattern until mat measures about 18", ending with a k row. **Next row:** K across and bind off loosely at same time.

**FINISHING:** Spray lightly with water or spray starch. Mark off a rectangle 12" x 18" on brown paper. Place paper on ironing board or hard surface for pinning. Using rustproof pins, stretch and pin place mat face down to size of rectangle. Spray back of mat until thoroughly saturated with spray starch. Let dry completely. Remove pins.

Cut a piece of backing 13" x 19" for each mat. Fold under ½" hem all around; blindstitch. Place knitted piece over hemmed fabric and neatly whipstitch piece together around edges.

# VINYL PICNIC PLACE MAT WITH POCKETS

Cut pockets, bind them with bias tape, sew to vinyl rectangle.

SIZE: 13″ x 19″.

MATERIALS: ⅜ yard clear vinyl; ⅜ yard ticking; 2½ yards ½″-wide single-fold bias tape.

TO START: From vinyl cut 13″ x 19″ rectangle for mat and two 5″ x 7″ rectangles for pockets. Following photograph, stitch bias tape over 2 adjacent edges of each pocket rectangle. Place pockets on mat as shown, matching uncovered edges to edges of mat. Stitch tape-covered long sides to mat, easing pocket for easy insertion of silverware. With right side facing upward, pin bias tape flat around outer edges, mitering at corners.

BOUND EDGES: Cut 1¾″-wide bias strip of ticking long enough to go around all sides plus 6″ to allow for corners and overlap at joining. If necessary, piece edging to obtain required length. Fold in and press ¼″ to ½″ on both long edges of binding strip. Fold strip in half lengthwise so that folds meet at inside along one edge (like bias tape).

Apply to edge by slipping strip over edge of mat; allow ⅛″ of tape to show around inner edge. Miter all corners and fold under ½″ at end to overlap beginning of strip. Machine-topstitch through both folds encasing edge of mat.

# BARGELLO-TRIMMED DESK SET

A pencil holder, notebook cover and the blotter borders are covered with a tailored design in quick-to-do bargello stitch.

**TO PREPARE CANVAS:** Draw outline of each piece on canvas, using following dimensions, leaving 3″ between pieces and at least 2″ around edges of canvas: 5¾″ x 16½″ for notebook cover, two 2¼″ x 18¾″ sections for blotter borders, 4″ x 10½″ (or size of your can) for pencil holder. Tape edges of canvas to prevent ravelling.

**BARGELLO:** Following diagram for pattern and execution of stitch, cover the marked areas with bargello stitch. Cut pieces apart, allowing 1½″ to 2″ borders. Block if necessary.

**FINISHING: Blotter:** Place bargello strips on matching pieces of cardboard, fold excess canvas along one long edge over board and glue. Cover large board with vinyl cut 1″ larger on all edges. Fold edges over board. Place bargello-covered borders at opposite ends of board, with folded edges facing inward. Fold remaining excess canvas over board and glue. Cut felt to fit back of board and glue. Slip blotter in place, trimming if necessary.

**Notebook Cover:** Place cardboard pieces on wrong side of embroidered areas of bargello strip, leaving ¾″ separation at center so that cover will fold. Turning in corners first, fold canvas excess over boards and glue. For lining, cut felt same size as bargello. For pocket, cut another felt piece the same width as lining and 7″ long. Stitch pocket over one end of lining, making ⅛″ seams. matching corners and leaving inner edge open for pocket. Glue lining to bargello. Slip cardboard backing of memo pad into pocket; fold cover over and weight with several books to train pad to stay closed.

**Pencil Holder:** Fold bargello wrong side out around can. Pin seam, matching pattern carefully. Sew seam as close to bargello as possible. Press seam open. Turn. Fold excess canvas around one edge to wrong side and press. Slip over can with folded edge at bottom; glue lightly around bottom. Fold excess canvas at top to inside of can and glue. Cut 2 vinyl circles to fit bottom of can; glue one to inside and one to outside of bottom. Line inside of can with strip of vinyl.

**MATERIALS:** 23″ x 28″ piece of double-thread (penelope) needlepoint canvas with 10 spaces per inch; 3-ply Persian-type needlepoint and crewel yarn, 90 yards each turquoise (color A) and magenta (B), 30 yards vermillion (C); tapestry needle; white glue; 25″-square piece of felt for blotter backing and notebook-cover lining; 23″ x 25″ piece of self-adhesive vinyl for blotter and pencil holder. **Blotter;** Double-thick matboard or heavy cardboard, one piece 18¾″ x 22¼″ and 2 pieces 2¼″ x 18¾″; blotter. **Notebook cover;** 2 pieces 5″ x 8″ heavy cardboard, 5¾″ x 8″ memo pad. **Pencil holder;** Tin can (we used 16-ounce size).

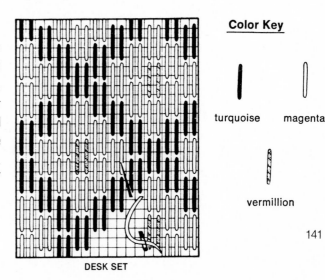

**DESK SET**

**Color Key**

| turquoise | magenta |
|-----------|---------|

vermillion

141

**MATERIALS:** 45"-wide quilted fabric (see note below to estimate yardage); cover-a-button kit with eight ¾"-diameter button molds.

**Note:** Measure top, sides and ends of locker. Buy enough turquoise to cut a piece for top and one for each side and each end, adding ¾" all around each piece. Buy enough red to cut 2"-wide welting strip to fit around top, piecing if necessary, and sixteen 2" x 4" pieces for tabs. From turquoise fabric, cut pieces ¾" larger all around than top, sides and ends of locker. From red fabric, cut 2"-wide welting strip, pieced if necessary, to fit around top.

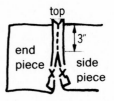

**TO SEW:** With right sides facing make ½" seam, stitching an end piece to a side piece for 3" (see diagram). Stitch other end piece to other end of side piece in same manner, then stitch remaining side piece to free ends of end pieces so that 4 pieces are joined in ring. Topstitch seam allowance flat at open edges (X on diagram).

With right side out, fold welting in half lengthwise; matching raw edges, pin around right side of top piece, easing around corners.

With right sides facing and welting sandwiched between, stitch top edge of a side piece to a long edge of top piece, then stitch an end piece to top piece and so on until all edges of top are joined to top edges of other pieces. Turn right side out and slip cover over locker. Mark correct length; turn under hem and topstitch.

Cut sixteen 2" x 4" pieces from red for tabs. Shape ends to points. Turn in all edges ¼" and press. Hold 2 pieces together, wrong sides facing, and topstitch all edges. Repeat to make 7 more tabs. Pin 2 tabs to each corner of cover. Make buttons and sew 2 to each tab, sewing through both tab and locker slipcover.

# FOOT LOCKER SLIPCOVER TO SEW

A storage trunk can double as a side table when disguised with a smart cover of quilted fabric trimmed with eight button tabs.

# CROCHETED SLEEVE FOR POT HANDLES

A clever kitchen notion works up fast in single crochet stitch.

**SIZE:** 5½" long.

**MATERIALS:** Lily Sugar-n-Cream (heavy cotton yarn), 1 (2.3-ounce) ball each hunter green No. 58 and dark rose No. 44; aluminum crochet hook size G (or international hook size 4:50 mm) or the size that will give you the correct gauge.

**GAUGE:** 4 sc = 1".

**HOLDER:** With green, ch 24. Join with sl st to form ring. **1st rnd:** Work 1 sc in each of next 23 ch; join with sl st in 1st sc. **2nd rnd:** Ch 1, sc in same sc as sl st, sc in each sc around (23 sc); join as before. **3rd and 4th rnds:** Repeat last rnd. At end of 4th end, drop green, attach rose. **5th and 6th rnds:** With rose, repeat 2nd rnd.

Working in sc rnds, work in stripe pattern of 3 rnds green, 2 rose, 4 green, 2 rose, 3 green, 2 rose and 2 green. At end of last rnd, with green, ch 8 for loop, sl st at base of loop; turn, work sc in each ch st of loop. Break off.

# PLANT HAMMOCK AND POTHOLDERS TO CROCHET, CALICO BOXES TO SEW

Cluster stitch provides a nice texture for the plant holder. You can work all three reversible potholders with only four ounces of yarn. The baskets are made in three useful sizes; they're stiffened with cardboard and tied with grosgrain.

PLANT HAMMOCK

**SIZE:** About 9"-diameter and 8" deep.

**MATERIALS:** Acrylic knitting-worsted-weight yarn, 1 (4-

ounce) skein each orange (color O), gold (G) and yellow (Y); aluminum crochet hooks sizes I and K (or international hooks sizes 5:50 mm and 7:00 mm) or the size that will give you the correct gauge.

**GAUGE:** On I hook, 2-dc cl + ch 1 ÷ 1".

**Note:** Work with 2 strands of color specified held together throughout.

**HOLDER:** With O, starting at center of base with size K hook, ch 6. Join with sl st to form ring. **1st rnd:** Ch 3, (y o, insert hook in ring, y o and draw lp through, y o and draw through 2 lp on hook) twice, y o and draw through all 3 lp on hook (1st 3-dc cl made); ch 2, * (y o, insert hook in ring, y o and draw lp through, y o and draw through 2 lp on hook) 3 times, y o and draw through all 4 lp on hook (another 3-dc cl made); ch 2. Repeat from * 6 times more; join with sl st in top of ch 3. **2nd rnd:** Sl st in next sp, ch 3, work 3-dc cl, ch 2 and 3-dc cl in same sp, ch 2, * work 3-dc cl, ch 2 and 3-dc cl in next sp (cl group made), ch 2. Repeat from * around (16 cl); join. **3rd rnd:** Change to size I hook. Sl st in next sp, ch 3, work 1st 3-dc cl in same sp, ch 2, work cl group in next sp, ch 2, * 3-dc cl in next sp, ch 2, cl group in next sp, ch 2. Repeat from * around (24 cl); join. **4th rnd:** Sl st in next sp, ch 3, work 3-dc cl in each sp, working 3 cl groups evenly spaced (27 cl); join. Break off O.

**5th rnd:** With G, sl st in next sp, ch 3, dc in same sp (1st 2-dc cl made), ch 2, * y o, insert hook in next sp, y o and draw lp through, y o and draw through 2 lp on hook, y o, insert hook in same sp, y o and draw lp through, y o and draw through 2 lp on hook, y o and draw through all 3 lp on hook (another 2-dc cl made); ch 2. Repeat from * around (27 cl); join. Repeating 5th rnd, work 4 more rnds G, 3 Y and 2 rnds O. **Last rnd:** Sc in each sc and st around; join. Break off.

**HANGING CORDS (make 3):** With Y and size I hook, crochet 32" chain. Sl st in 2nd ch from hook and in each ch across. Break off. Following photograph (page 143), fasten securely inside upper rows of holder.

**TASSEL:** Wrap 1 strand each O, G and Y around 5½" piece of cardboard 16 times. Cut strands at one end and remove cardboard. Open strands and tie together at center. Fold in half again and tie ½" to 1" from folded end. Trim ends to even length. Tie tassel to center of base.

### REVERSIBLE POTHOLDERS

**SIZE:** 5½" square.

**MATERIALS:** Orlon-acrylic knitting-worsted-weight yarn, 1 ounce each green, white, yellow and turquoise will make 3 reversible potholders; aluminum crochet hook size J (or international size 6.00 mm) or the size that will give you the correct gauge; white felt or heavy cotton fabric for lining; tapestry needle; three 1⅛"-diameter plastic rings.

**GAUGE:** 2½" in diameter after 1st rnd.

**Note:** 2 squares are used for each reversible potholder. For first color combination, follow first color suggested at beg of each rnd. For second combination, follow first color in parentheses; for third combination, follow second color in parentheses.

**SQUARE:** With green (yellow-turquoise), starting at center, ch 4; join with sl st to form ring. (Right side is always facing you as you work.) **1st rnd:** Sl st in ring, ch 4, (y o, insert hook in ring and draw up 1" lp, y o and draw through 2 lp on hook) twice, y o and pull through all 3 lp on hook, ch 1 (1st cl made); * (y o, insert hook in ring and draw up 1" lp, y o and draw through 2 lp on hook) 3 times, y o and pull through all 4 lp on hook, ch 1 (another cl made). Repeat from * until 12th cl is completed; join to top of 1st cl. Break off.

**2nd rnd:** With white (turquoise-white), make lp on hook and work 2 cl in each ch sp before each cl of last rnd (24 cl in all), ending last cl with ch 1; join as for last rnd. Break off.

**3rd rnd:** With yellow (white-green), sc in any ch-1 sp between cl of last rnd, * (ch 1, sc in next ch-1 sp) 4 times; work 8 dc in next ch-1 sp for corner, sc in next ch-1 sp. Repeat from * around, ending with 4th corner; join. Break off.

**4th rnd:** With turquoise (green-white), starting at 1st dc of any 8-dc corner group, * sc in each dc of corner, sc in next sc, (sc in top lp of ch 1, sc in next sc) 4 times. Repeat from * around; join and break off. Square should measure 5½".

Make another square using same colors.

**FINISHING:** For each potholder cut two 5¼" squares of felt or fabric for lining. With lining sandwiched between edges of crochet, pin or baste squares tog just over edge of lining. Sew all 4 sides with same color as last rnd. Place ring at corner and sew in place with matching yarn.

### CALICO BASKETS

**SIZES:** Small: 6" square x 2" deep; medium: 7½" x 2¼"; large: 9" x 2½".

**MATERIALS:** To make 8 baskets of each size you will need 45"-wide calico in 3 prints: 1¼ yard for small, 2 yards for medium, 2½ yards for large; five 22" x 28" sheets posterboard (shirt cardboard or stiff plastic can be substituted); 1¾ yard ⅜"-wide grosgrain ribbon for each basket; mat knife.

**TO MAKE BASKET:** (**Note:** Dimensions for small basket are outside parentheses, those for medium and large baskets are within parentheses.) On calico mark off two 11" (13"-15") squares. Following broken lines on diagram, mark wrong side of squares with pencil for fold lines. Cut out squares and cut rounded corners (first make cardboard pattern for 1 rounded corner and use it to trace others). Set pieces aside.

On posterboard mark off 5¾" (7¼"-8¾") square for bottom of basket and four 1¾" x 5¾"(2" x 7¼"-2¼" x 8¾") rectangles for sides. Cut out with mat knife.

Press fold lines on calico squares. Cut ribbon in 8 equal lengths. Place ribbons on right side of 1 calico square and pin end of each at a dot. Pin free ends of ribbons near center of calico so they won't get caught in stitching. Stitch calico squares together with right sides facing and ribbons sandwiched between, making ½" seam around 3 sides (leave 1 side open between dots). Trim seam; turn.

Insert posterboard pieces inside calico pocket, fitting each one within an area outlined by pressed fold lines. Turn under raw edges of opening and blindstitch. Topstitch along fold lines, being careful not to catch posterboard. Tie corner ribbons.

**CALICO BASKETS**

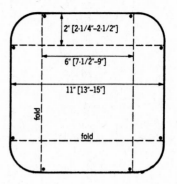

# TISSUE COVERS AND DRESS-HANGER COVERS TO CROCHET, SACHETS TO SEW

Tissue covers are single crochet; dress hangers are worked over two wire hangers; sachets consist of fabric, lace, potpourri.

**SIZE:** To cover tissue box 4½″ wide x 9½″ long x 3″ deep and standard toilet-tissue roll.

**MATERIALS:** Coats * Clark's Speed-Cro-Sheen (cotton knit and crochet thread), 3 (100-yard) balls for 1 large tissue-box cover and 2 balls for 1 toilet-tissue-roll cover; aluminum crochet hook size H (or international size 5:00 mm) or the size that will give you the correct gauge.

**GAUGE:** 7 sc = 2″.

**Note:** Use thread double throughout. Before starting, check size of tissue box and adjust number of stitches if necessary.

### TISSUE-BOX COVER

**FIRST HALF:** Starting at edge of center opening on top section, ch 54 to measure about 15½″ (this measurement is the length across top of box plus twice the depth). **1st row:** Sc in 2nd ch from hook and in each ch across (53 sc); ch 1, turn. **2nd row:** Sc in each sc across; ch 1, turn. Repeat last row until piece measures 2¼″ (half the width of top of box). Omit ch 1 at end of last row. Break off but do not turn.

Skip 1st 11 st (depth of box) and working in back lp only of each st, sc in each of next 31 sc (do not work in remaining 11 sc); ch 1, turn. **Last row** forms turning ridge on right side. Working through both lp, work even on 31 sc for 3″ (or depth of box). Break off. Make other half in same manner.

**FINISHING:** Holding both sections together with starting chains touching, sew seam at each end, leaving 6½" center opening (or match opening of tissue box). Sew side seams on each piece. **Border:** Sc evenly around lower edge, decreasing 4 st evenly spaced. Join and break off.

## TOILET-TISSUE-ROLL COVER

Starting at center of top, ch 3. Join with sl st to form ring. **1st rnd:** Work 6 sc in ring. **2nd rnd:** Work 2 sc in each sc around (12 sc). Do not join rnds, but mark end of each rnd. **3rd rnd:** * Sc in next sc, 2 sc in next sc. Repeat from * around (18 sc). **4th rnd:** * Sc in each of next 2 sc, 2 sc in next sc. Repeat from * around (24 sc).

Continuing in sc, inc 6 sc evenly spaced on each of next 5 rnds (54 sc). Piece should measure 5" in diameter. **10th rnd (turning ridge):** Working in back lp only of each st, sc in each sc around. Working through both lp, work around in sc for 4" (or desired depth). **Next rnd:** Sl st around. Break off.

## SACHETS

**SIZE:** 4" square, not including lace.
**MATERIALS: For each sachet:** Two 4½" squares fabric (10 sachets can be made from ¼ yard 45"-wide fabric); ½ yard ½"-wide ruffled lace; lace motif; ⅜"-wide grosgrain ribbon; potpourri.
**SACHET:** Cut two 4½" squares of fabric. Hand-sew lace motif on corner of 1 square. Press raw edges of square under ¼". Sandwiching lace between layers, baste edges of squares together along 3 sides. Stuff with potpourri; baste 4th side closed. Machine-zigzag over basting. Make bow from ribbon.

## COVERED DRESS HANGERS

**MATERIALS:** Rug yarn, bulky knitting yarn or knitting-worsted-weight yarn, 15 yards of rug or bulky yarn or 30 yards of knitting worsted (see Note below) will make 1 covered hanger; 2 wire coat hangers; aluminum crochet hook size H (or international size 5:00 mm); masking tape.
**Note:** If using knitting worsted, work with yarn double.
**CROCHETED COVER:** Cut 6" length of yarn and fold into 2 loops. Holding hangers together, tape loops to ends of hanger handles, having ¼" ends of loops extend beyond handle tips (see Diagram 1). Tie end of working yarn tightly around loops just beyond handle tips. With same yarn, make lp on crochet hook close to handle. Tape loose end of yarn to handle.

Holding 1 arm of hanger between your knees, with handle pointing up and toward you, work sl st around end of handle by bringing hook behind handle, yarn over handle, around hook and through lp on hook (Diagram 2). * With yarn behind handle, make another sl st by bringing hook over handle, yarn over hook and through lp on hook (Diagram 3). With yarn over handle and hook behind handle, make another sl st as for Diagram 2. Repeat from * until 5 or 6 sl st have been completed. Slide st close tog and close to handle tip. Continue making sl st in this manner, pushing them close tog to cover hanger well. Work along handle, arms and back to base of handle. Break off and tie around hanger. Tie 3 different-colored hangers tog with an 18"-long crocheted or twisted chain worked with 3 strands yarn.

**DRESS HANGER COVERS**

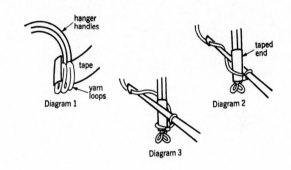

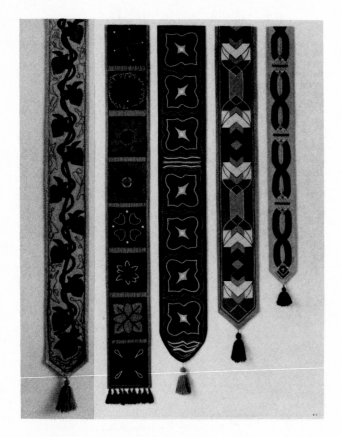

# FIVE APPLIQUÉD AND EMBROIDERED BELLPULLS

The long running patterns lend themselves to many purposes—decorating a narrow wall area; accenting a bedspread, bolster or headboard; dressing up a shelf or plain window curtains.

**MATERIALS:** Light- and medium-weight cottons and linens are used for all bellpulls. Fabrics of different textures such as rough-weave linen, smooth percale or broadcloth and tweed-type materials give effective results.

Cut fabric for each bellpull backing and lining, following individual directions. Note that 1½″ seam allowance at top of lining provides casing; allowance at other edges is ¼″.

**BELLPULL PATTERNS:** See How to Enlarge Patterns, page 8. Patterns include a whole repeat of some designs, half a pattern of symmetrical motifs, each block on the Blossoms bellpull and outlines of all shaped ends.

**TO MAKE APPLIQUÉ PATTERNS:** Shaded areas on drawings indicate appliqué. Where possible, two tones are used to distinguish adjacent pieces, not to indicate a change in color. Place tracing paper over enlarged bellpull pattern and outline pieces to be appliquéd, making only one tracing of each different piece. When a center line divides pieces, fold paper; trace and complete outline. Paste or rubber-cement tracings to thin cardboard. Cut out cardboard pattern. Place cardboard on right side of fabric (leaving ½″ between pattern pieces) and trace around it lightly with pencil. Cut fabric pieces, adding ¼″ seam allowance to all edges. Turn under allowances; baste and press.

Following pattern drawings and bellpull photographs, pin appliqué pieces to right side of backing; appliqué with blindstitch.

**TO SHAPE BELLPULL END:** Follow pattern drawing to trace and cut paper pattern for end. Pin to backing and shape fabric, allowing ¼″ for seams. Repeat for lining.

**EMBROIDERY:** Light lines on pattern drawings, simulating stitches, indicate embroidery. Key relates lines to stitch diagrams, illustrating working methods. (Also see Embroidery Stitch Diagrams, page 9.) Letters, which indicate colors of floss and yarn, correspond to those given in individual directions.

Work embroidery free hand, following pattern drawings and photograph. If a guide is preferred, transfer lines with carbon paper or mark lightly with pencil.

**FINISHING:** With right sides facing, stitch lining and appliqué backing together along sides and shaped end, leaving top end open. The 1½″ allowance at top of lining is for casing. Turn bellpull; press. Fold under ¼″ allowance at top of appliqué backing; blindstitch. **Casing:** Turn in seam allowance along long edge and ends, clipping at sides. Fold casing to wrong side and blindstitch long edge in place. Cut heavy cardboard or thin strip of wood to fit casing and slide it in place. Sew a small ring or yarn loop to center of casing for hanging bellpull. **Tassel:** Cut yarn the number of strands and length specified. Tie together at center. Fold in half and tie together again about ½" from fold. Attach to bellpull with ½" braided yarn strip.

## CABLE

**SIZE:** 5" x 44½", finished.

**MATERIALS:** 36" fabric: 1⅜ yards (or ⅜ yard if pieced) aqua for backing, ⅜ yard maroon for lining and appliqué, ⅛ yard each pink and blue, scraps of lavender and green for appliqué; 6-strand embroidery floss: 2 skeins each blue (A) and green (B), 4 skeins each pink (C) and orange (D); 1 ounce maroon sport yarn (E); sewing thread to match appliqué.

**TO START:** Cut backing to measure 5½" x 45" (piecing it if desired). Cut lining and piece it to measure 5½" x 46½". Cut point at one end of each as in General Directions. Make appliqué patterns; cut and prepare pieces.

Following pattern and photograph page 91, pin pieces in place.

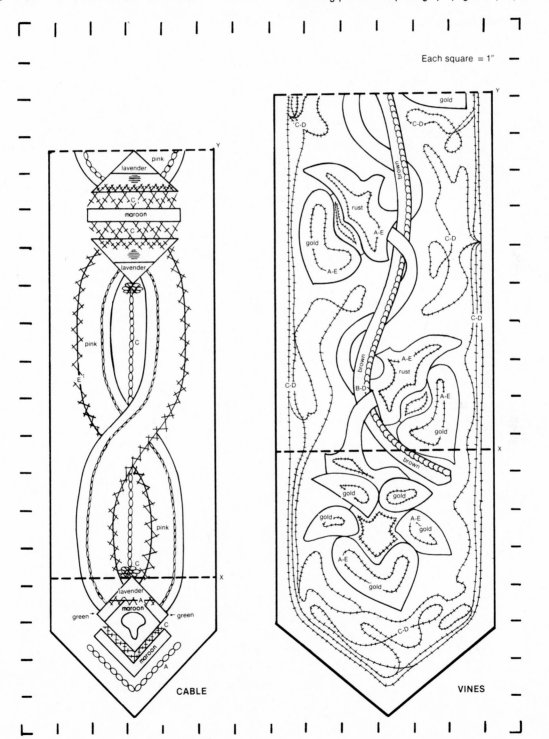

Each square = 1"

CABLE

VINES

149

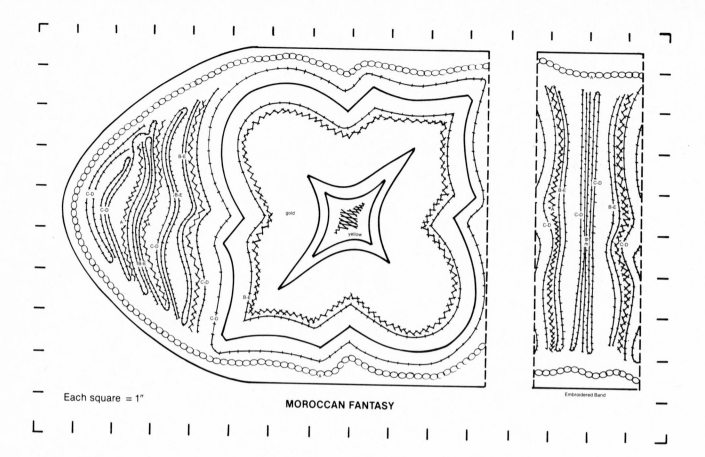

Each square = 1"

**MOROCCAN FANTASY**

Embroidered Band

Repeat design from X to Y twice more, then repeat from X to top end strip. Note that cable strips alternate colors and cross in opposite direction in each repeat of design. Sew appliqué in place.

Embroider bellpull as shown, using 6 strands each blue and green floss, 12 strands each pink and orange floss and 1 strand yarn.

**FINISHING:** See General Directions. For tassel cut 35 strands yarn 7" long. Complete tassel and sew to point.

### MOROCCAN FANTASY

**SIZE:** 8½" x 58", finish.

**MATERIALS:** 36" fabric: 1⅛ yards black for lining and backing, ½ yard gold and ¼ yard each orange and yellow for appliqué; 6-strand embroidery floss: 4 skeins pinks (A), 1 skein each white (B) and gold (C); knitting worsted, 1 ounce gold (D) and small amount white (E); sewing thread to match appliqué.

**TO START:** Cut backing and piece it to measure 9" x 58½". Cut lining and piece to measure 9" x 60". Cut point at one end of each as in General Directions. Make appliqué patterns; cut and prepare pieces. **Note:** Do not turn under allowances on yellow

pieces and outer edges of orange pieces as other appliqué will overlap them.

Pin, then appliqué yellow and orange pieces in place under center opening of each gold piece.

Following photograph page 91, appliqué seven gold pieces, alternating positions and leaving 3" for embroidered band between two pieces.

Embroider bellpull as shown, using 6 strands pink, 2 strands each white and gold and 1 strand yarn. For couching, work floss over yarn, matching colors.

**FINISHING:** See General Directions, page 148. For tassel cut 65 strands gold yarn 10" long. Complete tassel, typing it with braided white yarn. Sew to point.

### BLOSSOMS

**SIZE:** 8" x 63¾", finished.

**MATERIALS:** 36" fabric: ½ yard gold for backing, ⅝ yard green for lining, eight 7½" squares in black, gold and shades of green and brown for appliqué backing; eight 6½" squares in shades of pink, red, orange for appliqué; 6-strand embroidery floss:

150

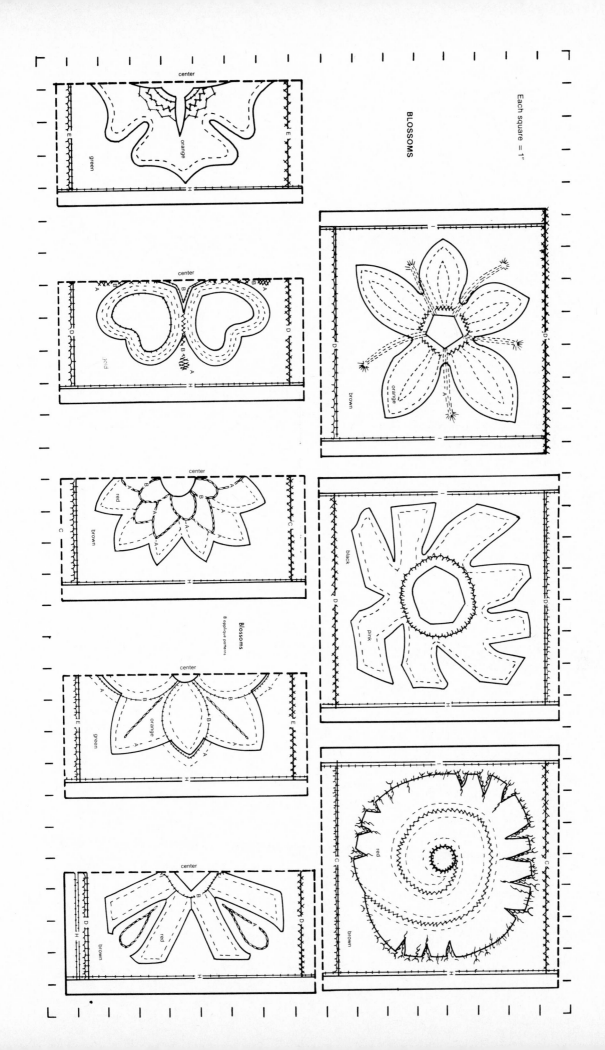

Each square = 1"

BLOSSOMS

center

green
orange

center

gold

center

red
brown

center

brown
orange

Blossoms
8 appliqué pattern

center

green
orange

center

brown
red

brown

orange

black

pink

red

brown

151

3 skeins each white (A) and black (B); small amounts of fingering yarn in light green (C), dark green (D), brown (E), pink (F), red (G), orange (H) and rust (I); sewing thread to match appliqué.

**TO START:** Cut backing and piece it to measure 8″ x 64¼″. Cut lining and piece it to measure 9½″ x 65¾″. Turn under and baste seams on 2 opposite edges of each 7½″ backing square for its top and bottom edges. Make appliqué patterns, making *full* patterns from the five half patterns shown. Cut and prepare pieces as in General Directions, using 6½″ squares for appliqué fabric. Following patterns and photograph, sew appliqué to each backing square.

Embroider appliquéd squares, using 3 strands floss and 1 strand yarn. Work running stitches with sewing thread the color of appliquéd pieces except where indicated otherwise. Work plain couching along sides with thread over yarn, matching colors. Embroider basted edges of squares later.

**FINISHING:** Pin squares evenly spaced onto right side of backing (see photograph for arrangement), leaving 1″ of backing free at bottom and ¼″ at top. Appliqué basted edges of squares. With right sides togehter, center backing on wider lining, with lower edges matching; seam lower edges and turn right side out. Fold to front the ¾″ of lining extending along each side, turn in ¼″ allowance and blind-stitch. Lining forms ½″ borders along sides. Complete embroidery.

Make casing at top as in General Directions. **Tassels:** Make 2 each pink, red, orange and 3 rust. For each tassel, cut 10 strands yarn 5″ long. Complete tassels and sew, evenly spaced, across end of bellpull.

### VINES

**SIZE:** 6½″ x 54″, finished.

**MATERIALS:** 36″ fabric: 1⅝ yards (or ½ yard if pieced) natural color for backing, ½ yard gold for lining and appliqué, ¼ yard rust and scraps of pink for appliqué; 1 package brown ½″-wide cotton bias tape for appliqué; 6-strand embroidery floss: 2 skeins each pink (A), green (B) and gold (C); 1 ounce gold knitting worsted (D) and small amount pink sport yarn (E); sewing thread.

**TO START:** Cut backing to measure 7″ x 54½″ (piecing if desired). Cut lining and piece it to measure 7″ x 56″. Cut point at one end of each as in General Directions, page 148. Make appliqué patterns; cut and prepare pieces. **Note:** Brown bias tape can be applied without a pattern. Do not turn under allowances on pink pieces; other pieces will overlap them.

Following pattern and photograph, pin pieces in place. Repeat

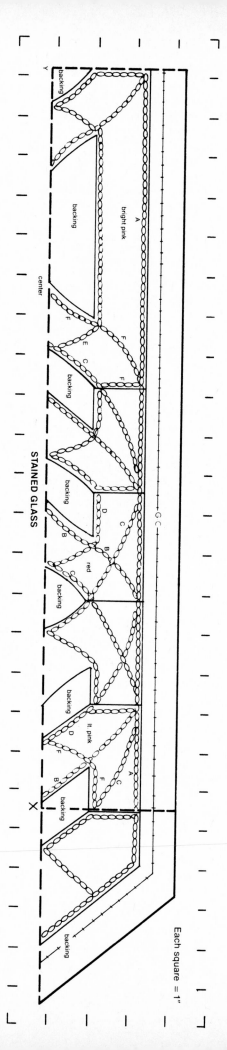

design from X to Y 3 times more, then repeat from X to top end of strip. Sew appliqué in place.

Embroider bellpull as shown, using 3 strands floss and 1 strand yarn throughout. Couch yarn with matching floss, working pink for flowers and leaves, gold for all remaining couching. Work green blanket stitch over gold yarn on brown stem.

FINISHING: See General Directions. For tassel cut 45 strands gold yarn 10". Complete tassel and sew to point.

### STAINED GLASS

SIZE: 7½" x 52½", finished.

MATERIALS: 36" fabric: 1½ yards (or ½ yard if pieced) gold for backing, ¾ yard bright pink for lining and appliqué, ⅛ yard each light pink, brown and red for appliqué; 6-strand embroidery floss: 2 skeins each maroon (A), brown (B), orange (C), gold (D), yellow (E), light pink (F); 1 ounce orange sport yarn (G); sewing thread.

TO START: Cut backing to measure 8" x 53" (piecing it if desired). Cut lining and piece it to measure 8" x 54½". Cut point at one end of each as in General Directions. Make *full* appliqué patterns from the half patterns shown. Note that gold backing shows through openings in appliqué. Cut and prepare pieces as in General Directions. Following pattern and photograph on page 91, pin, then sew appliqué. Repeat from X to Y once more along backing strip, then repeat from X again to top end of strip.

Embroider bellpull as shown, using 3 strands floss and 1 strand yarn. Couch orange yarn with orange floss.

FINISHING: See General Directions. For tassel cut 45 strands yarn 11" long. Complete tassel and sew to point.

# MORNING GLORY EMBROIDERED SHEET AND PILLOWCASE

Delicate vines make a charming pattern on plain bed linens. You embroider over a layer of special "vanishing" canvas which is removed by pulling canvas threads when your work is finished.

### GENERAL DIRECTIONS

CANVAS: The design is worked over special double-thread (penelope) "vanishing" needlepoint canvas that is basted to fabric. Double-thread canvas has 2 vertical threads and 2 horizontal threads per mesh and there are 2 types. One has interlocked vertical threads and loosely woven horizontal threads; the other has

## SHEET AND PILLOWCASE HEM

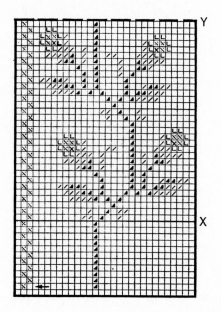

Y

X

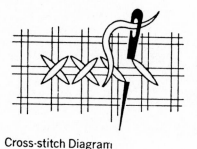

Cross-stitch Diagram

loosely woven vertical and horizontal threads. Be sure to buy the second type of canvas because all the threads must be loosely woven so they can be pulled out ("vanish") when the embroidery has been completed.

You can use any size canvas. We used canvas with 11 spaces per inch (which will make 11 cross-stitches per inch). If you use canvas with fewer spaces per inch than ours, your design will be larger, whereas a canvas with more spaces per inch will produce a smaller design.

**TO WORK CROSS-STITCH:** Cut piece of canvas slightly larger than the size of fabric area to be embroidered. Baste to fabric. Work with an embroidery hoop for soft fabrics and use 3 strands of 6-strand cotton floss throughout. Thread floss in needle and knot 1 end. Starting at lower end of border design, bring

needle, from wrong to right side, through fabric and center of a space in canvas (always work through the large spaces, not through the tiny ones where threads cross). Insert needle in next space diagonally above to the left; bring needle out in space directly below. Continue in this manner, making a row of diagonal stitches; then a row of cross-stitches as shown in diagram, below. Be careful not to catch the canvas threads with needle. Fasten on wrong side by weaving floss back and forth 2 or 3 times through stitches on wrong side of work. **Note:** Usually all stitches are crossed in the same direction. Our designer, however, has deliberately crossed some stitches in one direction and some in the opposite direction to give texture to the design.

When embroidery has been completed, soak piece in lukewarm water for a few minutes. While piece is still damp, use tweezers to pull out canvas threads in one direction; then pull out remaining threads. Rinse piece to remove from fabric any trace of "sizing" used to stiffen canvas. Press if necessary.

**TO FOLLOW CHART:** Follow the color key. Colors are represented by a symbol.

## SHEET AND PILLOWCASE

**MATERIALS:** Top sheet and pillowcase with plain hems; 3½"-wide strips of "vanishing" canvas with 11 spaces per inch (see Canvas under General Directions) to fit length of hems on sheet and pillowcase; 6-strand cotton embroidery floss—for a twin sheet and pillowcase we used D.M.C. in the following colors: 2 skeins light green No. 907, 2 skeins moss green No. 904, 1 skein light pink No. 963, 2 skeins candy pink No. 956, 1 skein American beauty No. 815; embroidery hoop.

**TO EMBROIDER HEM:** Remove stitching from hem and open out hem so that embroidery will be worked through only 1 thickness of fabric (when hem is folded and stitched again, after embroidery has been completed, the wrong side of embroidery will be hidden inside hem). Baste 3½"-wide strips of canvas along section of hem to be embroidered. Follow chart and work border (see arrow on chart) about ⅝" from fold line on hem. Work morning glory vine as shown on chart, then repeat from X to Y along hem. For pillowcase you may have to adjust last repeat to fit design around case; or embroider half of hem only.

**FINISHING:** Fold hem again and work a row of tight machine-zigzag stitches, or other decorative stitch, with contrasting-color thread; or work plain topstitching.

# NEEDLEPOINT-COVERED FOOTSTOOL

The Victorian design of birds and flowers is worked in tent or half cross-stitch; background and basket in mosaic and woven brick stitch, respectively. Design can also be used for a pillow.

**SIZE**: 8" high x 12⅛"-diameter.

**MATERIALS: Frame:** 12" x 36" piece ¾" plywood; 8" piece ¾"-diameter dowel; four 2¾"-diameter wooden balls; white glue; 1¼" finishing nails; plastic wood putty; pigmented-shellac primer; semi-gloss enamel; compass. **Needlework:** 18" square single-mesh needlepoint canvas with 14 spaces per inch; 3-ply Persian-type needlepoint and crewel yarn in the following colors: one 10-yard skein each medium fern (A), bronze (B), dark chartreuse (C), avocado (D), dark pink (E), light pink (F), blush pink (G), coral (H), orange (I), grapefruit (J), banana (K), turquoise (L) and amethyst (M) and four 40-yard hanks dark rose (N); #20 tapestry needle; masking tape. **Upholstery supplies:** 12"-diameter piece 3"-thick polyurethane foam or foam rubber; ½ yard 36"-wide muslin; 1⅛ yards 2½"-wide tassel fringe; special bonding adhesive; tacks or staples; tack hammer or staple gun.

## FOOTSTOOL FRAME

Mark and cut three 12"-diameter circles from ¾" plywood. Inside one 12" circle, use the same centerpoint to draw an 11"-diameter circle to make the cutting guideline for the ½" wide ring. Just inside and abutting guideline, drill several ⅛"-diameter overlapping holes for inserting the saber saw blade. Cut out ring. Save circle cutout and trim it to 10⅝"-diameter for cushion base.

Sand inside edge of ring smooth. With glue and 1¼" finishing nails, laminate the two 12" circles and ring together as shown in assembly detail (page 156). **(Note:** Make certain best side of ring faces up.)** Clamp pieces, wiping off any squeezed-out glue. When dry, unclamp and sand the entire outside edge smooth.

For legs, use a spade bit to drill a ¾"-diameter hole to 1¼" depth in each wooden ball. Cut four 2" dowel pegs, then coating one end of each with glue insert in balls as shown. Turn frame bottomside up and draw a circle 2" in from edge. Divide circle in quarters. Referring to jig detail, make a drilling jig from a 2" x 2" x 2" wood block as shown. At each quarter line on frame base, temporarily nail drilling jig in place as shown, and drill ¾"-diameter hole to ¾" depth. Remove jig and repeat for all leg holes.

Test-assemble legs in holes and check that legs are even and that the stool does not wobble; adjust if necessary. When satisfied, mark dowels, remove and then glue legs in place. Because the sides of stool are to be covered, they do not have to be finely finished. Fill any defects around the top rim with wood putty and sand well. Apply a single coat of pigmented-shellac primer to frame; let dry and sand lightly. Apply two coats of enamel; let dry.

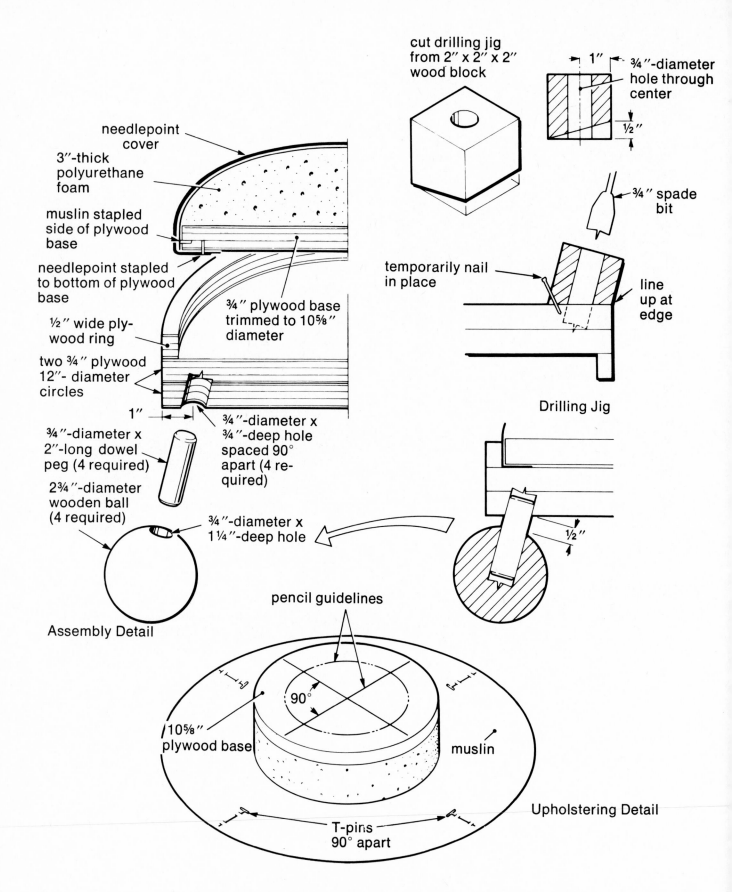

needlepoint cover

3″-thick polyurethane foam

muslin stapled side of plywood base

needlepoint stapled to bottom of plywood base

½″ wide plywood ring

two ¾″ plywood 12″- diameter circles

1″

¾″-diameter x 2″-long dowel peg (4 required)

2¾″-diameter wooden ball (4 required)

¾″ plywood base trimmed to 10⅝″ diameter

¾″-diameter x ¾″-deep hole spaced 90° apart (4 required)

¾″-diameter x 1¼″-deep hole

Assembly Detail

cut drilling jig from 2″ x 2″ x 2″ wood block

1″

¾″-diameter hole through center

½″

¾″ spade bit

temporarily nail in place

line up at edge

Drilling Jig

½″

pencil guidelines

90°

10⅝″ plywood base

muslin

T-pins 90° apart

Upholstering Detail

156

**woven brick stitch**

**mosaic stitch**

COLOR CHART

**Color Key**

| | | | | | | |
|---|---|---|---|---|---|---|
| ◩ Orange (I) | | ▲ Amethyst (M) | | ▣ Med. fern (A) | | ◎ Light pink (F) |
| ─ Grapefruit (J) | | ◿ Turquoise (L) | | ◪ Dark chartreuse (C) | | △ Dark pink (E) |
| ◉ Bronze (B) | | ◺ Banana (K) | | ⦂ Avocado (D) | | |
| ⊺ Coral (H) | | ■ Dark rose (N) | | ⦂ Blush pink (G) | | |

157

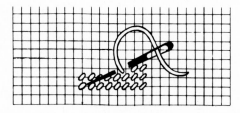

**Tent stitch**

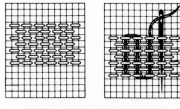

**Woven brick stitch**

## NEEDLEPOINT COVER

**TO START:** Prepare needlepoint canvas by binding edges with masking tape to prevent raveling and to seal off the spiky mesh ends that may catch the yarn as you work. Also find center of canvas by basting a line from the center of one edge to the center of opposite edge, being careful to follow a row of spaces. Then baste another line from center of third edge to center of fourth edge. Basting threads will cross at center. From centerpoint, use a compass to draw a 16″-diameter circle guideline.

**YARN:** The yarn specified separates into three strands. Use two strands together, unless otherwise specified. Work with yarn cut into 18″ lengths.

**STITCHES:** The center motif of morning glories, roses, birds and basket handle are worked in tent stitch (if desired, work motif in half cross stitch which uses less yarn).

The background behind the center motif is worked entirely in mosaic stitch. To work body of basket use the woven brick stitch. Refer to the stitch diagrams.

**CHART (page 157):** Where tent stitch is used, each space on chart indicates one stitch. Where long stitches covering several spaces are used (woven brick and mosaic for basket and background) each long stitch is indicated by stitch sample.

**TO WORK NEEDLEPOINT:** To begin, find center stitch on chart and work it in the center of the canvas. Continue to follow chart, working center flowers and bird motif first. When center motif is complete, work basket in woven brick stitch. Fill in background with continuous mosaic stitch.

**BLOCKING:** With pencil, ruler and compass draw a 16″-diameter circle on brown wrapping paper; then tack the paper to a hard surface. Dampen needlepoint (or wet it thoroughly if it is badly out of shape). Stretch and tack it at 1″ intervals to the board following the circle outline on paper. Allow to dry for at least 2 days before removing tacks.

## UPHOLSTERING FOOTSTOOL

Divide the 10⅝″-diameter plywood cushion base into equal quarters with compass, ruler and pencil. Trim needlepoint canvas to an 18″-diameter circle and muslin to a 16″-diameter circle. Divide both canvas and muslin into quarters, using large bank or T-pins to mark quarter sections as shown.

Use plywood cushion base to trace circle on 3″ polyurethane foam. Cut foam to size using a serrated-edged knife. Attach foam to base with special bonding adhesive, following manufacturer's directions. Center foam base on muslin, lining up quarter marks as shown in the upholstering detail. Pull muslin up and over base at one quarter mark; staple or tack in place. Repeat at opposite quarter mark, then at remaining two marks. Check that muslin is taut and evenly overlapped to back in relation to the quarter mark, if not, remove staples and adjust. Continue pulling muslin and stapling, working with pairs of opposite quarters. Frequently check top surface to make certain that all ripples are pulled out. Trim muslin to edge of back.

Following procedure described above, cover cushion with needlepoint, stapling it into back ½″ to 1″ from edge of base. Before starting wipe the wrong side of needlepoint with a damp cloth. To help pull the heavy needlepoint canvas over base edge, use a pair of slip-joint pliers to grasp edge of needlepoint. Always staple through worked canvas into base for strength.

To finish edge of frame, cut tassel fringe slightly longer than frame circumference. Center and glue fringe as in photograph, overlap ends, then trim for a neat butt joint. Use pins to hold fringe in place until dry. Push cushion into frame.

# THREE-PANEL MACRAMÉ SCREEN

Holland sisal cord is knotted on horizontal wooden dowels interspersed with medallions made of covered embroidery hoops or wire bent into circles. The macramé panels are fitted into the frames of a do-it-yourself screen available at lumberyards.

The two outer panels are alike, the center panel is knotted in a different pattern. Either of these two patterns would make a handsome wall hanging or room divider if it were left unframed and suspended from its top dowel.

**Note:** In the accompanying directions, abbreviations are used to identify the knots. Letters refer to the three general categories of knots illustrated. Numbers which appear next to the letters refer to the individual knot in that category, which are illustrated on page 164–168.

SK #1 is Lark's Head.

  SK-Starting Knot
  BK-Basic Knot
  VOBK-Variation on Basic Knot

### SCREEN FRAME

**SIZE:** Horizontals and verticals for do-it-yourself screen frames are available in various lengths. Frame dimensions are for macramé panels 16″ x 65½″. Use ¾″ double-action brass screen hinges for assembly.

**MATERIALS: One frame:** For horizontals, two pieces of 1⅛″ x 1⅝″ pine 16″ long. For verticals, two pieces of 1⅛″ x 1½″ pine 70¼″ long; ⅞″-diameter dowel 16″ long; twelve 2″ x #10 flat-head wood screws.

**TO START:** See frame detail (page 160) for construction. Cut verticals slightly longer than finished dimensions so they can be sanded even after frames are assembled. To mark location of horizontal pieces and top and bottom dowels, mark center points of screw holes on edge of one vertical. Then stack verticals together with outside edges facing up and transfer marks with a square. Using a 13/64″- diameter twist drill, drill verticals and countersink rails for screws.

Place screen members on a flat surface. Using an awl, mark location of screw holes on ends of horizontal members. Predrill horizontals with a 9/64″ drill. Apply white glue to ends of horizontals and screw frame together. Let dry and sand surfaces even. Stain or paint frame.

Cut dowels to fit frame; predrill top (see outer panel directions) and bottom dowels. Attach bottom dowel only to frame ¾″ above horizontal.

### OUTER PANEL

**MATERIALS:** One panel: 1200′ of 3-ply Holland sisal cord; scissors; rubber bands; white glue; masking tape, 16″ long dowels, one ⅞″ in diameter, for top, eleven ⅜″ in diameter and two 3/16″ in diameter; pairs of embroidery hoops, two oval 4½″ x 8¾″, two pairs 5″ in diameter; galvanized wire; two screw eyes;

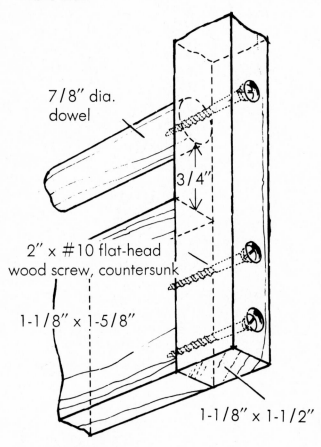

7/8" dia. dowel

3/4"

2" x #10 flat-head wood screw, countersunk

1-1/8" x 1-5/8"

1-1/8" x 1-1/2"

four "C" clamps; blunt needle.

**TO START:** Use three circuits of galvanized wire to form a 9" diameter circle. Completely wrap it and each pair of embroidery hoops with masking tape to prevent the cord from slipping when being knotted around the hoops and ring. Measure out two 10' lengths of sisal and then measure out twenty 52' lengths of sisal by placing the four "C" clamps in a square 13' apart and winding sisal a full circuit around them five lengths at a time. Remove cord from clamps by cutting the side at which the winding was begun. Continue winding several lengths at a time until there are twenty in all. Mark the center point of each cord with a piece of masking tape. Roll up each strand end into a neat bundle, held by a rubber band.

Hang one ⅞" dowel at a convenient height by inserting screw eyes into dowel ends and suspending by string.

**Row 1:** Fold a 52' length of cord in half at center, forming loop. Place loop over dowel and tie a Double Clove Hitch with Picot (SK #2). Continue knotting with all doubled cords until there are 40 strands on dowel (see chart, page 169). Even up knots on dowel. Glue first and last knots in place to keep them from slipping off.

**Row 2:** Place a 3/16" dowel directly below the first dowel. Tie Horizontal Clove Hitches (VOBK #9-Step A) around dowel, beginning with center strands 20 and 21. Make the second row of knots very close to the first. Continue to work out from the center, first knotting one side and then the other until row is completed. Glue end knots in place.

**Row 3:** Place a ⅜" dowel directly below previous row and repeat Row 2.

**Note:** If the macramé is to be mounted in a frame, take the work down from its hanging position and remove screw eyes from the dowel ends. Following instructions for screen frame, screw dowel to frame.

Continue to knot.

**Section A:** Step 1: Following chart, use strands 5 and 6 to tie two loose Half Hitches (BK #1) around anchor cords 7 and 8 and then around 1 and 2.

Step 2: Use strands 3 and 4 to tie loose Half Hitches around anchor cords 1 and 2 and then around 7 and 8.

Step 3: Continue across tying four more groups of Half Hitches and using eight strands for each group.

**Row 4:** Place a ⅜" dowel ¾" below Row 3 and repeat Row 2.

**Row 5:** Place a 3/16" dowel directly below previous row and repeat Row 2.

**Section B:** Step 1: Following chart, tie ten rows of Alternating Square Knots (VOBK #22). Begin by using strands 19 and 22 to tie a Square Knot around anchor cords 20 and 21.

Step 2: Continue to tie Square Knots, adding one more knot to each succeeding row until the tenth row has ten Square Knots across.

**Row 6:** Place ⅜" dowel 7⅛" below Row 5 and repeat Row 2.

**Row 7:** Use 10" length of sisal to tie one row of Vertical Clove Hitches (VOBK #10-Step A). Glue end knots. When glue has dried, cut off excess cord.

**Row 8:** Place a ⅜" dowel directly below Row 7 and repeat Row 2.

**Section C:** Step 1: Make the Double Alternating Lark's Head Braid (VOBK #3) on left side by tying 12 pairs of Lark's Heads, using strands 1 through 8. Repeat for right side of panel, using strands 33 through 40.

Step 2: Place the oval embroidery hoop 1½" below Row 8 and use strands 20 and 21 to tie Clove Hitches around it. Continue to tie Clove Hitches around upper half of hoop by working from the center out, using strands 19 back through 9 and strands 22 through 32.

Step 3: Use strands 13 through 16 and 25 through 28 to tie a

Gathering Knot (VOBK #23) around anchor cords 17 through 24.

Step 4: Following chart, allow strands 9 through 12 and strands 29 through 32 to loop slightly before tying them in Clove Hitches around hoop.

Step 5: Use strands 13 through 28 to finish tying Clove Hitches around bottom edge of hoop.

**Row 9:** Place a ⅜" dowel 7½" below Row 8 and repeat Step 2.

**Section D:** Use strands 1 and 2 to form an Alternating Half Hitch Chain (VOBK #7), made with two loops by hitching strand 2 on 1 and then 1 on 2. Continue across, tying 19 more Half Hitch Chains.

**Row 10:** Place a ⅜" dowel 1¼" below Row 9 and repeat Step 2.

**Section E: Step 1:** To begin the Spiral Half Square Knot Braid (VOBK #17) on the left, use strands 1 and 4 to tie six Half Square Knots around anchor cords 2 and 3 which make one complete Spiral. Continue across for two more Spirals, using strands 5 and 8 around 6 and 7 and strands 9 and 12 around 10 and 11.

Step 2: **Note:** Keep numbering across in progression as each Spiral is worked. Use strands 3 and 6 to tie a Square Knot (BK #3—Version 1) around anchor cords 4 and 5, and strands 7 and 10 around 8 and 9.

Step 3: Repeat Steps 1 and 2 each two more times.

Step 4: Tie two more complete Spirals, using strands 1 and 4 around anchor cords 2 and 3, and strands 5 and 8 around 6 and 7.

Step 5: Use strands 3 and 6 to tie a Square Knot around anchor cords 4 and 5 and strands 9 and 12 around 10 and 11 (see chart, page 169).

Step 6: Tie one more complete Spiral, using strands 1 and 4 around anchor cords 2 and 3.

Step 7: To tie the Spiral Half Square Knot Braid on the right, renumber the last twelve cords in reverse from 12 back to 1 and repeat Steps 1 through 6.

Step 8: Place the 5" embroidery hoop 2" below Row 10 and use strands 20 and 21 to tie two Clove Hitches around it. Continue to tie Clove Hitches around upper half of hoop by working from the center out, using strands 19 back through 13 and 22 through 28.

Step 9: Tie one Alternating Square Knot (VOBK #22) by using strands 19 and 22 around anchor cords 20 and 21.

Step 10: Tie two Square Knots by using strands 17 and 20 around 18 and 19, and strands 21 and 24 around 22 and 23.

Step 11: Repeat Steps 9 and 10 until there are seven rows in all.

Step 12: Use Strands 17 through 24 to tie Clove Hitches around bottom of hoop.

Step 13: Allowing strands 16 back through 13 to loop slightly, tie more Clove Hitches around bottom of hoop.

Step 14: Repeat Step 13 using strands 25 through 28.

Step 15: Place the 9" wire ring 1" below the embroidery hoop. Use strands 20 and 21 to tie two Clove Hitches around the ring. Continue to tie Clove Hitches around upper part of hoop by working from the center out, using strands 19 back through 7 and 22 through 34.

Step 16: To begin the diamond pattern in the ring, use strands 21 through 33 to tie Clove Hitches around anchor cord 20.

Step 17: Use strands 19 back through 8 to tie Clove Hitches around anchor cord 21.

Step 18: Use strands 22 through 32 to tie Clove Hitches around anchor cord 19.

Step 19: Use strands 18 back through 9 to tie Clove Hitches around anchor cord 22.

Step 20: Use strands 23 through 31 to tie Clove Hitches around anchor cord 18.

Step 21: Use strands 17 back through 10 to tie Clove Hitches around anchor cord 23.

Step 22: Follow chart to weave pairs of strands over and under each other for center of diamond.

Step 23: **Note:** Keep numbering across in progression as the rows are worked. To begin the bottom half of the diamond pattern, use strands 31 back through 24 to tie Clove Hitches around anchor cord 18.

Step 24: Use strands 10 through 17 and former anchor cord 18 to tie Clove Hitches around anchor cord 23.

Step 25: Hook strand 32 around anchor cord 18 and then use to tie a Clove Hitch around anchor cord 19. Continue to tie Clove Hitches, using strands 31 back through 24 and former anchor cord 23 around anchor cord 19.

Step 26: Hook strand 9 around anchor cord 23 and then use to tie a Clove Hitch around anchor cord 22. Continue to tie Clove Hitches, using strands 10 through 17 and former anchor cords 18 and 19 around anchor cord 22.

Step 27: Hook strand 33 around anchor cord 19 and then use to tie a Clove Hitch around anchor cord 20. Continue to tie Clove Hitches, using strands 32 back through 24 and former anchor cords 23 and 22 around anchor cord 20.

Step 28: Hook strand 8 around anchor cord 22 and then use to tie Clove Hitch around anchor cord 21. Continue to tie with strands 9 through 17 and former anchor cords 18, 19 and 20 around anchor cord 21.

Step 29: Hook strand 7 around anchor cord 21 and tie a Clove Hitch around ring.

Step 30: Hook strand 34 around anchor cord 20 and tie a Clove Hitch around ring.

Step 31: Continue to tie strand 8 through 33 in Clove Hitches around ring.

Step 32: To complete bottom half of the Spiral part at left side of Section E, repeat Steps 5 back through 1 and then finish the Spiral part of Section E on the right side.

**Note:** To complete rest of panel, continue with Rows and Sections not shown in chart.

**Row 11:** Place a ⅜" dowel 25" below Row 10 and repeat Row 2.

**Section F:** Repeat Section D.

**Row 12:** Place a ⅜" dowel 1¼" below Row 11 and repeat Row 2.

**Section G:** Repeat Section C.

**Row 13:** Place a ⅜" dowel 7½" below Row 12 and repeat Row 2.

**Row 14:** Repeat Row 7.

**Row 15:** Repeat Row 6.

**Section H:** Tie seven rows of Alternating Square Knots with first row having ten Square Knots across.

**Row 16:** Place ⅜" dowel 5¼" from 15 and repeat Step 2.

**Row 17:** Tie Clove Hitches around bottom ⅞" dowel which has already been inserted in the frame.

**TO FINISH:** Work at the back of the panel. Lift each cord and apply glue to the dowel underneath. Give cord one final tug to tighten knot. Let glue dry and cut excess cord.

### CENTER PANEL

**MATERIALS:** 1200' of 3-ply Holland sisal cord; rubber bands; white glue; masking tape; 16" long dowels, one ⅞" in diameter for top, eleven ⅜" in diameter, and six 3/16" in diameter; five pairs of embroidery hoops 5" in diameter; galvanized wire; two screw eyes; four "C" clamps.

**TO START:** Repeat the To Start section for the Outer Panel, omitting one 10' length of sisal cord.

**Row 1:** Repeat Row 1 of Outer Panel.

**Row 2:** Repeat Row 2 of Outer Panel

**Row 3:** Repeat Row 3 of Outer Panel.

**Note:** If the macramé is to be mounted in a frame, take the work down from its hanging position and remove screw eyes from the dowel ends. Following instructions for screen frame, screw top dowel into frame.

Continue to knot.

**Section A:** Repeat Section A of Outer Panel.

**Row 4:** Repeat Row 4 of Outer Panel.

**Row 5:** Repeat Row 5 of Outer Panel.

**Section B: Step 1:** Following chart, tie ten rows of Alternating Square Knots (VOBK #22). Begin by tying ten Square Knots across.

Step 2: Continue to tie Square Knots, decreasing each succeeding row by one knot until the tenth row has one knot.

**Row 6:** Repeat Row 6 of Outer Panel.

**Section C: Step 1:** Use pairs of strands across to tie twenty Alternating Half Hitch Chains (VOBK #7), each made with three loops. On first chain hitch strand 2 around strand 1, 1 around 2, 2 around 1.

Step 2: Hitch strand 3 around strand 4, 4 around 3, 3 around 4.

Step 3: Continue across, repeating Steps 1 and 2.

**Row 7:** Place ⅜" dowel 1½" below Row 6 and repeat Row 2.

**Section D: Step 1:** Use strands 1 through 4 and strands 37 through 40 to tie an Alternating Lark's Head Braid (VOBK #2) on each outer edge. Each braid is tied with 12 Lark's Heads.

Step 2: Place one 5" embroidery hoop 1" below Row 7 and use strands 12 and 13 to tie two Clove Hitches around it. Continue to tie Clove Hitches around upper half of hoop by working from the center out, using strands 11 back through 5, and 14 through 20.

Step 3: For center of circle, begin by using strands 11 and 14 to tie a Square Knot around anchor cords 12 and 13.

Step 4: Use strands 11 and 12 to tie an Alternating Half Hitch Chain made with two loops. Repeat with strands 13 and 14 in reverse.

Step 5: Repeat Step 3.

Step 6: Repeat Step 4.

Step 7: Repeat Step 3.

Step 8: Use strands 11 through 14 to tie Clove Hitches around hoop.

Step 9: Allow strands 10 back through 5 to loop slightly, and then use them to tie Clove Hitches around hoop.

Step 10: Repeat Step 9, using strands 15 through 20 to cover hoop completely.

Step 11: To work the right ring, renumber the sixteen unworked strands 5 through 20; repeat Steps 2 through 10.

**Row 8:** Place ⅜" dowel 7½" below Row 7 and repeat Row 2.

**Row 9:** Place 3/16" dowel directly below Row 8 and repeat Row 2.

**Section E: Step 1:** To make left outer Chevron of Chevron Clove Hitches (VOBK #13), tie strands 5 through 8 around anchor cord 4.

**Step 2:** Use strands 3 back through 1 to tie Clove Hitches around anchor cord 5.

**Step 3:** Use strands 6 through 8 and former anchor cord 4 to tie Clove Hitches around anchor cord 3.

**Step 4:** Use strands 2 and 1 and former anchor cord 5 to tie Clove Hitches around anchor cord 6.

**Step 5:** To make four more Chevrons of Clove Hitches, renumber each group of eight strands across 1 through 8 and repeat Steps 1 through 4, four more times.

**Row 10:** Place a 3/16" dowel 2¾" below Row 9 and repeat Row 2.

**Row 11:** Place ⅜" dowel directly below Row 10 and repeat Row 2.

**Section F: Step 1:** Tie six rows of Alternating Square Knots (VOBK #22), starting first row with ten knots.

**Step 2:** For seventh row, follow chart and begin at outer edge to tie four Square Knots across. Leave eight strands unworked and tie four more Square Knots across.

**Steps 3 through 10:** Continue tying Square Knots as on chart, until fifteen rows are worked.

**Step 11:** Place 9" wire ring directly below Alternating Square Knots and use strands 20 and 21 to tie Clove Hitches around it. Continue to tie Clove Hitches on upper half of ring, using strands 19 back through 6 and 22 through 35.

**Step 12:** Center 5" embroidery hoop within 9" ring and use strands 20 and 21 to tie two Clove Hitches around it. Continue to tie Clove Hitches on upper half of hoop, using strands 19 back through 13 and 22 through 28.

**Step 13:** To complete left side of hoop, use strand 20 to tie a Clove Hitch directly below knot 13. Continue using strands 19 back through 13 to tie Clove Hitches directly below each other (see chart, page 170). Leave strands loose enough to form swirl.

**Step 14:** To complete right side of hoop, use strand 21 to tie a Clove Hitch directly below knot 28. Continue using strands 22 through 28 to tie Clove Hitches directly below each other (see chart). Leave strands loose enough to form swirl.

**Step 15:** To complete left side of 9" ring, use strand 6 to tie a

Clove Hitch directly below itself. Continue, using strands 12 back through 7 to tie Clove Hitches directly below each other (see chart). Leave strands loose enough to form swirl.

**Step 16:** To complete right side of 9" ring, use strand 35 to tie a Clove Hitch directly below itself. Continue, using strands 29 through 34 to tie Clove Hitches directly below each other (see chart). Leave strands loose enough to form swirl.

**Step 17:** Use strands 13 through 28 to complete tying Clove Hitches around ring.

**Step 18:** To complete Section F, repeat Steps 9 back through 1.

**Note:** To complete rest of panel, continue with Rows and Sections not shown on chart as follows:

**Row 12:** Place ⅜" dowel 20¼" below Row 11 and repeat Row 2.

**Row 13:** Repeat Row 10.

**Section G:** This is like Section E but the Chevron Clove Hitches are worked upside down.

**Step 1:** To make the first Chevron on the left side, use strands 7 back through 5 to tie Clove Hitches around anchor cord 8.

**Step 2:** Use strands 2 through 4 and former anchor cord 8 to tie Clove Hitches around anchor cord 1.

**Step 3:** Use strands 6,5 and former anchor cord 1 to tie Clove Hitches around anchor cord 7.

**Step 4:** Use strands 3,4 and former anchor cords 8 and 7 to tie Clove Hitches around anchor cord 2.

**Step 5:** To make four more Chevrons of Clove Hitches, renumber each group of eight strands across 1 through 8 and repeat Steps 1 through 4 four more times.

**Row 14:** Place 3/16" dowel 2¾" below Row 13 and repeat Step 2.

**Row 15:** Repeat Row 9.

**Section H:** Repeat Section D.

**Row 16:** Place ⅜" dowel 7½" below Row 15 and repeat Step 2.

**Row 17:** Repeat Row 7 of Outer Panel

**Row 18:** Place ⅜" dowel ½" below Row 17 and repeat Step 2.

**Section I:** Repeat Section H of Outer Panel.

**Row 19:** Repeat Row 16 of Outer Panel.

**Row 20:** Repeat Row 17 of Outer Panel.

**TO FINISH:** Work at the back of the panel. Lift each cord and apply glue to the dowel underneath. Give cord one final tug to tighten knot. Let glue dry and cut excess cord.

## MACRAMÉ KNOT DIAGRAMS

*Our Macramé drawings are divided into three types: Starting Knots, Basic Knots, Variations on Basic Knots (which include chains and braids).*

### STARTING KNOTS

1. **Lark's Head**: Usually worked in a series around a cord, dowel or similar stable unit which is termed holding line. Lark's Head is used to start work when keeping an exact width is not important. Place knot loosely on holding line as in Step A. Pull tight as in Step B.

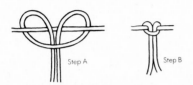

2. **Double Clove Hitch with Picot**: This is worked in a series around a holding line. Slip a Lark's Head backward around holding line; loop cord ends around holding line, forming Half Hitches as in Step A. Pull knot tight with center loop at top forming picot, as in Step B.

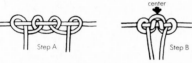

### BASIC KNOTS

**Note**: For clarity in most knot diagrams we show the knots originating from one of the two standard starting knots, tied around a holding line.

1. **Half Hitch**: A simple turn used in chains and braids. A Half Hitch can be worked in either direction.

2. **Clove Hitch**: This knot is actually two Half Hitches, and mastering it is absolutely essential. Any piece that must be strong is made with Clove Hitches, which also help stiffen edges.

3. **Square Knot**: Execute this knot very deliberately while

learning it. After the passes have been mastered, considerable speed can be developed.

**Version 1** is used when cords are in thick bundles. Work with 4 strands as in Step A. Place 1 under 2 and 3; hold. Bring 4 under 1, over 3 and 2, through loop at right. Pull up. Following Step B, place 4 over 2 and 3; hold. Bring 1 over 4, under 3 and 2, through loop at right. Pull up as in Step C.

To make knot in reverse (not shown in diagram) start with 4 under 3 and 2; hold. Bring 1 under 4, over 2 and 3, through loop at left. Pull up. Place 1 over 3 and 2; hold. Bring 4 over 1, under 2 and 3, through loop at left.

**Version 2** is used when cord ends are not tied in bundles. Following Step A, loop strand 1 over 2 and 3; put fingers down through loop, under 2 and 3; grasp at points X and pull them underneath strands 2 and 3 and over loop, as in Step B. Following Step C and still holding loops, pull strand 4 through these loops. Following Step D, hold strands, pull outward as shown, then tighten top half and then bottom half of knot. Pull up, as in Step E.

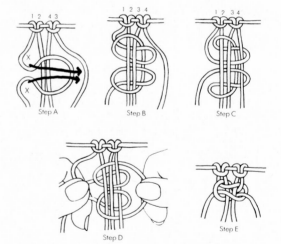

4. **Overhand Knot**: This can be used decoratively in a series or alone in combination with a tassel. It also can be tied at cord ends to prevent fraying. To position this knot exactly, make a loose Overhand Knot in the general area; place a large straight pin in opening at exact position, tighten cord around it and remove pin.

**Version 1**, Step A, shows Overhand Knot being executed with one strand, and Step B shows it tightened. **Version 2** is executed with two strands, and **Version 3** is one strand worked around an anchor cord.

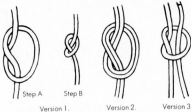

Step A   Step B

Version 1.   Version 2.   Version 3.

## VARIATIONS ON BASIC KNOTS
## INCLUDING CHAINS AND BRAIDS

For our purposes, a chain is defined as a series of strands looped alternately over each other; a braid consists of strands looped over an anchor cord or cords.

**1. Lark's Head Braid:** Using one strand as a tying cord, tie as many Lark's Heads as needed around the anchor cord. Note last Lark's Head on diagram: One half of knot is worked at a time throughout.

**2. Alternating Lark's Head Braid:** Using strand 1 as a tying cord, tie a Lark's Head around strands 2 and 3. Next use strand 4 to tie a Lark's Head around strands 3 and 2, directly under the first Lark's Head. Repeat, alternating right and left outer strands.

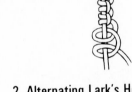

**3. Double Alternating Lark's Head Braid:** Eight strands are used. Strands 2 and 3, 6 and 7, are anchor cords while 1 and 4, 5 and 8 are tying cords. With strand 1, tie a Lark's Head around 2

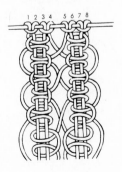

and 3. With 8, tie a Lark's Head around 6 and 7; with 4, tie a Lark's Head around 6 and 7; with 5, tie a Lark's Head around 2 and 3. Repeat, always crossing strand 5 over strand 4. This braid can be widened indefinitely by adding four strands or multiples of four strands.

**4. Half Hitch Braid:** Using one strand as a tying cord, tie as many Half Hitches as needed around the anchor cord. This braid can be kept flat or allowed to twist very attractively.

**5. Alternating Half Hitch Braid:** Work with four strands. Using strand 1 as a tying cord, tie a Half Hitch around strands 2 and 3. Next, use strand 4 to tie a Half Hitch around 3 and 2. Repeat, alternating strands 1 and 4.

**6. Triple Half Hitch Braid:** Using strand 1 as a tying cord, make a Half Hitch around strand 2; make another around strands 2 and 3 and then around strand 2 again. Using strand 4, make a Half Hitch around strand 3, around 3 and 2, then around 3. Repeat, alternating strands 1 and 4.

**7. Alternating Half Hitch Chain:** Work with two strands by passing left strand around right strand, making a Half Hitch. Pass right strand around left in same manner. Repeat, alternating knots. This chain curves easily.

**8. Two Strand Alternating Half Hitch Chain:** Work the same as No. 7 but tie with two strands at the same time. This chain also can be tied with three or more strands which make a very decorative chain.

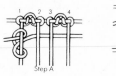

**9. Horizontal Clove Hitch:** Fasten an anchor cord directly below and parallel to holding line. Use pin at right end and pull cord taut. Fasten but do not cut. Following Step A use strand 1 to tie a Clove Hitch around anchor cord; pull tight. Following Step B continue knotting across. Insert pin, bring anchor cord around it to turn corner neatly. Continue making Clove Hitches. This knot can be worked from left or right. Note: Area to be knotted can be made as wide as needed by adding more Double Clove Hitches with Picot to holding line.

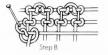

Step A   Step B

**10. Vertical Clove Hitch:** This is begun like No. 9 except that the anchor cord is fastened at the left and becomes a tying cord. Following Step A, use anchor cord to tie a Clove Hitch around strand 1. Following Step B tie knots across for second row. Insert pin, bring anchor cord around it and begin knotting for third row. Can be worked from right or left.

Step A   Step B

**11. Diagonal Clove Hitch:** This is worked like No. 9 except that anchor cord is turned and held on a diagonal. Tighten each knot as it is tied.

**12. Double Diagonal Clove Hitch:** This is begun like No. 11. For the second diagonal row, use strand 4 of the previous row as an anchor cord; tie Clove Hitches around it. The last Clove Hitch is tied with the anchor cord of previous row. Tighten each knot as it is tied.

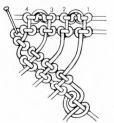

**13. Chevron Clove Hitch:** This is made with any multiple of two strands. We use 8 strands. Following Step A use strands 2, 3 and 4 to tie Clove Hitches around anchor cord 1, keeping it at an angle. Use strand 7 to tie a Clove Hitch around anchor cord 8.

Following Step B use strands 6 and 5 to tie Clove Hitches around anchor cord 8. To finish center, tie 8 in a Clove Hitch around anchor cord 1.

Following Step C tie 3, 4 and 8 around anchor cord 2. Tie 6 around anchor cord 7.

Following Step D use 5 and 1 to tie Clove Hitches around 7. To finish center, use 2 to tie Clove Hitch around 7.

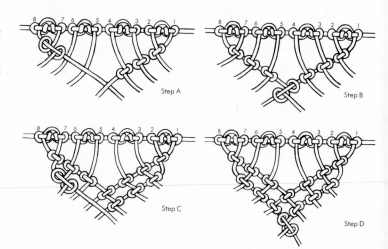

Step A   Step B

Step C   Step D

**14. Alternating Clove Hitch Braid:** Work with four strands. Use strand 1 to tie a Clove Hitch around anchor cords 2 and 3. Next, use strand 4 to tie a Clove Hitch around 3 and 2. Repeat, alternating strands 1 and 4.

**15. Square Knot Braid:** Work with four strands. Following Step A, use strands 1 and 4 to tie a series of Square Knots around anchor cords 2 and 3. Step B shows knots tightened.

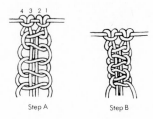

**16. Two Strand Square Knot Braid:** Work with eight strands. Use strands 1, 2 and 7, 8 in pairs to tie a series of Square Knots around anchor cords 3, 4 and 5, 6.

**17. Spiral Half Square Knot Braid:** This braid will automatically spiral around its anchor cords as it is worked. Work with 4 strands. To tie a Half Square Knot place strand 1 under 2 and 3; bring 4 under 1, over 3 and 2 and through loop formed as in Step A. With the same strands tie 5 more Half Square Knots as in Step B. Note that the sixth Half Square Knot completes one spiral. While working be sure to keep cords 1 and 4 going in the same direction.

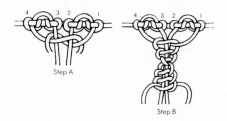

**18. Looped Square Knot Braid:** Work with four strands the same as the Square Knot Braid but form loops on outer edges by working cord around a dowel or pencil.

**19. Knotted and Looped Square Knot Braid:** Work with four strands the same as the Square Knot Braid but tie an Overhand Knot with anchor cords between each pair of Looped Square Knots.

**20. Knotted Loop Square Knot Braid:** Work with four strands the same as the Looped Square Knot Braid but tie an Overhand Knot in each loop before making the next Square Knot.

**21. Beaded Knot Braid:** Work with four strands. Following Step A, use strands 1 and 4 to make a Square Knot around anchor cords 2 and 3. Leave an opening the size of one knot and tie three more Square Knots. Following Step B bring anchor cords up,

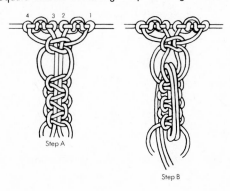

through opening and down again. Following Step C pull cords tight to form a bead on top. Following Step D, use strands 1 and 4 to tie a Square Knot below bead.

The size of the bead may be enlarged by increasing the number of Square Knots made in Step A after the opening. With five, six or more Square Knots, the bead becomes a ring.

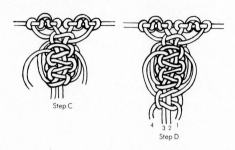

Step C

Step D

**22. Alternating Square Knots:** Work with at least eight strands (or twelve, as shown), or any multiple of 4 strands. Tie rows of Square Knots. First row: Use strands 1 and 4 to tie knot around 2 and 3; tie strands 5 and 8 around 6 and 7, strands 9 and 12 around 10 and 11. Second row: Tie strands 3 and 6 around 4 and 5, 7 and 10 around 8 and 9. Repeat first and second rows. Note that strands 2 and 11 remain anchor cords throughout.

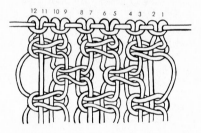

**23. Gathering Knot:** This is worked with a Square Knot that can be tied with any number of strands around any number of anchor cords. It is shown with two pairs of strands tied around six anchor cords.

 Clove Hitch

 Lark's Head

 Double Clove Hitch with Picot

 Alternating Half Hitch

 Square Knot

 Gathering Knot

 Square Knot Braid

 or  Spiral Half Square Knot Braid

168

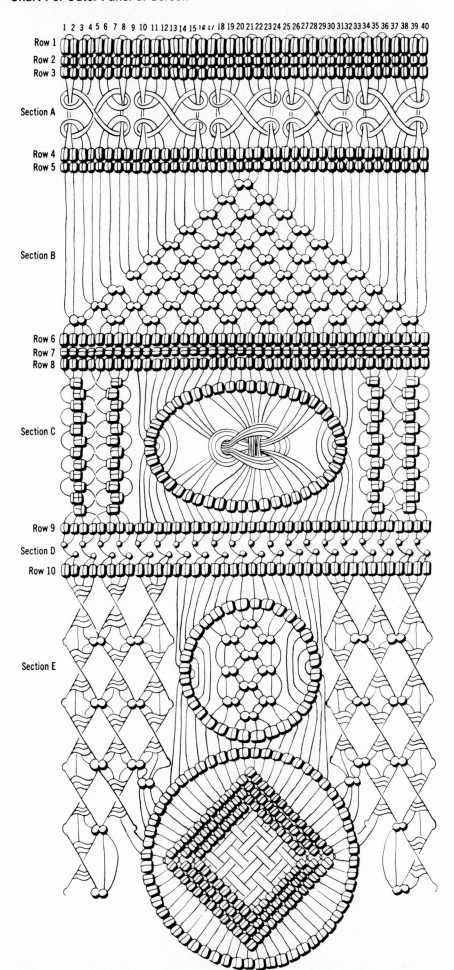

1 2 3 4 5 6 7 8 9 10 11 12 13 14 15 16 17 18 19 20 21 22 23 24 25 26 27 28 29 30 31 32 33 34 35 36 37 38 39 40

Row 1
Row 2
Row 3

Section A

Row 4
Row 5

Section B

Row 6
Row 7
Row 8

Section C

Row 9

Section D

Row 10

Section E

1 2 3 4 5 6 7 8 9 10 11 12 13 14 15 16 17 18 19 20 21 22 23 24 25 26 27 28 29 30 31 32 33 34 35 36 37 38 39 40

Row 1
Row 2
Row 3

Section A

Row 4
Row 5

Section B

Row 6

Section C

Row 7

Section D

Row 8
Row 9

Section E

Row 10
Row 11

Section F

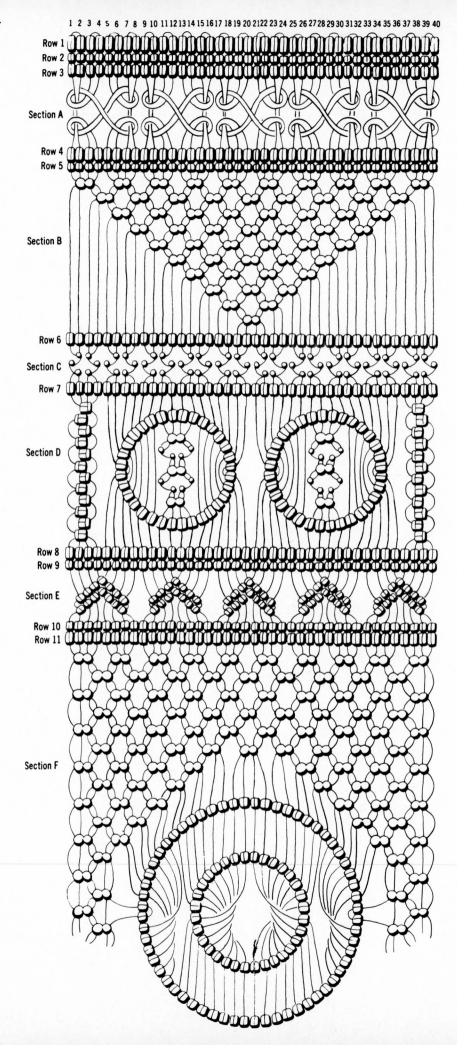

# MACRAMÉ ROMAN WINDOW BLIND

Dyed nylon parachute cord i sknotted around horizontal wooden dowels to make a lacy filigree pattern that lets sun through.

Refer to chart symbols and knot diagrams given with directions for the Three Panel Macramé Screen, pages 164, 165, 166, 167 and 168. In the directions that follow below, abbreviations are used to identify the knots. Letters refer to the three general categories of knots illustrated on pages 164–168, numbers refer to the individual knots within those categories. For example, SK #1 is Lark's Head.

SK—Starting Knot
BK—Basic Knot
VOBK—Variations on Basic Knot

**SIZE:** The window blind shown is 32" x 40". See Note for adjusting size.

**MATERIALS:** 1600' of nylon parachute cord; two "C" clamps; household dye; rubber bands; white glue; two large screw eyes; 32" dowels, ten ⅜" diameter and ten 3/16" diameter.

**Note:** To adjust size to fit your window, place "C" clamps farther apart and cut longer cords. Repeat pattern rows and sections until shade is desired length. You will need an additional pair of dowels for each pattern section added.

**TO START:** Measure out fifty 31' lengths of cord by placing two "C" clamps 15½' apart and winding cord a full circuit around them five lengths at a time. Remove cord from clamps by cutting the side at which the winding was begun. Continue winding several lengths at a time until there are fifty. Mark the center point of each cord by tying a loose Overhand Knot (BK #4). Roll up each strand into a neat bundle held by a rubber band.

Measure 25' cord for pull. Dye all cords.

Hang one ⅜" dowel from a convenient working height by inserting a screw eye into each dowel end and suspending it by strings.

**Row 1:** Undo the Overhand Knot on each cord and fold cord in half, forming loop in center. Place loop over dowel and tie a Double Clove Hitch with Picot (SK #2). Continue knotting with all doubled cords until there are 100 strands on dowel measuring 32" in width. Glue the end knots.

**Row 2:** Place a 3/16" dowel directly below first dowel. Tie Clove Hitches (Horizontal Clove Hitch, Step A—VOBK #9) around dowel, beginning with center strands 50 and 51, being certain that the second row of knots is very close to the first (see chart). Continue to work out from the center, first knotting one side and then the other until row is completed. Glue end knots in place.

**Section A: Step 1:** To make Looped Square Knot Braid (VOBK #17), use strands 1 and 4 to tie a Square Knot around anchor cords 2 and 3, placing the knot ¾" below Row 2. Tie 4 more Square Knots, placing each knot ¾" below the previous one.

**Step 2:** Continue across, tying four more Looped Square Knot Braids, skipping 20 strands between each. Tie strands 25 and 28 around anchor cords 26 and 27; 49 and 52 around 50 and 51; 73 and 76 around 74 and 75; 97 and 100 around 98 and 99.

**Note:** Each group of 20 unworked strands is to be tied into a diamond shape (see chart and photograph). The two outer diamonds are worked like the left-hand one in chart, and the two inner diamonds are worked like the right-hand one in chart.

**Step 3:** To make left outer diamond, use strand 15 to tie a

171

Clove Hitch (VOBK #13) around strand 14. Cords 14 and 15 are now anchor cords.

Step 4: Use strands 13 back through 5 to tie Clove Hitches around anchor cord 15.

Step 5: Use strands 16 through 23 to tie Clove Hitches around anchor cord 14.

Step 6: Use strands 16 through 22 to tie Clove Hitches around anchor cord 13.

Step 7: Use strands 12 back through 6 to tie Clove Hitches around anchor cord 16.

Step 8: Use strands 9 and 10 in pairs and 19 and 20 in pairs to tie a Gathering Knot (VOBK #23) around anchor cords 11, 12, 17, and 18.

Step 9: Use former anchor cord 13 and strands 22 back through 17 to tie Clove Hitches around anchor cord 23.

Step 10: Use strands 7 through 12 and former anchor cord 23 to tie Clove Hitches around anchor cord 6.

Step 11: Use former anchor cords 14 and 13, strands 22 back through 17 and former anchor cord 6 to tie Clove Hitches around anchor cord 24.

Step 12: Use former anchor cord 16, strands 7 through 12 and former anchor cords 23 and 24 to tie Clove Hitches around anchor cord 5.

Step 13: To make right outer diamond, renumber the 20 unworked strands on far right, 5 through 24, and repeat Steps 3 through 12.

Step 14: To make diamond just left of center, use strand 39 to tie a Clove Hitch around strand 38. Cords 38 and 39 are now anchor cords.

Step 15: Use strands 37 back through 29 to tie Clove Hitches around anchor cord 39.

Step 16: Use strands 40 through 47 to tie Clove Hitches around anchor cord 38.

Step 17: Use strands 40 through 46 to tie Clove Hitches around anchor cord 37.

Step 18: Use strands 36 back through 30 to tie Clove Hitches around anchor cord 40.

Step 19: Use strands 31 and 36 to tie two Square Knots (BK #3) one under the other around anchor cords 32 through 35.

Step 20: Use strands 41 and 46 to tie two more Square Knots, one under the other, around anchor cords 42 through 45.

Step 21: Use former anchor cord 37 and strands 46 back through 41 to tie Clove Hitches around anchor cord 47.

Step 22: Use strands 31 through 36 and former anchor cord 47 to tie Clove Hitches around anchor cord 30.

Step 23: Use former anchor cords 38 and 37, strands 46 back through 41 and former anchor cord 30 to tie Clove Hitches around anchor cord 48.

Step 24: Use former anchor cord 40, strands 31 through 36 and former anchor cords 47 and 48 to tie Clove Hitches around anchor cord 29.

Step 25: To make right inner diamond, renumber the 20 remaining unworked strands, 29 through 48, and repeat Steps 14 through 24.

Row 3: Place a ⅜" dowel 6" below Row 2. Tie Clove Hitches around dowel, starting at center and working out. Glue end knots in place.

Row 4: Place a 3/16" dowel directly below Row 3. Tie Clove Hitches around dowel, starting at the center and working out. Keep this row close to Row 3. Glue end knots.

Section B: This straight fall of cord alternates with the knotted sections. To lengthen or shorten blind, add or subtract to these straight sections.

Row 5: Repeat Row 3.

Row 6: Repeat Row 4.

Section C: Step 1: To begin left end section of Alternating Square Knots (VOBK #22), work one row of four Square Knots ¾" below Row 6 as follows. Use strands 1 and 4 to tie a Square Knot around anchor cords 2 and 3; 5 and 8 around 6 and 7; 9 and 12 around 10 and 11, and 13 and 16 around 14 and 15.

Step 2: Work a second row of three Square Knots ¾" below first as follows: Tie strands 3 and 6 around anchor cords 4 and 5; 7 and 10 around 8 and 9; 11 and 14 around 12 and 13.

Step 3: Repeat Step 1.

Step 4: Repeat Step 2.

Step 5: Repeat Step 1.

Steps 6 through 10: For right end section of Alternating Square Knots, renumber the last 16 strands on the far right 1 through 16 and repeat Steps 1 through 5.

Step 11: To begin the left one of the three groups of Double Diagonal Clove Hitches (VOBK #12), use strands 18 through 26 to tie Clove Hitches around anchor cord 17, and 35 back through 27 around anchor cord 36.

Step 12: Use strands 19 through 26 and former anchor cord 17 to tie Clove Hitches around anchor cord 18.

Step 13: Use strands 34 back through 27 and former anchor cords 36 and 18 to tie Clove Hitches around anchor cord 35.

Step 14: Use strands 19 and 20 and strands 33 and 34 to form two Alternating Half Hitch Chains (VOBK #7), each made with 3 loops.

172

Step 15: Use strands 21 and 22 and strands 31 and 32 to form two Alternating Half Hitch Chains, each made with 9 loops.

Step 16: Use strands 23 and 24 and strands 29 and 30 to form Alternating Half Hitch Chains, each made with 7 loops.

Step 17: Use strands 25 and 26 and 27 and 28 to form Alternating Half Hitch Chains, each made with 3 loops.

Step 18: Use former anchor cord 17 and strands 26 back through 19 to tie Clove Hitches around anchor cord 35.

Step 19: Use former anchor cord 36 and strands 27 through 34 to tie Clove Hitches around anchor cord 18.

Step 20: Use strands 26 back through 19 and former anchor cord 35 to tie Clove Hitches around anchor cord 17.

Step 21: Use former anchor cord 37, strands 28 back through 34 and former anchor cord 18 to tie Clove Hitches around anchor cord 36.

Steps 22 through 32: To knot the center group of Double Diagonal Clove Hitches, skip four strands and renumber the next twenty strands 17 through 36. Repeat Steps 11 through 21.

Steps 33 through 43: To knot the right group of Double Diagonal Clove Hitches, skip four strands and renumber the next twenty strands 17 through 36. Repeat Steps 11 through 21.

Step 44: Use the four unworked strands on the left to make a Square Knot Braid. Use strands 37 and 40 to tie a Square Knot around anchor cords 38 and 39, ¾" below Row 6.

Step 45: Tie another Square Knot about 4" below first one, using same strands as used in Step 44.

Step 46: Use the four unworked strands on the right to tie another Square Knot Braid, repeating Steps 44 and 45.

**Row 7:** Repeat Row 3.

**Row 8:** Repeat Row 4.

To complete knotting window blind, repeat Section B, Row 3, Row 4, Section A, Row 3, Row 4, Section B, Row 3, Row 4, Section C, Row 3 and Row 4 for length needed, ending with Rows 3 and 4.

**TO FINISH:** Work loose ends into back with a blunt needle; glue to hold and trim off excess cord.


### INSTALLING BLIND

**MATERIALS:** Five cup hooks, four (six or eight) curtain rings; awning cleat; twelve wood knobs for dowel ends; parachute cord (dyed to match blind); white glue; paint.

See back view of blind. Glue wood knobs to dowel ends and paint them. Tie or sew curtain rings to ⅜" dowel, which is second from the bottom, one ring about 3" from each end. Repeat on every other ⅜" dowel.

Insert cup hooks and cleat as shown; hang blind, run cord through curtain rings and cup hooks; tie ends.

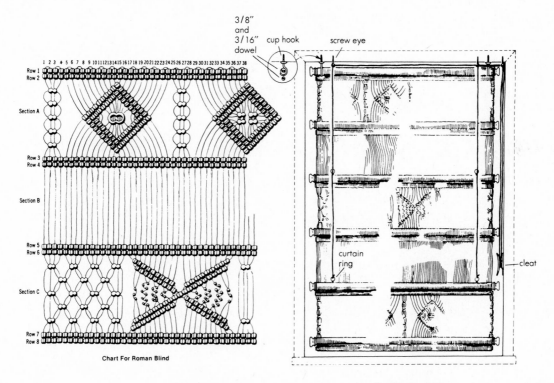

Chart For Roman Blind

Installing Blind, Back View

# YARN SOURCES

If you have trouble in obtaining any of the yarns specified in these projects, write to the following addresses for information on mail-order sources:

*Aunt Lydia*
*Dawn Sayelle*
    America Thread Co.
    Hi Ridge Park
    Stamford, Connecticut 06905

*Brunswick*
    Brunswick Yarns
    230 Fifth Avenue
    New York, New York 10001

*Bucilla*
    Bucilla Yarns
    30–20 Thomson Avenue
    Long Island City, New York 11101

*Coats & Clark*
*J. & P. Coats*
*Red Heart*
    Coats & Clark
    75 Rockefeller Plaza
    New York, New York 10019

*D.M.C.*
    D.M.C. Corporation
    107 Trumbull Street
    Elizabeth, New Jersey 07206

*Elsa Williams*
    Elsa Williams
    445 Main Street
    West Townsend, Massachusetts 01474

*Jute-Tone*
*Lily*
    Belding Lily Co.
    Shelby, North Carolina 28150

*Kentucky*
    January & Wood Co.
    Maysville, Kentucky 41056

*Lion Brand*
    Lion Brand Yarn Co.
    1270 Broadway
    New York, New York 10001

# PHOTOGRAPHY CREDITS

| | |
|---|---|
| Ben Calvo, *Woman's Day* Studio | All photographs except as follows: |
| Sigrid Owen | Pages 73, 100 |
| Carmen Schiavone | 12, 14, 15, 16, 20, 21 |
| | 24, 25, 26, 27, 46, 51 |
| | 104, 123, 141, 153 |
| Gordon E. Smith | 74, 110, 114, 116, 118, 125 |

# DESIGNER CREDITS

| | | | |
|---|---|---|---|
| Barbara R. Ackerman | Pages 126 | Lura LaBarge | 104 |
| Carolyn Ambuter | 46, 155 | Patti Lawrence | 72 |
| Cindy Lea Arbelbide | 41 | Bella Lentsch | 69 (Coming-Up-Roses Pillow) |
| Pat Bartlett | 73 | Annette Lep | 20 |
| Lorraine Bodger | 107 | Caroline McLoughlin | 100 |
| Helen Bullett | 26 | Clara Migliori | 143 (Plant Hammock) |
| Theresa Capuana | 29 | Charlotte Patera | 65 |
| Taffy Cayce | 21 | Marianne Peters | 67 (Honeycomb Puff Pillow) |
| Madeleine Chisholm | 102 | George Pfiffner | 159, 171 |
| Barbara Christopher | 39 | Bertha Powers | 17 |
| Flavia deVergara | 67, (Rainbow-and-Cream Pillow) | Beatrice Rasquin | 143 (Pot Sleeve) |
| William Dissler | 23 | Marjorie W. Rhind | 148 |
| Claudia Ein | 24 | Hilda Roennspiess | 134 |
| Helen Farrar | 69 (Nine-Times-Lavender Pillow) | Harry Schmidt | 36 |
| Gloria Fein | 122 | Ann Schwiebert | 141 |
| John Gordon | 130 | Holly Shaw | 75 |
| Sara Gutierrez | 51, 53 | Mavis Smith-Heap | 114 |
| Anne Halliday | 98 | Jane Truitt | 80 |
| Carol Hasselriis | 25 | Marilyn Wein | 54, 76, 112, 132, 135, 136 |
| Solweig Hedin | 60 | | 138, 140, 142, 146, (Sachets) |
| Laurel Hobbs | 143 (Calico Baskets) | *Woman's Day* Staff | 12, 14, 15, 16, 33, 54 |
| Binny Ipcar | 27 | | 74, 77, 110, 111, 116, 118 |
| Marjorie Kratz | 123 | | 120, 121, 125, 139, 143(Potholders), |
| | | | 146 (Tissue and Dress-Hanger Covers) |

# Index